SETH FINN

Media
Gratifications
Research
Current Perspectives

Edited by
Karl Erik Rosengren
Lawrence A. Wenner
Philip Palmgreen

SAGE PUBLICATIONS Beverly Hills London New Delhi

For information address:

SAGE Publications, Inc.
275 South Beverly Drive
Beverly Hills, California 90212

SAGE Publications India Pvt. Ltd.
M-32 Market
Greater Kailash I
New Delhi 110 048 India

SAGE Publications Ltd
28 Banner Street
London EC1Y 8QE
England

Printed in the United States of America

Library of Congress Cataloging in Publication Data

Main entry under title:

Media gratifications research.

   Bibliography: p.
   Includes index.
   1. Mass media—Audiences—Research—Addresses, essays,
lectures.   I. Rosengren, Karl Erik.   II. Wenner,
Lawrence A.   III. Palmgreen, Philip.
P96.A83M43 1985   302.2′34′072   85-2308
ISBN 0-8039-2471-2

FIRST PRINTING

CONTENTS

FOREWORD

IT IS PERHAPS both ironic and uniquely appropriate that, true to the assumptions of the research tradition it sought to assess, Blumler and Katz's volume *The Uses of Mass Communications* (1974) has been subject to various and often conflicting interpretations and uses by members of its scholarly "audience." The editors of this influential work themselves viewed the collection of essays as an attempt to come to grips with many of the issues—theoretical, methodological, and substantive— that beset the uses and gratifications tradition as it experienced a renaissance in the late 1960s and early 1970s. Critics of the approach largely viewed this attempt as a failure, and pointed to the volume (minus its critical essays by Elliot and by Carey and Kreiling) as the final feeble volley from a misguided band of researchers who could now be expected to retreat in disarray into scientific obscurity.

Those more sympathetic to the approach, however, arrived at a more benevolent reading of the text and consequently put it to a very different use. These readers viewed the often brilliant expositions of issues and criticisms alike as a challenge, and many were inspired to grapple in bold and innovative ways with the particularly formidable obstacles impeding an understanding of the audience experience with mass communication. Not that the continuing upsurge in uses and gratifications research over the last decade can be attributed entirely to the influence of Blumler and Katz's benchmark volume, but the ideas expressed therein have played a major role in setting the agenda for such research and have provided the dominant conceptual and ideological framework within which debate about the merits of the approach continues.

Whatever its roots, such has been the scope and volume of research into audience uses of the mass media in recent years that the resurgence of uses and gratifications research that prompted the Blumler and Katz assessment pales by comparison. Except for a less ambitious "midcourse correction" attempted in the form of a special issue of *Communication Research* edited by David Swanson in 1979, the trajectory of this stage of the media gratifications paradigm has gone largely uncharted. We arrived at this conclusion more or less independently a few years ago, and at the 1983 meeting of the International Communication Association in Dallas, discussions among ourselves and various other scholars revealed a great deal of interest in a new stock-taking enterprise. This led to our issuing invitations to an international field of authors to submit essays on a wide range of theoretical and methodological issues, new research paradigms, and key research areas. The response, both from authors connected to the Blumler and Katz volume and from many others more recently attracted to the media gratifications area, was gratifying beyond our expectations.

The result is a collection of essays very much in the tradition of the "Analytical Perspectives" portion of *The Uses of Mass Communications.* So many were the conceptual, methodological, and substantive issues clamoring for attention that we decided early on to forgo primarily empirical contributions (which constituted a major portion of the Blumler and Katz work) in favor of essays that are expository, critical, and analytical. We also asked our authors to probe the value of synthesis and merger—of various theoretical strands and research traditions, of uses and effects, of micro and macro perspectives, of survey, experimental, and ethnographic modes of inquiry—for we are convinced that such *eclectic synthesis,* and not eclecticism per se, is responsible for much of the vitality that permeates current media gratifications research. We have also endeavored, particularly in opening and closing chapters by ourselves and by Blumler, Katz, and Gurevitch, to provide an updated perspective on earlier research, to examine the present state of theoretical and methodological development, and to point out the roads that seem to offer the most promising vistas for the future. Other authors, perhaps writing ten years hence in a similar volume, will best be able to determine how well we have succeeded, but we hope that the ideas expressed in the following pages will have some impact on the development of media gratifications theory and research. We are also decidedly optimistic about where such research might lead us, and we hope that others, after a thoughtful reading of the essays in this book, will be inclined to share in that optimism.

—*Philip Palmgreen*
Karl Erik Rosengren
Lawrence A. Wenner

PART I
LOOKING BACK

Chapter 1

USES AND GRATIFICATIONS RESEARCH:
The Past Ten Years

Philip Palmgreen
Lawrence A. Wenner
Karl Erik Rosengren

TEN YEARS IS A LONG TIME in the history of mass communication research. In a field where the concerns of research scientists and critical analysts are remarkably varied and often tied to the rapid changes in the technological structure of the media themselves, it is remarkable that a line of research based on a relatively simple premise has continued to flourish. The guiding premise behind media gratifications research was neither new nor revolutionary when posed in Blumler and Katz's landmark volume *The Uses of Mass Communications* in 1974. It suggested simply that we "ask not what media do to people, but ask what people do with media." This transposition voiced the concerns of many mass communications researchers who felt the need for a shift to a vision of the mass communication process that more clearly embraced the concept of an active audience. Such a shift of vision is consonant with Kuhn's (1962) notions about the role that transformation plays in the theory-building process, although the phrase "shift of paradigm" is perhaps too grandiose as a description of what occurred.

Although this shift of vision was clearly not a new idea in 1974 (certainly not outside the United States), it was relevant to a considerable number of new reseachers who used the basic tenets of the uses and gratifications approach as posed in the Blumler and Katz volume as a point of departure. In assessing the impact of that volume, it is important to note the infusion of these researchers' ideas into the mix of thoughts about media use and how that use intervenes in the process of media effects. Without such an infusion there would have been little movement of the bandwagon, and we would have little justification to be writing here about the past ten years of media gratifications research.

There is a certain irony, of course, in proclamations that the uses and gratifications approach has become a major research tradition within mass communication. While proclamations of this kind are becoming increasingly common (Palmgreen et al., 1980, 1981; Roberts and Bachen, 1981; Swanson, 1979a, 1979b), there is a parallel tendency for almost none of these proclamations to go without the almost requisite reference to the considerable criticism that has been levied at the position (Anderson and Meyer, 1975; Carey and Kreiling, 1974; Elliot, 1974; Lometti et al., 1977; Messaris, 1977; Swanson, 1977, 1979b). It is difficult to conceptualize this constant defense of one's own backside as a position of strength. Indeed, to an outsider, researchers in the tradition may well have appeared as a train of flagellants, always gratefully accepting new whips from whoever happens to pass by.

Still, there is no question that gratifications research has proliferated over the past ten years, and that the vested interests of its proponents have been countered by a loyal opposition of critics with their own paradigmatic biases. By being continually shot at—and shooting back—those waving the uses and gratifications banner have proved to themselves and to their opponents that they are alive and kicking. As Kuhn (1962) has shown in some detail, such conflicts are at the heart of developing scientific theory.

DEVELOPMENT OF THE
MEDIA GRATIFICATIONS PARADIGM

While currently enjoying popularity, media gratifications research has developed much like anything else in social science—slowly, and tending to plod along a relatively uncharted course. One of its redeeming features no doubt has been its longevity, much of which might be attributable to the flexibility of the approach and the reluctance of its practitioners to become fenced in, either through premature modeling or through external criticism. Viewed another way, it could be said that media gratifications research was "slow out of the starting gate." This slow start can be traced to two factors.

First, the dominance of the "effects" focus in pre- and post-World War II communication research tended to overshadow the concern with individual differences in gratifications inquiries. Second, and certainly related, was that the early phases of development in media gratifications research were rather lacking in explicit or broad-based statements regarding the theoretical assumptions of the position. The dawdling nature of the first phase of development was characterized by Blumler and Katz (1974: 13) as providing "insightful *description* of audience subgroup orientations to selected media content forms."

While the early descriptive research (Berelson, 1949; Herzog, 1944; Suchman, 1942; Waples et al., 1940; Warner and Henry, 1948; Wolfe and Fiske, 1949) was hampered by conceptual and methodological shortcomings, these attempts at gratifications inventories were refined in a new generation of descriptive studies that ushered in "operationalization" as the second phase of development in media gratifications research.

It is interesting to note that the transitional studies of this second phase (Freidson, 1953; Himmelweit et al., 1958; Johnstone, 1961; Maccoby, 1954; Riley and Riley, 1951; Schramm et al., 1961), which Blumler and Katz (1974: 13) suggest emphasize "operationalization of the social and psychological variables presumed to give rise to differentiated patterns of media consumption," were not designed primarily to study gratifications, but rather the relationship between peer and familial integration and media use. This capacity of the gratifications approach to be applied to a variety of research areas with differing theoretical assumptions continues to be one of its strong points.

The operationalization phase also marked the beginning of concern with typologies in media gratifications research. Most influential has been the fourfold typology (surveillance, correlation, socialization, entertainment) of a functionalist bent posed by Lasswell (1948) and refined by Wright (1960). Decidedly focused on the utility of media-person interactions rather than the maintenance of equilibrium within a system, later studies that developed typologies (Blumler and McQuail, 1969; Katz, Gurevitch, and Haas, 1973; McQuail et al., 1972) signaled convergence on individual differences over more traditional functionalist concerns. In fact, McQuail et al. (1972: 155) consciously avoid the language of functionalism and attempt a "new start" by outlining a "typology of media-person interactions" that consists of the varying forms of diversion, personal relationships, personal identity, and surveillance.

These more systematic attempts at typologies during the latter part of the operationalization phase combine with a number of attempts at articulating the elements of media gratifications research (Blumler et al., 1971; Katz et al., 1974; Lundberg and Hultén, 1968; Rosengren, 1974) to introduce the third phase of development, which Blumler and Katz (1974: 13) characterize as "attempts to use gratification data to provide explanations of such other facets of the communication process with which audience motives and expectations may be connected." Since "explanations" in social science go hand in hand with theory building, this third phase of development in media gratifications research merits particular attention.

SOME BASIC ASSUMPTIONS

During the third phase of development, thinking about the media gratifications process matured. Many assumptions of the approach crystallized, a number were revised or realigned, and substantial strides were taken toward theoretical integration. No doubt most influential to this crystallization process was the Katz et al. (1974: 20) description of the uses and gratifications approach as one concerned with "(1) the social and psychological origins of (2) needs, which generate (3) expectations of (4) the mass media or other sources which lead to (5) differential patterns of media exposure (or engagement in other activities), resulting in (6) need gratifications and (7) other consequences, perhaps mostly unintended ones."

This now classic précis and an elaborated conceptual scheme by Rosengren (1974) outlined the general dimensions of a paradigm for uses and gratifications research. These paradigmatic statements developed as an outgrowth of a set of axiomatic assumptions that tended to guide a preponderance of media gratification inquiries. Statements of these assumptions have been made elsewhere (Katz et al., 1974; Lundberg and Hultén, 1968; Wenner, 1977) and derive key elements from a number of studies (see especially Katz, Gurevitch, and Haas, 1973; McQuail et al., 1972; Rosengren and Windahl, 1972). Briefly, among the most important of these assumptions are that (1) the audience is active, thus (2) much media use can be conceived as goal directed, and (3) competing with other sources of need satisfaction, so that when (4) substantial audience initiative links needs to media choice, (5) media consumption can fulfill a wide range of gratifications, although (6) media content alone cannot be used to predict patterns of gratifications accurately because (7) media characteristics structure the degree to which needs may be gratified at different times, and, further, because (8) graftifications obtained can have their origins in media content, exposure in and of itself, and/or the social situation in which exposure takes place. These assumptions hold in a climate in which judgments about the cultural significance of media are suspended.

DEVELOPMENT OF
MEDIA GRATIFICATIONS THEORY

While these statements of paradigm and working assumptions are of undeniable importance as basic to the development of media gratifications research during this third phase, there has been debate concerning two overriding and related issues: (1) the role of theory in uses and gratifications studies, and (2) the relation of functionalism to media gratifications research. The debate has largely been resolved among adherents of a gratifications approach, but there is no doubt that this resolution has been accelerated by the varied criticism directed at gratifications research (Anderson and Meyer, 1975; Carey and Kreiling, 1974; Elliot, 1974; Lometti et al., 1977; Messaris, 1977; Swanson, 1977, 1979b), most of which addressed the functionalism and theory issues among other questions about central assumptions and method.

As Blumler (1979: 11) has succinctly pointed out, "There is no such thing as *a* or *the* uses and gratifications theory, although there are plenty of theor*ies* about uses and gratifications phenomena." A variety of "multitheory" schemas have been developed, illustrating diverse integrative theoretical strategies that occupy the gamut between microtheory and macrotheory. Among these we see McQuail and Gurevitch's (1974) view that gratifications research may be pursued from structural/cultural, action/motivation, or even "functional" positions; Wenner's (1977) observation that gratifications research could be approached through the multidimensional integration of affiliation, utilitarian, and consistency theories; Rosengren and Windahl's (1977) assessment of gratifications research as integrating the three mass communications theories of individual differences, social categories, and social relations as posed by DeFleur (1966); and McGuire's (1974) well-explicated argument relating some sixteen theoretical positions to gratifications research.

The development of these broad-based theoretical frameworks has yielded recently to more explicit theoretical constructions concerning expectancy-value relationships to gratifications (Babrow and Swanson, 1984; Blood and Galloway, 1983; Galloway and Meek, 1981; Palmgreen and Rayburn, 1982, 1983, 1984; Rayburn and Palmgreen, 1983, 1984; Van Leuven, 1981), transactional processes of gratifications and effects (McLeod and Becker, 1974, 1981; Wenner 1982, 1983a), and the dimensions of audience activity (Levy, 1983; Levy and Windahl, 1984; Windahl, 1981). These developments signal, as Windahl (1981) has suggested, that uses and gratifications research is at yet another crossroads.

Over the past ten years, there has been a change from isolated ad hoc studies that attempted explanations to sustained efforts within explicit theoretical and methodological frameworks. We believe this signals a fourth phase of development in media gratifications research; one that is concerned explicitly with formal *theory* building and testing. Looking back on it from today's perspective, the critical attack on media gratifications research as being "atheoretical" has dissolved in the face of theoretical advances made along several fronts in the last decade by uses and gratifications researchers. While these advances have been uneven and often lacking in coordination, the result has been the emergence of a rather complex theoretical structure, the outlines of which recently have been sketched by Palmgreen (1984a, 1984b). Building on earlier efforts by McLeod and Becker (1981), Weibull (1983c), Rosengren (1974), and others, Figure 1.1 relates the Palmgreen model to a broader theoretical framework. While Palmgreen's model was devised to integrate what is known about media gratification processes with research in related areas (primarily expectancy-value theories), Figure 1.1 may be regarded as an attempt to locate gratification processes within an overall societal perspective.

Space does not permit detailed discussion of each set of relationships depicted in Figure 1.1. An obvious feature of the general model, however, is its rather complex causal structure. Ten years ago, Blumler and Katz (1974: 16), again in the foreword to their 1974 volume, expressed the hope that uses and gratifications research could "be detached from its former functionalist moorings." It would appear that this has been achieved successfully, although terminological evidence of the functionalist heritage still remains.[1] Most varieties of functionalism have in common the attempt to explain a social pattern or behavior (structure) in terms of the effects or consequences (functions) of the pattern or behavior (Cancian, 1968; Stinchcombe, 1968). An examination of the model should make it clear that this is not the main form of uses and gratifications explanations. The general model presented here, while taking into account the feedback from gratifications obtained to those sought, also considers (among other things) the social psychological origins of needs, values, and beliefs, which give rise to motives for behavior, which may in turn be guided by beliefs, values, and social circumstances into seeking various gratifications through media consumption and other nonmedia behaviors. The gratification processes are seen as taking place within a field of interaction between societal structures and individual characteristics, an interaction calling forward specific realization of the potentials and restrictions inherent in those structures and characteristics.

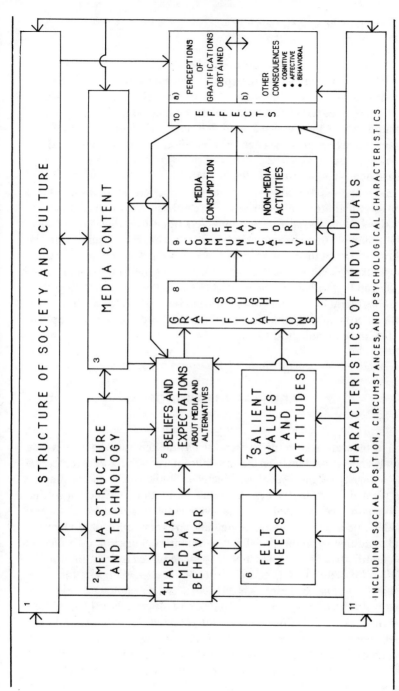

Figure 1.1   A General Media Gratifications Model

STRUCTURE OF SOCIETY AND CULTURE

1

2 MEDIA STRUCTURE AND TECHNOLOGY

3 MEDIA CONTENT

4 HABITUAL MEDIA BEHAVIOR

5 BELIEFS AND EXPECTATIONS ABOUT MEDIA AND ALTERNATIVES

6 FELT NEEDS

7 SALIENT VALUES AND ATTITUDES

8 GRATIFICATIONS SOUGHT

9 MEDIA CONSUMPTION BEHAVIOR / NON-MEDIA ACTIVITIES

10 EFFECTS
a) PERCEPTIONS OF GRATIFICATIONS OBTAINED
b) OTHER CONSEQUENCES
• COGNITIVE
• AFFECTIVE
• BEHAVIORAL

11 CHARACTERISTICS OF INDIVIDUALS INCLUDING SOCIAL POSITION, CIRCUMSTANCES, AND PSYCHOLOGICAL CHARACTERISTICS

17

Mirroring the complex nature of the phenomena under study, the model is multivariate and nonrecursive. The many arrows and boxes of the model may appear bewildering, but we believe they represent a minimum of concepts and relations to be included, if these complex phenomena are to be grasped at all. It is not particularly difficult to add boxes and arrows to the model. (For instance, we have not included any arrows directed toward other arrows, symbolizing the interaction effects often found in cases such as this one.)

In such a multivariate structure, no single element can assume a central explanatory role. Certainly the emphasis is not on gratifications obtained, as it must be in a traditional functional explanation (Cancian, 1968), nor is undue prominence given to needs. If any concept in the theoretical structure can be said to be central it is the gratifications sought from media exposure, thus underscoring the motivational nature of uses and gratifications theory. Yet the model makes clear that gratifications sought cannot be viewed in isolation, connected as they are in both antecedent and consequent fashion to a host of media, perceptual, social, and psychological variables.

RESEARCH FINDINGS

The theoretical structure represented by the general model has arisen slowly and painstakingly on the shoulders of a body of studies representing a variety of theoretical perspectives. While these studies may be aggregated in diverse ways, a useful conceptual scheme for sifting through the accumulated empirical evidence is suggested by the general model. Space limitations again preclude an examination of all elements and relationships in the model, but six major categories of research may be identified that are aligned more or less along a causal continuum. We shall follow this rough causal ordering in discussing, in turn, the research findings in these areas: (1) social and psychological origins of media gratifications; (2) expectancy-value approaches; (3) audience activity; (4) gratifications sought and obtained; (5) gratifications and media consumption; and (6) gratifications and media effects. As we shall see, many of these studies have begun to bridge certain important gaps observed by Blumler, Katz, and others a decade ago, while others point the way down new and promising paths of inquiry.

SOCIAL AND PSYCHOLOGICAL ORIGINS
OF MEDIA GRATIFICATIONS

John W. C. Johnstone (1974: 35), in a study of social integration and mass media use among adolescents, observed that "members of mass audiences do not experience the media as anonymous and isolated individuals, but rather, as members of organized social groups and as participants in a cultural milieu." This is a view shared by the majority of uses and gratifications researchers who "have always been strongly opposed to 'mass audience' terminology as a way of labelling the collectivities that watch TV shows, attend movies, and read magazines and newspapers in their millions" (Blumler, 1979: 21). According to this view, then, many of the media-related needs and requirements of individuals spring from their location in and interaction with their social environment.

Empirical Studies of Social Origins

Research has slowly begun to map certain features of the role of social context in generating motivations for media consumption (boxes 4, 8, and 11 in Figure 1.1). At least twenty studies may be identified that furnish empirical evidence on the role of demographic and social circumstances. In about half of these studies this examination has been largely exploratory, unguided by specific hypotheses grounded in theory, though in some cases informal "expectations" are voiced (for example, Becker and Fruit, 1982; Davis and Woodall, 1982; Greenberg, 1974; Hur and Robinson, 1981; Kippax and Murray, 1980; Lometti et al., 1977; Lull, 1980a; McQuail, 1979; Peled and Katz, 1974; Rubin, 1981a; A. Rubin and R. Rubin, 1982b). In most of these investigations the social origins of gratifications were not a primary focus of the study, and empirical data on the influence of demographic (in most cases) and social variables on gratifications is presented in subsidiary fashion. Only in a few cases are ex post facto explanations of observed relationships attempted. Still, these studies establish at a minimum that a variety of gratifications sought and obtained do have empirical ties with such variables as age, education, sex, income, family communication patterns, length of residence, discussions with others, and membership in organizations. In most cases the theoretical nature of these relationships awaits explanation.

A number of other studies have approached the question of social origins of gratifications via more theoretical avenues (Blumler, 1979; Brown et al., 1974; Hedinsson, 1981; Johnsson-Smaragdi, 1983; Johnstone, 1974; Nordlund, 1978; Palmgreen and Rayburn, 1979; Roe, 1983a, 1983b; Rosengren and Windahl, 1972, 1977; Rubin and Rubin, 1981). For example, Rosengren and Windahl (1977), working from a functional and compensatory theoretical framework, hypothesized and found support for a relationship between low potential for social interaction and parasocial interaction with mass media content. A study by Johnstone (1974), while not measuring gratifications directly, illustrates well the use of both compensatory and facilitative theorizing to postulate certain gratifications (escape, social orientation) as variables that intervene between social-structural variables and media consumption. Roe (1983a) proceeded from a similar structural-cultural perspective, but employed a more qualitative methodology, in examining the social uses that Swedish adolescents make of videocassettes. Roe demonstrates how social demands, interests, and expectations can lead to facilitative uses of a mass medium to promote social integration.

At least two conclusions about the social origins of media-related gratifications seem warranted. First, sufficient empirical evidence has now accumulated so that it is possible to state that many uses of the mass media do appear to have their origins in societal structure and social processes. Second, we are only beginning to understand the nature of the theoretical linkages. Certainly Katz et al. (1974) and Levy (1977b) are correct in observing that no general theoretical framework exists linking gratifications to their social origins. However, we might ask where else in mass media research such a general theory exists, and in any case, is it fair to apply such a standard at this stage? If theory is treated more as a goal than as an evaluative standard, then some limited progress has been made. Blumler's (1979) concepts of normative influence, social opportunity, and subjective social adjustment, along with Johnstone's (1974) and Roe's (1983a) concept of social orientation, have received some empirical support and deserve further elaboration and testing. Other concepts, such as social integration and life cycle seem equally promising. Whatever the conceptual framework, many more theoretical studies of social origins are needed if the uses that audience members make of the mass media are to be placed in their proper social and cultural context.

Psychological Origins

Psychological factors may also provide the motivational stimulus or point of origin for much media use. This is hinted at by Blumler's "subjective adjustment" to the social situation, but the topic has received its only extensive theoretical treatment in McGuire's brilliant essay on the psychological motives for media use. His sixteen-cell classification scheme for human motives highlights the relevance of a large number of psychological theories for understanding the cognitive and affective underpinnings of media consumption. Consistency, attribution, complexity, and various personality theories are among those McGuire examines for their usefulness in generating hypotheses about media gratifications.

Few studies, however, have traced empirical connections between gratifications and their psychological roots, and these have been limited to the examination of personality variables (Nordlund, 1978; Rosengren and Windahl, 1977) or attitudes (Greenberg, 1974; Hur and Robinson, 1981). It is true that more recent approaches to gratifications phenomena have been distinctly cognitive in nature. This is particularly true of the expectancy-value approach (treated later in this chapter), which includes such psychological concepts as beliefs, values, and perceptions (perceived gratifications obtained). These variables, though, are conceptualized as being in close causal proximity to gratifications sought, and are not in any sense thought of as causally more distant "origins" of media motivation. Thus McGuire's call goes largely unheeded a decade after it was issued.

AN EXPECTANCY-VALUE APPROACH

A concept central to most models of uses and gratifications phenomena is that of "expectancy." Numerous authors have employed the term (for example, see Katz et al., 1974; McLeod and Becker, 1981; Mendelsohn, 1974; Peled and Katz, 1974), and it is a key element in Katz et al.'s (1974) précis of the uses and gratifications approach presented earlier. Indeed, the concept of audience expectations concerning the characteristics of the media and potential gratifications to be obtained is essential to the uses and gratifications assumption of an active audience. If audience members are to select from among various media and nonmedia alternatives according to their needs, they must have some perceptions of the alternatives most likely to meet those needs.

Until recently, however, theory development in the area suffered from the lack of a rigorous conceptualization of expectancy. Expectations have been variously defined as probabilities of satisfaction assigned by audience members to various behaviors (McLeod and Becker, 1981), as audience demands upon the media (Peled and Katz, 1974), as affective anticipations regarding the prospects of particular events having certain consequences (Mendelsohn, 1974), and as gratifications sought (Katz et al., 1973).

Substantial conceptual clarification results if one adopts an expectancy-value approach to uses and gratifications, as certain authors (Babrow and Swanson, 1984; Blood and Galloway, 1983; Galloway and Meek, 1981; Palmgreen and Rayburn, 1982, 1983, 1984; Rayburn and Palmgreen, 1983, 1984; Van Leuven, 1981) recently have advocated.[2] Although the various theories under this label differ somewhat in their emphases (Atkinson, 1957; Fishbein, 1963; Fishbein and Ajzen, 1975; Rotter, 1954; Tolman, 1932; Vroom, 1964), all view behavior, behavioral intentions, or attitudes (or all three) as a function of (1) *expectancy* (or belief)—that is, the perceived probability that an object possesses a particular attibute or that a behavior will have a particular consequence; and (2) *evaluation*—that is, the degree of affect, positive or negative, toward an attribute or behavioral outcome.

Palmgreen and Rayburn (1982, 1983, 1984; Rayburn and Palmgreen 1983, 1984) have been exploring the interrelationships among beliefs, evaluations, gratifications sought, gratifications obtained, and media exposure (boxes 5, 7, 8, 9, 10a in Figure 1.1). Their research indicates that expectations of media characteristics are important factors influencing motives to seek associated gratifications, which in turn influence media consumption. Such consumption results in the perception of certain gratifications obtained, which then feed back to reinforce or alter an individual's perceptions of the gratification-related attributes of a particular newspaper, program, program genre, or whatever, as depicted in the general model. For instance, if a person values "information about current issues and events" positively and believes (expects) that television news possesses such information, he or she will be motivated to seek such information from television news (boxes 5, 7, 8). Assuming that television news is available to the audience member, exposure to television news programming should result. If the audience member obtains the expected information, this outcome (GO) will feed back to reinforce the initial belief about this program attribute (feedback arrow from box 10a to box 5). If he or she obtains the information at a lower or higher level than expected, then his or her associated belief should be altered, with a consequent change in motivation to seek information about current issues from television news.

An expectancy-value approach thus helps explicate certain fundamental gratification-consumption processes. It also possesses a number of other theoretical ramifications for such processes, which Palmgreen and Rayburn explore in Chapter 3.

Audience Activity

Uses and gratifications researchers have long been opposed to the old "hypodermic needle" concept of a passive media audience absorbing uncritically and unconditionally the symbolic output of all powerful media. Instead, uses and gratifications researchers have argued that audience members confront their experience actively, taking from it in accordance with the particular gratifications they pursue and the perceived abilities of the various media sources to satisfy these gratifications. Although this assumption has been criticized severely by some (for example, Elliot, 1974), it still constitutes one of the essential theoretical underpinnings of the approach. Rosengren has characterized uses and gratifications research as a finalistic or purposive approach based on a voluntaristic perspective, as opposed to media effects research that is more causal and deterministic in nature (Rosengren, 1984; Rosengren et al., 1983).

As Blumler (1979) has observed, it is unfortunate that uses and gratifications researchers have treated the concept of audience activity more as an "article of faith" than as an empirical question deserving of investigation. One of the reasons for this neglect, according to Blumler, is the "extraordinary range of meanings" associated with the activity concept, including utility, intentionality, selectivity, and imperviousness to influence. Swanson (1977, 1979b) adds still another connotation in insisting that audience activity be equated with the process of constructing meaning from message elements.

Building upon these and other interpretations, Levy and Windahl in Chapter 6, and in an earlier empirical study (Levy and Windahl, 1984), have mounted the most serious attempt to date to conceptualize and investigate empirically what is undeniably a complex, multidimensional construct. They conceive of a typology of audience activity constructed from two dimensions. The first dimension, *audience orientation,* is qualitative in nature and consists of three levels: (1) selectivity, (2) involvement, and (3) utility. Borrowing from Blumler (1979), they posit a second and *temporal* dimension that subdivides activity based on its occurrence before, during, or after exposure. The result is a potentially rich, ninefold typology that suggests a number of research questions, including those about the frequency with which different types of activity occur, the relationships among these types of activity, the implications of activity types for media effects, and the distribution of activity levels across media and audience subgroups.

From a theoretical standpoint, however, one of the most important findings of the Levy and Windahl (1984) study is that measures of gratifications sought and obtained were related consistently and positively to three different measures of activity (boxes 8, 9, 10a). That is, the more audience members were motivated in their use of television news and the more they perceived various types of gratification, the more active they were in their television news consumption.

Studies of Medium and Content Choice

While studies that have attempted direct measurement of audience activity are few (see also Levy, 1978b, 1983), indirect evidence is available from several studies that speak to various aspects of the activity question. For example, if activity is guided by motivations for media use and expectations concerning different media channels, audience members should differentiate among these channels on the basis of gratifications sought and/or obtained. There is a good deal of empirical evidence that supports this hypothesis. In a classic study of Israeli media use, Katz, Gurevitch, and Haas (1973) showed via multidimensional scaling that audience members differentiated among five different media on the basis of perceived gratifications obtained (boxes 2, 3, 9, 10a, Figure 1.1). Lometti et al. (1977), also using multidimensional scaling, showed that respondents differentiated among six media and two interpersonal channels along three dimensions. Similar empirical data on the ability of audience members to distinguish among different media on the basis of gratifications sought or obtained are provided by

Peled and Katz (1974), McLeod and Becker (1981), Becker and Fruit (1982), de Bock (1980), and Mendelsohn and O'Keefe (1976).

Lometti et al. (1977) have noted that such studies confound medium and content characteristics. While this may be true, such investigations do show that gratifications and media choice are related, providing empirical evidence for the "selectivity" and "utility" aspects of activity identified by Levy and Windahl. Still other studies, though, have "controlled" for type of medium by investigating the relationship of gratifications to content choice *within* a single medium. A. Rubin and R. Rubin (1982b) found through canonical analysis that viewing of daytime serials and game shows was associated with seeking of companionship, relaxation, arousal, habit, and passing the time. By comparison, viewing of TV news, documentary magazines, and talk shows was associated most strongly with an information-learning motive. Other studies that relate gratifications to choice of content within a medium are Nordlund (1978), Rubin (1981a, 1983), and Palmgreen et al. (1981). A few studies have failed to find evidence of gratification-related audience activity (Bantz, 1982; Kippax and Murray, 1980; Lichtenstein and Rosenfeld, 1983), but these appear to possess methodological difficulties (see Palmgreen, 1984b).

Activity and Meaning

We have said that information processing or the assigning of meaning to message elements is also an important dimension of audience activity. Garramone (1983) experimentally investigated the influence of "motivational set" on the processing of a televised political commercial. Subjects in an "issue set" learned more issue information and were more confident of their learning than those in an "image set." Those in the image set paid greater attention to the video portion of the ad, had greater confidence in their recall of video information, and were more likely than issue attenders to base personality inferences on information contained in the ad. McLeod and Becker (1981) have presented similar experimental evidence of the influence of motivations on the processing of media material. While the evidence is preliminary, it indicates audience members do actively process media content, and that this processing is influenced by motivation.

OTHER EMPIRICAL STUDIES

The selection of media sources, and thus audience activity of this type, is constrained by the number of possible choices the audience member has at his or her disposal (arrow from box 3 to box 9). Evidence is beginning to emerge that developments in communication technology that provide audience members with a greatly expanded repertoire of choices are also resulting in increased levels of selectivity (boxes 2, 3, 5, 8, 9). Heeter et al. (1983) examined channel selection data from 172 subscribers to a Florida interactive cable system. The head-end computer scanned channel-changing behavior once a minute continuously for one week. A great deal of channel changing took place, with a mean of 34 changes per household per day. Analysis of minute-by-minute changes showed change peaks on the hour and half hour, but significant levels of channel changing occurring throughout the hour. Although such data cannot relate such changes to audience motives and expectations, they do indicate that cable viewers are highly active in the process of selecting programs. Similar evidence of activity is found in a study of video recorder use by Levy and Fink (1984), who concluded that, in using video recorders for time-shifting and library-building purposes, VCR users are actively altering the broadcast schedule. They also observed that "recording and replay can be interpreted as an attempt by VCR users to maintain and perhaps increase those gratifications associated with certain types of television programs" (Levy and Fink, 1984: 59).

Finally, Barwise et al. (1982) studied 18,000 viewing diaries in New York City, Los Angeles, and San Francisco, gathered over a three-year period. Contrary to the earlier work of these authors, which has been widely cited as evidence of nonselectivity in the television audience (Goodhardt and Ehrenberg, 1969; Goodhardt et al., 1975), this study indicated a "marked degree of program loyalty." While availability acted as a constraint, repeat-viewing levels averaged 50 percent for most program types. About 60 percent of those viewing one episode of a program are viewing TV at the time the next episode is shown. Of these, 90 percent are engaged in repeat viewing. Repeat viewing levels were much higher than could be accounted for by *channel* loyalty. While still contending that the first stage of the viewing decision—whether to watch—is passive, Barwise et al. (1982: 27) conclude that the second-stage decision—what to watch—"does not seem so passive. Viewers do not just pick a program at random."

GRATIFICATIONS SOUGHT AND OBTAINED

In the early to mid-1970s, a number of media scholars (for example, Greenberg, 1974; Katz et al., 1973; Lometti et al., 1977) stressed the need to distinguish between the motives for media consumption or gratifications sought (GS) and the gratifications perceived to be obtained (GO) from this experience (boxes 8 and 10a). Research until then had neglected the distinction empirically, and thus an important theoretical link was being ignored. Whether the motivations that lead an individual to media consumption are equivalent to the perceived outcomes of that consumption should have important ramifications for future media behavior, as well as for media evaluation (McLeod et al., 1982).

In the past five years a considerable amount of research has been directed at examining the relationship between GS and GO and the combined and independent impact of these variables on media consumption and effects (Levy and Windahl, 1984; McLeod and Becker, 1981; McLeod et al., 1982; Palmgreen and Rayburn, 1979, 1984; Palmgreen et al., 1980, 1981; Rayburn and Palmgreen, 1983, 1984; Rayburn et al., 1984; Wenner, 1982, 1983a). One major finding of this research is that individual gratifications sought display moderately strong correlations (.40-.60) with corresponding gratifications obtained (Levy and Windahl, 1984; McLeod et al., 1982; Palmgreen et al., 1980; Rayburn and Palmgreen, 1983, 1984; Rayburn et al., 1984; Wenner, 1982, 1983a). This, combined with the generally much lower incidence of correlations observed between noncorresponding GS and GO, lends considerable support to a feedback model relating gratifications sought and obtained (by way of beliefs and expectations about the media; arrows from boxes 10a to 5 to 8).

On the other hand, gratifications sought are separable empirically as well as conceptually from gratifications obtained. There are several reasons for this conclusion. First, despite the "moderately strong" label that conventional usage would attach to the GS-GO correlations noted above, there is still considerable variance (65 percent to 85 percent) that GS and GO measures do *not* share. Gratifications sought and obtained do influence, but do not determine, one another. Second, the dimensions of GS and GO have been found to differ in some studies (McLeod et al., 1982; Palmgreen et al., 1980). Third, mean levels of gratifications sought often differ from mean levels of gratifications obtained. Fourth, at least two studies have found that GS and GO contribute independently to variance in media consumption and effects measures (arrows from box 8 to boxes 9 and 10b, and between boxes 10a and 10b) (Wenner, 1982, 1983a). As Roberts and Bachen (1981) point out, such findings clearly argue against any teleological criticism that any gratification sought must necessarily be obtained.

Illuminating the nature of the relationship between what people seek from media experience and what they obtain is, of course, one important contribution to uses and gratifications theory resulting from GS-GO research. An equally important result, however, is the finding that GS and GO are related in different ways to such variables as exposure, program choice, media dependency, and beliefs and evaluations of media attributes. For example, Palmgreen et al. (1981) found that GS generally did not discriminate between viewers of the three major American television network news programs, while a GO discrepancy model was highly successful in predicting news program choice. This finding was replicated for the most part in a study conducted by Rayburn et al. (1984) of morning news programs. Wenner (1982, 1983a), using a "transactional" hierarchical regression approach, showed that GS and GO contribute separately to variance in television news exposure and dependency, after the inclusion of demographic and exposure measures. Also, as discussed previously in connection with expectancy-value approaches, gratifications sought are influenced by both beliefs (expectancies) about and evaluations of media attributes, while perceived gratifications obtained are essentially unrelated to evaluative assessments, though they are strongly related to beliefs.

It is clear from these and other GS-GO research findings that researchers must distinguish between gratifications sought and obtained conceptually, operationally, and analytically. In the past, failure to make this distinction has often led to errant conclusions and conceptual confusion. Also, while investigations may focus on either concept, current GS-GO research demonstrates that separate measurement of both GS and GO within the context of the same study often leads to richer interpretations and increased understanding of the processes of audience-media interaction.

GRATIFICATIONS AND MEDIA CONSUMPTION

Research on the relationship between gratifications (both sought and obtained) and media consumption falls into two main categories: (1) typological studies of media gratifications (boxes 8 and/or 10a), and (2) studies that investigate the empirical association between gratifications sought and/or obtained on the one hand and measures of media exposure or medium or content choice on the other (boxes 8, 9, and 10a).

Typological studies, as noted earlier, are at the core of the first two phases of the uses and gratifications tradition and have as their main purpose the identification of types of motives for media consumption. Regarding the second study type, a survey of the literature reveals more than twenty investigations that show empirical associations between various gratification measures (both sought and obtained) and media exposure, medium choice, and content choice (Becker, 1976; Becker and Fruit, 1982; Blood and Galloway, 1983; Blumler and McQuail, 1969; Davis and Woodall, 1982; Greenberg, 1974; Hedinsson, 1981; Hur and Robinson, 1981; Kippax and Murray, 1980; McLeod and Becker, 1974; McLeod et al., 1979, 1982; McQuail, 1979; Nordlund, 1978; Palmgreen and Rayburn, 1979; 1982; Palmgreen et al., 1981; Peled and Katz, 1974; Rosengren and Windahl, 1972; Rubin, 1981, 1983; A. Rubin and R. Rubin, 1982b; Wenner, 1983a). While only one of the above-cited studies provides data of a longitudinal nature (Blood and Galloway, 1983) and the evidence is thus primarily correlational, when combined these investigations provide rather impressive documentation of the ability of a wide variety of gratifications indices to predict a still wider variety of media consumption measures in diverse settings ranging from peacetime presidential campaigns to media use in a war zone.

The majority of research to this point concerns television, including total TV exposure; exposure to different program content types, such as television news, debates, and quiz shows; public television viewing, and viewing of specific programs (such as *Roots*). Studies also show that gratifications are related to program choice. The published research does not relate exclusively to television, however. Kippax and Murray (1980) found that perceived gratifications obtained from each of five different media generally were positively related to exposure to the five media. Other studies that relate gratifications and needs to exposure to newspapers, radio, and other media include McLeod et al. (1979), Nordlund (1978), Rosengren and Windahl (1972), Kline et al. (1974), and Becker and Fruit (1982). The Becker and Fruit study also provides evidence that audience members' comparisons of gratifications obtained from different media are related to medium choice. Respondents' evaluations of newspapers and television (relative to one another) concerning the ability of these media to satisfy local and national information needs were related to choice of one or the other medium for either local or national news.

In general, the various media consumption studies show low to moderate correlations (.15-.40) between the gratification measures and consumption indices. While not large, the observed correlations are in the range of those generally found in cross-sectional surveys of mass media behavior, including "effects" studies. Also, approximately half the studies cited employed statistical controls, sometimes multiple controls, for a variety of demographic, exposure, and political variables. Thus data from studies in the United States, Britain, Sweden, Israel, and Australia are supportive of the key postulate that mass media consumption is motivated by gratifications associated with the consumption experience. Moreover, the research evidence speaks strongly against univariate or bivariate motivational schemes, since several investigations have found consumption predicted by multiple motivations. While much media consumption may be accidental, and though consumption is certainly constrained by such factors as availability and work schedule, as Bogart (1965) and others have contended, it is clear that motivation also plays a substantial role.

GRATIFICATIONS AND MEDIA EFFECTS

Earlier we noted Katz et al.'s (1974) conclusion a decade ago that hardly any empirical or theoretical effort had been expended in attempts to examine the relationship, if any, between motives for media use and subsequent effects (arrow between boxes 8 and 10b, arrow between boxes 10a and 10b). More recently, Blumler (1979) decried the lack of theoretical advancement brought about by an "exceedingly spare" list of published gratifications-by-effects studies. Windahl (1981) has also called for a merger of the effects and uses and gratifications traditions and has proposed a "uses and effects" model that treats the interactive outcome of media content and media use as "conseffects."

A review of the literature reveals that this long-desired merger, if not actually realized, has at least reached the point of serious negotiations. At least twenty empirical studies of a "uses and effects" variety may now be enumerated, two-thirds of which have appeared in the past five years (Becker, 1976; Blumler and McQuail, 1969; de Bock, 1980; Garramone, 1983; Greenberg, 1974; Hedinsson, 1981; Hur and Robinson, 1981; McLeod and Becker, 1974; McLeod et al., 1974, 1977, 1980; Nordlund, 1978; Roe, 1983b; Rosengren and Windahl, 1977; Rubin, 1981a, 1983;

A. Rubin and R. Rubin, 1982b; Weaver, 1980; Wenner, 1982, 1983a; Windahl et al., 1983).

These studies have shown that a variety of audience gratifications (again, both sought and obtained) are related to a wide spectrum of media effects, including knowledge, dependency, attitudes, perceptions of social reality, agenda-setting, discussion, and various political effects variables. Most of the investigations employed statistical controls for media exposure and/or demographic and other variables, with several using multivariate techniques, such as hierarchical regression, canonical correlation, multiple classification analysis, and structural equation modeling. The likelihood of spuriousness is therefore greatly reduced. In the studies using hierarchical regression (McLeod and Becker, 1974; McLeod et al., 1977; Wenner, 1982, 1983a) gratifications accounted for additional effects variance after the introduction of exposure and other control variables. In addition, at least three studies using self-report gratification measures have employed panel designs (Blumler and McQuail, 1969; McLeod and Becker, 1974; McLeod et al., 1977), with gratifications sought predicting later media effects. Another study involving inferred gratifications also used a panel design (Roe, 1983b). Cross-cultural validation stems from the fact that the investigations were carried out in four countries (United States, Great Britain, Sweden, and the Netherlands). Although the majority of the studies are about television, several of them provide data on newspapers.

Tests of a Theoretical Perspective

Blumler (1979: 15-16) criticized the few, mostly exploratory, uses and effects studies that had appeared until then for the lack of a theoretical perspective, for "feeding a number of audience orientations into the computer at the gratifications end and seeing what emerges at the effects end." Unfortunately, this still constitutes a reasonably accurate description of some uses and effects studies. While gratifications are often shown to enhance or mitigate effects, the theoretical nature of the relationship is sometimes neglected or treated only ex post facto.

In an attempt to stimulate a more theoretical approach, Blumler (1979) offered three hypotheses, based on a tripartite classification of commonly observed gratifications: (1) *Cognitive motivation* will facilitate information gain; (2) *diversion and escape motivations* will favor audience acceptance of perceptions of social situations in line with portrayals frequently found in entertainment materials; and (3) *personal identity motivations* will promote reinforcement effects.

Some empirical evidence has now accumulated that is relevant to each of these hypotheses. Regarding the hypothesis that cognitive or surveillance motivations should promote learning, McLeod and Becker (1974) found that surveillance was the strongest motivational predictor of knowledge gains during a political campaign. Similarly, McLeod et al. (1980) report that the surveillance motive predicted knowledge of an economic crisis, while communication utility did not. In a related vein, Atkin et al. (1973) and Atkin and Heald (1976) found that persons who viewed political ads for informational as opposed to "captive audience" reasons learned more about each candidate.

Two rare (for uses and gratifications research) *experimental* investigations cited previously in connection with audience activity also lend support to Blumler's hypothesis. Garramone (1983) and McLeod and Becker (1981) manipulated the motivational set with which subjects approached media content. The results of these studies support the survey findings in demonstrating that cognitive motivations of different types do affect learning from media materials. At the same time, they provide validational evidence for the self-report measures employed in the surveys.

The evidence available on the *diversion* hypothesis is not supportive, however, and suggests that the hypothesis should be reformulated. In four studies the strongest motivational correlate of the perceived content realism of television was an *information* (about life) motive (Greenberg, 1974; Rubin, 1979, 1981a, 1983). Viewing for escape or to forget, on the other hand, was either unrelated or related only weakly to perceived realism. In retrospect, it makes sense that those who perceive that television is an accurate reflection of life should also be those most likely to seek information about life from the medium. Content perceived as true to life, on the other hand, should hold little attraction for those seeking escape from their daily cares. Notice, however, that this hypothesis treats perceived television reality as a perceptual variable related to motives for media use, rather than as an effect of exposure. It should also be noted that the studies cited deal with the *perceived* reality of media portrayals. Such perception is not necessarily correlated with more objectively determined influence of, or learning from, such portrayals. Further investigations of Blumler's hypothesis that employ such objective measures are needed.

Finally, no direct data are available on Blumler's *personal identity* motivation hypothesis. This is partly due to the very broad nature of this audience orientation, as it seems to encompass reinforcement, identification, and parasocial interaction gratifications. Partial and indirect evidence is provided by Blumler and McQuail (1969) and McLeod and Becker (1981), who found that those seeking reinforcement during election campaigns manifested selective exposure to content about their own candidates. Some evidence of selective retention by reinforcement seekers was also found by McLeod and Becker.

CHALLENGES FOR THE FUTURE

From an integrative, theoretical perspective, the efforts of uses and gratifications researchers to come to grips with media consumption processes have not been in vain. Yet this progress should not breed complacency in the face of the many serious challenges that remain and that are certain to develop. Examining the general gratifications model presented earlier has heuristic value in identifying these challenges. It is obvious from such an examination that our knowledge of different conceptual areas is very uneven. Although additional research is needed in all these areas, some have received substantial empirical attention while others have been largely neglected. The "psychological characteristics" of box 11 (Figure 1.1), and the corresponding arrow to box 8, are included largely on the basis of reputation and McGuire's (1974) persuasive discussion of their relevance. Much additional research is obviously needed here. Also, while recent research on the social origins of gratifications has done much to negate the charge that gratifications research ignores social context, we are only beginning to understand the ways in which social-structural variables influence the matrix of values, needs, beliefs, and social circumstances that molds media behavior.

The recent trend toward more theoretically oriented studies must also be continued. An emphasis on variance explanation and post hoc theorizing still characterizes too many uses and gratifications investigations. General "expectations" must be replaced by directional hypotheses, and hypotheses must be grounded in well-articulated theoretical rationales. This is not to say that all investigations should follow the hypothetico-deductive model. There is certainly always a need, especially in new substantive areas, for exploratory studies of a descriptive nature. Careful conceptualization within the framework of ethnomethodological studies of media use can also contribute much to theoretical advancement (see James Lull's chapter in this volume). But whatever the approach, researchers should consider carefully the theoretical relevance and implications of their findings if the ultimate goal is a deeper understanding of processes of media consumption.

NEW COMMUNICATION TECHNOLOGIES

A major challenge that confronts uses and gratifications researchers is that of adapting and molding the current conceptual framework to deal with new communication technologies. Very little uses and gratifications research has addressed this issue, and yet it is a crucial one if we are to gain a better insight into the uses people have for cable television, teleconferencing, videocassettes, videotext, and other new communication systems. In addressing such issues, researchers should not be wedded to gratification typologies that the very changes under study may have rendered incomplete, if not obsolete. Williams and his associates in Chapter 13 examine in some detail the usefulness of approaching the communications revolution from a uses and gratifications perspective.

SOCIAL CHANGE

In a related and broader vein, researchers must realize the potential of the uses and gratifications approach to investigate processes of social change linked to mass communication. Given the nature of uses and gratifications theory that has evolved, charges by critics a decade or more ago that uses and gratifications research could only support the status quo now seem curiously outmoded. Carey and Kreiling (1974) and Elliot (1974) argued that (1) the uses and gratifications approach was based on functionalism; (2) functional theories deal with static, equilibrating systems and cannot accommodate change; and (3) policymakers could therefore maintain that current media structures were "functional" for audience members and no change in these structures was required.

Arguments have been advanced against each of these contentions by several authors (for example, see Blumler, 1979; Mendelsohn, 1974; Pryluck, 1975; Rosengren, 1974). In particular, we have contended here that current uses and gratifications theory is not functional in nature, unless one is willing to accept a radically altered definition of the term. Moreover, an examination of the general gratifications model of Figure 1.1 reveals several potential sources of change both in audience consumption behavior and in media structure and content. Of particular relevance is that perceived discrepancies between gratifications sought and obtained, which are frequently observed empirically (Palmgreen and Rayburn, 1979; Palmgreen et al., 1981; Rayburn et al., 1984; Wenner, 1982), may motivate changes in media consumption behaviors to reduce these discrepancies. Such changes in turn will stimulate changes in media content and structure in responsive media systems (boxes 8, 10, 2, 3). The empirical evidence cited earlier on gratifications sought and obtained does not support the critics' unrealistic assumption of the media's nearly perfect provision of the gratifications that audience members are seeking.

Change may also result from variations in the social and cultural milieu in which media use is embedded (see Melischek et al., 1984). Political and economic trends and upheavals bring with them substantial and sometimes radical alterations in needs, values, beliefs, social circumstances, and the structure and content of the mass media. The rapid evolution of media technology also forces individuals in modern society to confront a constantly varying and expanding array of choices. We would thus expect changes in both media consumption behaviors and media structures to be the norm rather than the exception. Maintenance of the status quo would be indicated only under circumstances in which gratifications obtained match those sought in a steady, unchanging environment, in the absence of reasonable alternatives and with unresponsive media systems.

Current uses and gratifications theory thus posits that change will arise from the dynamic interaction of an active, resourceful audience with responsive and equally resourceful media systems, within the context of fluctuating social, political, and economic environments. Where these conditions hold, uses and gratifications theory has the potential to provide new and fruitful insights into media-related social change.

A MULTIVARIATE COMPARATIVE MODEL

The general gratifications model presented earlier is based on the collective findings of a large number of uses and gratifications studies and research in related fields. While such first-generation multivariate procedures as factor analysis, multidimensional scaling, multiple regression, and canonical correlation have been employed, the great majority of investigations have been concerned with only limited portions of the general model. In many cases, only isolated, bivariate relationships are explored, albeit often with statistical controls. Such studies, of course, have the potential to provide an intensive view of the limited topic under investigation, but they do not provide a test of the multiple elements of the model as an integrated theoretical system. The process may be likened to examining an elephant through a magnifying glass: One may learn much about various parts of the anatomy, but it may be difficult to discern the nature of the beast.

What is needed in addition are studies that test large multivariate models incorporating indicators of many of the variable groupings in the general model less and that specify the complex relationships among these variables in a priori fashion. Only in this way may a true test of integrative models be accomplished. As Rosengren (1984) has discussed in detail, recent developments in second-generation multivariate procedures such as linear structural equation modeling now make this possible in uses and gratifications research. Procedures such as LISREL (linear structural relations) and PLS (partial least squares) have the capacity to handle large numbers of manifest and latent variables simultaneously, with either cross-sectional or panel data, and to carry out formal tests of alternative models. Their measurement models also provide a powerful means of improving the measurement of gratifications and related variables (see Hedinsson, 1981; Johnsson—Smaragdi, 1983; Roe, 1983b; Rosengren, 1984; Rosengren et al., 1983, for illustrations of LISREL in uses and gratifications studies).

Such techniques may also aid in the development of a *comparative* model of gratifications, media consumption, and media effects. The selection of a particular medium or interpersonal source does not occur in isolation, but involves a complex cognitive and affective comparison of the available alternatives. While a number of studies reviewed in this chapter have compared gratifications across different channels, none have attempted in a formal multivariate model to associate relative assessments of different media objects to media consumption, its origins, and its effects. Such a model introduces formidable measurement and analytical difficulties, which linear structural equation techniques can help overcome. While the development of such a model may be some years away, it has the potential to provide a much deeper understanding of the macro and micro forces governing individuals' use of modern mass media.

NOTES

1. There remains a tendency for most uses and gratifications researchers to employ the term "function" as a synonym for "gratification." This is unfortunate to the extent that it implies the sought gratification is "good" (or "functional") for the individual. The same difficulty is attached to the term "dysfunction." Such evaluative judgments have nothing to do with the task of explaining media consumption per se, although they are important in examining the broader ramifications of such consumption for the individual and society. It would aid the task of theorizing if uses and gratifications researchers would minimize the use of the terms "function" and "dysfunction" in favor of the less evaluative terms "gratification" and "avoidance."

2. Lundberg and Hultén (1968) provide an early example of the use of a conceptualization similar to expectancy-value theory, though the authors do not draw an explicit connection. Respondents rated the perceived importance to them of certain goals, and the perceived instrumentality of the media in helping them achieve these goals. A multiplicative index of the two measures predicted reported media use successfully.

PART II

PERSPECTIVES ON THEORETICAL ISSUES

THE SOCIAL CHARACTER
OF MEDIA GRATIFICATIONS

Jay G. Blumler

THE SOCIOLOGICAL CREDENTIALS of the uses and gratifications tradition of mass communication research are rather like those (in times past) of a marriage in Gretna Green or a divorce in Mexico: valid for some, but not universally accepted.

In part, this may be due to the evident patchiness of published work on the social forces that impel people to turn to the mass media for the gratification of certain needs. Even sympathetic commentators seem obliged to note that on this front the uses and gratifications portfolio of accomplishment is still somewhat thin. According to McLeod and Becker (1981), for example:

> The locations in social structure of motive patterns and of the ability to use media content to achieve satisfaction is an inadequately researched issue. Surely the harsh realities of being poor, of living in decaying cities, and the like have some connection to media uses and gratifications and their effects.

Palmgreen (1984b) has also concluded that "many more theoretical studies of social origins are needed if the uses which audience members make of the mass media are to be placed in their proper social and cultural context."

More fundamentally, however, the uses and gratifications approach has been tarred by sociologically minded critics with a brush of "mentalism." Elliott (1974), for example, has depicted its conceptual

AUTHOR'S NOTE: Many ideas in this chapter were first aired in discussion with Professor Denis McQuail.

framework as incorrigibly "individualistic" and "asocial." In the eyes of Bouillin-Dartevelle (1978), "the social significance of uses of mass media seems to have escaped the majority of researchers who have followed this method." According to Morley (1980), "Uses and gratifications is an essentially psychologistic problematic, relying as it does on mental states, needs and processes abstracted from the social situation of the individuals concerned."

Are such accusations just? On the one hand, the central concerns of uses and gratifications researchers (including the terminology through which these have been expressed) do sound personal, individualistic, even utilitarian. They focus on the audience member's media *uses* and *gratifications*. It is as if, when he or she has an itch (for escape perhaps), *Dynasty* will scratch it. (Or, if in need of reminiscence, *Coronation Street* may do the trick; for reassurance that the world is still in one piece, following the news would serve; and if loneliness is the problem, then almost any broadcast with chatty and attractive personalities should suffice.) Furthermore, different media are said to be patronized for their varying capability of satisfying such requirements—as if they were merely means to the realization of personal desires. (Such a thoroughgoing utilitarianism also structures relations between the prototypical professional communicator [C] and the gratification-seeking audience member [B] postulated in Westley and MacLean's (1957) influential model for communications research. It may be recalled that the former was there conceived as someone who was obliged, through competition for audience attention with other Cs, to select material "appropriate to B's need satisfactions or problem solutions.")

On the other hand, many authors of uses and gratifications studies have maintained that, when pursuing the sources of audience orientations, they were at least equally concerned with social as with personality variables (with "extra-individual characteristics" as with "intra-individual characteristics," in Rosengren's, 1974, terms). Before a cumulative tradition of such work had even been established, Merton (1949) had declared:

> Gratifications derived from mass communications are not merely psychological: they are also a product of the distinctive social roles of those who make use of those communications.

And, more recently, Katz et al. (1973) have claimed:

> Viewing the media in this way permits one to ask not only how the media gratify and influence individuals but how and why they are differentially integrated into social institutions. Thus, if individuals select certain media, or certain types of content, in their roles as citizens, or consumers,

or church members, we gain insight into the relationship between the attributes of the media (real or perceived) and the social and psychological functions which they serve.

The aim of this chapter is to explore the issues posed by this conflict of perspective. Have uses and gratifications researchers significantly short-changed the social dimensions of audience experience? If so, what explains such neglect, and can it be put right? Is the uses and gratifications approach inherently asocial? Or can it be tailored to do full justice to the nature of the audience member as a social being? Such questions cannot be tackled without undertaking a certain amount of conceptual analysis. But first certain features of the attempts that have so far been made to study the impact of social circumstance on audience behavior should be noted.

THE RESEARCH RECORD

On the face of it, uses and gratifications scholars do appear to have been faithful to their own social brief, as it was defined in the approach's classic paradigm:

> They are concerned with 1) the social and psychological origins of 2) needs, which generate 3) expectations of 4) the mass media or other sources, which lead to . . . [Katz et al., 1974].

It is true that the time for merely exploratory effort is past: More theoretically guided studies are needed, focusing especially on the postulated impact of a wider and more imaginatively conceived range of social variables than those standard demographics of age, sex, and social status on which some investigators still too sparely rely. Nevertheless, a number of researchers have managed to trace the "social origins" of at least those media gratifications that they have been able to measure. Neither has theory development been neglected, and the literature now offers some overarching perspectives on the processes by which *varieties* of social circumstances might engender certain media-related needs. Blumler (1979), for example, proposed three such mechanisms: (1) normative influences on what individuals aim to get out of media fare; (2) the facilitation by socially distributed life chances (such as a higher education or frequency of social contact) of a richer involvement in media materials; and (3) the need to compensate via media consumption for a relative lack of socially distributed life chances given more abundantly to others (as in, say, lack of company, leisure outlets and resources, or a satisfying job). Other frameworks of comparable generality have been expounded by Rosengren and Windahl (1972), Johnstone (1974), Nordlund (1978), Dimmick et al. (1979), A. Rubin and R. Rubin (1982), and Roe (1983b). Meanwhile, as Palmgreen (1984b) points out, empirical research "has slowly begun to map certain features of the role of social context in generating motivations for media consumption."

However, two broad outcomes, as well as several decided biases (or limitations), of much "social origins" research have not yet received the attention they merit. The former may be illustrated by selected results from a wide-ranging survey that was fielded in Britain in 1975 at the Leeds University Centre for Television Research in cooperation with the Audience Research Department of the BBC.[1]

As explained in Blumler (1979), this was based on a sample of approximately 1000 adults who (1) endorsed a set of 32 gratification statements as true or not true of their uses of newspapers, of television as a medium, and of 4 recently viewed TV programs, and (2) answered many detailed questions about their social situations. Guided by factor analyses, the 32 gratification statements were reduced to 4 types of media satisfaction, scores for the attainment of each of which were assigned to each respondent: surveillance, curiosity, diversion, and personal identity.

The first major pattern in the findings worth stressing is the complex latticework of social influences on media gratifications disclosed. They could be pictured as a set of different mazes—often meaningful but certainly intricate.

For one thing, the social factors associated with media satisfactions differed according to the individual's stage of life at the time. This feature is illustrated by Table 2.1, showing which background variables emerged from AID analyses as the best discriminators between high-scoring and low-scoring individuals for each of the four gratification areas in uses of television and the press made by full-time workers, nonworking housewives, and retired people, respectively. It can be seen that, whatever the focus of media satisfaction, the most powerful background discriminant was rarely the same in even two of the three subsamples. Thus diversion seeking from television was most strongly associated with a lack of organizational affiliation among retired people; with lower educational background among housewives; and with an instrumental attitude toward work among the fully employed. For surveillance seeking from television, being housebound was the most powerful discriminator among housewives and the retired, whereas among full-time workers age (being older) was most powerful.

TABLE 2.1
AID Analyses of Social Position by Media Satisfaction Scores,
First Splitting Variables

	Television	*Press*
Diversion		
Full-time workers	instrumental work values	foreign travel (−)
Housewives	education (−)	age
Retired	organizational affiliations (−)	geographical mobility
Surveillance		
Full-time workers	age	occupational status
Housewives	frequency of getting out (−)	foreign travel
Retired	frequency of getting out (−)	geographical mobility
Curiosity		
Full-time workers	organizational affiliations	education
Housewives	geographical mobility (−)	geographical mobility
Retired	foreign travel	foreign travel
Personal Identity		
Full-time workers	age	worry about job loss
Housewives	age	car ownership (−)
Retired	education (−)	geographical mobility

And for satisfying personal identity needs through television, the best predictor among the retired was a limited education, but among housewives and the fully employed it was a function of age (being older).

In addition, the impact of social situation on media satisfaction differed according to the medium concerned. Of twelve television-press comparisons shown in Table 2.1, only two yielded the same best predictors. Among the retired, for example, diversion seeking from television was best explained by lack of organizational membership but in press use it was shown to be by experience of geographical mobility; among housewives, a need for diversion from television was most closely associated with a limited education, but age (being older) as the primary factor when the same satisfactions were sought from newspaper reading; and among the fully employed workers, having an instrumental attitude toward work best explained uses of television for diversion, while lack of travel abroad went most strongly with diversion scores for press use.

Moreover, very few social position variables were related to gratification variables in a straightforward or linear fashion. Those that did so were familiar and unsurprising, for example, a tendency for more men to derive cognitive satisfactions from media use than women (and vice versa for noncognitive satisfactions); a usually positive correlation of educational background with surveillance concerns and an inverse association with diversion concerns; and a tendency for surveillance scores to rise as people grew older (at least until they reached retirement age).

More commonly, the impact of a social factor tended to depend on the presence or absence of other conditions. For example, we had postulated that people not gainfully employed would be more likely than those working full time to seek diversion from media fare. But in the Leeds survey, such a relationship applied only to male respondents, who (particularly if they were less educated, sick, disabled, or retired) were more likely to seek diversion gratifications from television. No such pattern emerged for women. Men were left with time on their hands, while women could still be fully occupied in housework or looking after the children.

Another case in point is the role of geographical mobility; a greater number of recent residential moves were associated with a greater need for surveillance, diversion, and personal identity, notably from newspaper reading. This finding was more pronounced among retired people, for whom it was more a manual than a nonmanual phenomenon. Such contingencies suggest that mobility is more disruptive for older people, who may find it more difficult to make new friends at an advanced age, and for manual workers, some of whom may either be more dependent on local contacts for their social satisfactions or lack the confidence that special efforts to forge new contacts will succeed.

Yet another striking example has previously been reported by Blumler (1979): the significance for certain media gratifications of not having a telephone in the house. Sometimes associated with higher diversion and personal identity scores, this was more significant for individuals who stayed at home all day—housewives and retired people—than for full-time workers. Among such housebound sample members, it mattered more for individuals of nonmanual than of manual background, a class distinction that was particularly marked among the housewives. It was as if the deprivation arising from not having a telephone was felt more keenly by middle-class women, many of whom may use it as an instrument of daily social contact.

The disposition of an audience to project a certain requirement onto a certain medium is thus quite a composite conglomerate. Diversion seeking from television, for example, is a product of pressures stemming from myriad sources. With "social origins," then, it is not simply that many roads lead to Rome. It is also that there are many Romes and most of the roads are full of bends and forks!

Perhaps two implications follow from such results. One is methodological. When investigating the social factors productive of media gratifications, we should not normally look for the best linear predictor from several possible independent variables. Instead, we should be tracing the social origins of audience gratifications through interactive contingencies, such that certain variables may prove influential when other conditions are met. For this purpose, whole-population sampling may be less appropriate than more specialized sampling approaches, based on the prior identification of potentially formative junctures in people's life circumstances, holding them constant, and examining the influence within them of a range of theoretically pertinent social differences on individuals' media motivations and uses. A. Rubin and R. Rubin (1982a) have demonstrated the richness of findings that such a strategy can yield, in their investigation among the elderly of relations between sociodemographic characteristics, so-called contextual factors of social and communication environment, and viewing motivations.

The tangled tracery of social paths to media gratifications may also have implications for that merger of uses and gratifications and effects traditions, which has been called for by (among others) McLeod and Becker (1974) and Windahl (1981). There is perhaps something anomalous about the contrast between the multiple "causation" of media gratifications from the social side and their presumed uniformity of impact on the effects side:

Social origins   Gratification   Effect

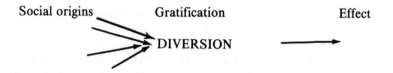

DIVERSION

Since diversion seekers, for example, are a very heterogenous group, we may not be able to take for granted that with a unitary measure for it, high scorers will all be (and react) the same.

A second outcome of the Leeds findings to be emphasized is the prominence among them of homologous or facilitatory linkages between social background characteristics and gratification scores (as distinct from compensatory scores). Such connections spanned several domains of life experience. In work, those with expressive occupational values were also more keen to derive cognitive satisfactions from media use. The number of organizations joined by respondents—trade unions, religious, charitable, professional, political, business, civic, educational, sports and social groups—also seemed to operate as a stimulant to information seeking. There was a greater sensitivity to the cognitive potentials of the media shown by workers whose experience had been broadened by foreign travel. And in some sample subgroups, estimated frequency of social contact and desire for more social contact ran the same way—chiefly reflecting a greater readiness on the part of the more sociable respondents to throw themselves personally into media consumption (shown by high scores for personal identity). A connection between these results might be found in the notion of commitment, as if a preparedness to invest some meaning through commitment in what one did in one domain (vocational, organizational, or recreational) had implications for a similar investment in media activity.

Such patterns could have implications for the very role of social factors in the classic uses and gratifications paradigm—for what they reflected seemed less to be instances of social *origins* of media needs than cases of a concordance between certain constellations of social *experience* and certain satisfactions sought from media experience. In other words, we might need to distinguish between two distinct models of how social situation may relate to media gratification. If so, the differences could be charted as follows:

Social Origins	*Social Experience*
causal sequence to needs	no necessary causal sequence
mainly compensatory processes	mainly facilitatory processes
adjustment model, such that the individual accommodates to environmental constraints with the help of the media	integrative model, such that what one is like and how one lives in certain spheres is carried over into how one uses the media

This observation serves to introduce several other little-noticed limitations in the attempts made to date to find out how social factors shape audience motives for media use. First, study of the impact of social position on media gratifications depends entirely on prevailing gratifications models. We can use social variables only to explain those gratifications that we have so far conceptualized, dimensionalized, and measured.

Second, research on the social sources of audience expectations has been heavily slanted toward the medium of television. This is understandable, since the revival of the uses and gratifications approach in the 1960s more or less coincided with the rapid and wholesale diffusion of television and the heavy inroads it made into virtually everybody's leisure time. It is an empirical bias nevertheless—and possibly a severely distorting one. For one thing, television is a distinctive medium, tending to offer something for everyone more or less at once. Content boundaries are widely drawn, multifunctional needs, interests, and tastes are served, and heterogeneous audiences result. The goods concerned are so presented as to encourage audiences to sample a varied diet. It is thus a kaleidoscopic medium par excellence, and what viewers get is a smorgasbord. For another, there is some evidence that television is regarded by many audience members (typically its heaviest viewers) as catering best to their least essential needs (diversion, escape, passing time) in contrast to more involving cognitive and identity needs. Thus it is very different in organization and service from those media that group and segregate contents within firmly defined compartmental bounds, encouraging audiences to sample within rather than across streams (as in radio, cable TV, and many magazines).

Third, social factors have chiefly been conceived as *initiating* background influences in the gratifications process. Although, in principle, they should play a part at every stage in the chain (see Rosengren, 1974: 27), they have usually been treated merely as instigators of a process, which, once under way, is played out largely at the intrapersonal level.

IN REVISIONIST SPIRIT: SOCIALIZING THE USES AND GRATIFICATIONS APPROACH

Taken together, these biases help to explain why the uses and gratifications approach may be accused fairly of having neglected certain social processes that significantly shape the media expectations of audience members. Two such omissions are considered in detail in the following sections of this chapter. In my view, the defects involved are corrigible. Although certain modifications of the uses and gratifications outlook are called for, their adoption is fully compatible with the essential elements of the approach: some priority of regard and valuation for the nature of the audience experience as understood by the media consumer himself or herself; stress on the potential of the individual to engage "actively" with at least some of the media materials in his or her life; interest in audience dispositions as governors of media exposure and mediators of communication effect.

THE LOSS OF SOCIAL IDENTITY

Consider two characterizations of the uses and gratifications approach to mass communication research. For Katz (1979), it is about the selectivity of personal interest and how the media are impressed "into the service of individual needs and *values.*" In Palmgreen's (1984b) view, an important concern should be how "social-structural variables influence the matrix of *values*, needs, *beliefs* and social circumstances which molds media behavior" (emphasis added in both cases). When such statements are related to published gratifications research, it is at once apparent that social values and beliefs rarely feature among accounts of audience motivation. Yet when investigators have encountered such a mainspring of audience orientation, meaningful and exciting results have sometimes emerged.

Various blindspots explain this gap. First, and most important, the main dimensions of audience gratification and concern have not made a separate space for a notion of *social identity*. Though apparently an ingredient in the McQuail et al. (1972) typology (for example, in the category of "value reinforcement"), it was subsequently lost to view. Second, on the social origins side of research, little attention has been paid to the *social group memberships and affiliations*, formal and subjective, that might feed audience concerns to maintain and strengthen their social identities through what they see, read, and hear in the media. Third, the *forms of media output* that might best gratify such needs have largely been ignored.

Loss of a "social identity" motivation for media use is partly due to the fact that certain early gratification typologies, on which later investigators often drew, had failed to find a home for it. For example, the otherwise insightful work of Rubin (1983) on viewing motivations leans heavily on the Greenberg (1974) schema of learning, habit, arousal, companionship, relaxation, escape, and passing time. Rubin's addition to that list of a "social interaction" category— comprising the items (1) Because it is something to do when friends come over, (2) So I can talk with other people about what's on, (3) So I can be with other members of the family or friends who are watching—is only a limited step in the required direction. Although social utility functions may be involved in communication-for-social-identity, they could not be said to embody the heart of that concept.

Another reason for neglect of social identity needs is their submergence in so-called *personal identity* clusters. According to Blumler (1979), the personal identity function stands for "ways of using media materials to give added salience to something important in the audience member's own life or situation," among which valued social attachments should be prominent. Yet in the very Leeds research that was intended to explore the social origins of mass media satisfaction, personal identity was measured using the following items:

(1) It sometimes reminds me of past events in my life.

(2) It shows what others are thinking about people like me.

(3) It gives me support for my ideas.

(4) I sometimes find examples of how to get on with others.

(5) It makes me wish I were like some of the people I see or read about.

(6) I can imagine myself in situations I see or read about.

(7) It makes me feel as if I really know the people I see or read about.

One can faintly discern a "social" component floating amid such statements—especially in "It gives me support for my ideas"—but it is quite diluted by the more personal elements.

On the face of it, the mapping-sentence strategy followed by Katz et al. (1973) and replicated with minor revisions by Kippax and Murray (1980) should have captured social identity impulses for media use. The authors assembled as comprehensive a list as possible of "social and psychological needs said to be satisfied by exposure to the mass media." They also classified those needs by certain "facets," including needs likely to perform "an integrative function," related to "strengthening contact with family, friends and the world." But some of the socially loaded items in their 35-statement inventory were worded in rather general terms and abstracted from any concrete affiliation (such as, "To feel that I am influential"; "To feel that others think as I do"; "To spend time with friends"; "To learn how to behave among others"). Although other items did refer to more specific collectivities, they comprised only the family and the Israeli state, giving the list a "sociopolitical bias" acknowledged by Katz et al. (1973) themselves.

Actually such a bias applies to the entire uses and gratifications field, not just the Israeli research. That is, we probably know most about how people project their social identities into their media expectations and uses in two of their roles: as family members (as in the work of Lull, 1980b) and as citizens (stemming from the line of research into political communication gratifications initiated by Blumler and McQuail, 1968, and summarized for later replication and extensions in Becker, 1979; McLeod and Becker, 1981). Yet a host of other roles emerging from the elaborately differentiated structure of modern society has virtually been ignored in uses and gratifications research. One reason for such neglect may be the pressure to operationalize and quantify gratification measures that dominated much of the tradition's more systematic phase from the early 1960s onward. This encouraged the design of surveys of sampled audience members' orientations to media generally. Correspondingly, less attention was paid to those more focused forms of media content (such as individual programs, magazines, and newspapers) in which possessors of certain social identities are more likely to find reflections and confirmations of their own roles. Fascination with television also played a part. As a national medium, attracting highly heterogeneous audiences viewing at home, television is most likely to address those roles that are more or less universally shared—namely, those of family membership and citizenship.

If we continue to tolerate such a bias, however, we will be able to tell only half the social story of the modern communications revolution, which, according to Carey (1969), has both centripetal and centrifugal dimensions. The former is reflected in the rise of national media, which "allowed individuals to be linked, for the first time, directly to a national community without the mediating influence of regional and other local affiliations." Although they include a certain amount of specialist material, such media chiefly "give public and identifiable form to symbols and values of national identity and also block out of public communication areas of potential conflict." For its part, the centrifugal dimension emerged from "the development of specialised media of communication located in ethnic, occupational, class, regional and other 'special interest' segments of the society." And though "virtually unstudied," such minority media are "in many ways more crucial forms of communication."

SOME LESSONS FOR THE FUTURE

What positive lessons for future work follow from these observations? *First*, uses and gratifications researchers should return more often to the qualitative drawing board before settling on dimensions, items, and scales for quantitatively measuring media motivation. When doing so, they should endeavor especially to listen for expressions of social identity concerns and for indications of the vehicles through which they are being met. An example of what can emerge may be seen in past research on political television that employed the originally qualitatively based item, "To remind me of my party's strong points." This proved to be quite strongly associated in meaningful patterns with such variables as voters' partisanship levels (in attitudes toward their own and opposing parties), stability of voting behavior (within and across campaigns), knowledge levels, media preferences, and selectivity of exposure to campaign communication (Blumler and McQuail, 1968; Blumler et al., 1976).

Second, we should now be aiming to study more often those audience-content relations in which social identity concerns are most likely to be involved. For such a purpose, we should be looking at the readers of newspapers with characteristic editorial profiles (such as *The*

Washington Post rather than "the press"), fans of certain value-laden programs (not "television viewing" generally) and subscribers to those specialist magazines and journals that decorate news agents' shelves in such profusion nowadays. Given that many of these publications appear to admit readers to a sort of community that has its own rites, standards, pecking orders, models of excellence, leaders of fashion, reasons for pride in a pursuit or a way of life, and problematic concerns, they should also offer a wealth of socially relevant gratifications for inquiry to tap.

The potential of such an approach can be gleaned from past radio research in the Blumler et al. (1970) study of regular listeners to the long-running British soap opera, *The Dales*. This concluded that much of the program's appeal to fans "derived from its fidelity to a view of social reality that would conform to their own notions and experiences." The role of listeners' values surfaced in two of the study's six gratification clusters—labeled *reinforcement of family values* (including items such as "It's nice to know that there are families like the Dales around today"; "It reminds me of the importance of family ties"; and "It puts over a picture of what family life should be like") and *reinforcement of the social role of women* (including "It is free from the bad language you get so much of on TV"; "It makes a pleasant change from all the violence in society these days"; and "It is a way of being nosey without harming anyone"). Moreover, scores on those two clusters were associated most strongly with relevant social background particulars:

> An interest in using *The Dales* to reinforce one's sense of the value of family ties is found not only among older and more conservative-minded women, but also among the more lonely listeners, and among those women who, while deriving from large families of origin, were residing at the time of the interview in small households (in some cases no longer having a man in the house).

Also of interest was a certain feature of the value-reinforcement mechanism that the study uncovered. This seemed to entail not so much a cozy immersion of the audience in a program cocoon as a complex role of reassurance for listeners who saw themselves living in a world where what they stood for was often challenged in other parts of their social and communication environment. Similar relations among social identity, awareness of challenge to it from other quarters, and ways of using supportive media materials have surfaced from several ostensibly quite different pieces of research. For example, the Blumler and Mc-Quail (1968) study of political television gratifications concluded:

> A desire for reinforcement . . . was allied to a high degree of sensitivity to the key issues at stake in the 1964 election—regardless of the party that had projected them into the limelight.

It can be discerned in Roe's (1983a) finding that Swedish adolescents used video cassettes to exercise autonomy from parents and adults and to present an anti-establishment profile. It probably plays a part as well in the reactions to sports programs of loyal fans following the fortunes of their team against opponents (Gantz, 1981).

Third, sampling strategies should be devised that are designed to trace social identity needs in media consumption. One approach might concentrate on the members of a given group (ethnic, religious, trade union, professional, civic, political, or the like) whose affiliations and communication patterns might be connected. This approach might aim to tap (1) the varying salience and meanings of membership to different individuals and their associations with (2) the kinds of group-related communications they follow (especially mass media and interpersonal sources), (3) the place of the latter in their overall patterns of media use, and (4) the uses and gratifications (including social identity concerns) associated with such consumption. Another approach might place emphasis on the patrons of a given communication vehicle presumed to offer some form of social identity satisfaction. Here attention might focus on distinctions of background and outlook between individuals using such material in identity-strengthening ways and those looking for other satisfactions. The spread of cable television might offer opportunities to try yet another approach. Since most systems offer several different strands of relatively homogeneous programming, a cable-spanning study could aim to identify the uses and gratifications associated with different channels and how, if at all, they can be related to the social identities that matter to audience members.

Fourth, there is probably more than one form of matrix interconnecting identities and interests, and their reasons for using related communications. Groups could vary on such dimensions as being narrowly specialist or potentially more all-encompassing; their acceptability to or rejection by other groups in society; being self-sufficient or having claims on the rest of society; whether internally homogeneous or more differentiated; the nature of the principal unifying bond; and how in-group communication is organized. It follows that efforts should be made to generate typologies of different categories of group-based identities, including the sorts of communication needs that might flow from them.

One building block for such a scheme might be found in the work of Lewis (1981), who writes about "group set identities" centering on "taste cultures." In his view, many such "taste cultures" consist of shared "cultural choices" that function "both to entertain, inform and beautify life and to express values and standards of taste and aesthetics." Much of the discussion is illustrated by stylistic preferences in such cultural forms as music, drama, dress, and art. A quite different category is suggested by the case of magazines for homosexuals, which Carey (1969) treats as typifying how minority media organize scattered members of sectional groups into audiences. To their readers, such magazines are said to offer

> an encompassiong ideology, and explanation of their behaviour and an argument stipulating their relationship to the larger society. . . . In the pages of such publications are formulated the policies, complaints and aspirations of the group; friends and enemies are identified along with evidence of their goodness and badness. . . . In *One* and the *Mattachine Review* one finds rationalisations for the position of homosexuals and justifications couched in legal, moral and historical terms; . . . [as well as] legal articles pleading the case for the civil liberties of homosexuals.

In this example, the publications seem to pivot on more broadly political concerns (though lifestyle preferences would also be conveyed). Of course, many other publications, broadcast programs, and special sections of newspapers seem to cater to people grouped in yet another way—as devotees of some less specific pursuit, including anglers, gardeners, racing car drivers, microcomputer users, and do-it-yourselfers.

These examples suggest that group-based communication might center on one or more of three axes. For one type, aesthetic values, elements of taste and style, and notions of how most enjoyably to be playful could be uppermost. Its dedicated followers would be thought of as connoisseurs. For another type, the focus would be on specific interests, hobbies, and leisure activities, and those most fully involved would be thought of as experts. In yet another type, social purposes, loyalties, claims, and problems would be central, and the most committed members would be thought of as militants or activists. It is also intriguing to note some correspondence between these distinctions and the trichotomous gratification typologies that have emerged from much work on mass media audiences: *diversion* (corresponding perhaps to the playful axis); *cognitive* satisfactions (knowing how to pursue sports, hobbies, and other activities); and *identity* per se (most analogous to the social commitment dimension). People doing research into the social identity gratifications underlying communication patterns might therefore expect to find different balances of similar needs among individuals aligned with different types of groups.

Fifth, and finally, it should be noted that all this presupposes a pluralistic organization of society, containing many subsidiary groups and cultures. In such a society, many affiliations are formed without overt attempts to incorporate them all under some assumed-to-be superior and all-embracing loyalty. Moreover, freedom of association gives rise to a multitude of communication organs and messages, many of which are visible and available to all. No group's publications reach only its own members, unless special steps have been taken to ensure privacy.

Three consequences stem from such arrangements. First, any single individual may "belong" to a number of such groups, and he or she will value memberships and roles more highly than others. Measures of members' levels of identification with such groups, if they can be obtained, should therefore filter the types and amounts of gratification sought from their publications. Second, because everyone is exposed to communication from groups with loyalties different from, and perhaps opposed to, his or her own, special needs for in-group communication to reinforce its own value system may often arise (as noted in several examples above). Third, however, in a pluralistic society, it is almost as if some social identities are "offered for sale," while corresponding media fare seems at times to invite consumers to don and play with group identities and styles different from those they have previously assumed. This applies to some taste cultures (such as pop music for all generations perhaps) and may even play a part in persuasive communication. A certain amount of "identity volatility" is thus promoted by pluralistic communication arrangements. Consequently, the detection of shifts over time in audience gratifications for different specialist and minority interest publications and media materials could help keep us in touch with significant sociopolitical system changes as well.

THE ROLE OF THE AUDIENCE MEMBER

Social factors have often appeared in the extreme left-hand box of models of the uses and gratifications process. In such cases, they are visualized as doing little more than giving birth to the needs that are then directed to media and nonmedia alternatives for satisfaction.

Yet social factors may play on the uses and gratifications system at many more levels than just that of the stimulation of media needs, and it is time we took this more fully into account. For example, social conditions may affect the availability (via resources, preparation, and custom) of so-called functional alternatives to media sources of satisfaction. Or they may shape the relationship between media and nonmedia sources. In some social settings, media sources may complement, enrich, or express in different forms what nonmedia sources do—instead of offering only alternative outlets for what the latter could supply. In addition, social variables may mediate the relationship, which might be closer for certain types of people than others, between gratifications sought and obtained. In one test of such a possibility in election campaign conditions, McLeod et al. (1982) looked at the influence of age and time of voting decision on the validity of drive reduction and exposure learning models of relationships between political gratifications sought and received. In other cases other variables might be influential. Better-educated individuals, for example, reared to be critical, might be especially sensitive to discrepancies between what media contents seem to promise and what they actually offer. Media addicts (indiscriminate and unselective users) might encounter a lot of material falling short of their expectations. People suffering from social alienation (a condition that can be defined in terms of heightened awareness of a divorce between what should be and what is) might also be quick to find media fare disappointing.

Without some reconceptualization in social terms of the nature of audience members themselves, however, the most fundamental objections to research in this vein cannot be met. In most uses and gratifications models, audience members are merely vessels into which motives pour and out of which media behaviors flow. Yet this leaves out a vital element in the sequence of uses and gratifications processes—the notion of audience roles. This concept suggests the prescription for people in different social circumstances and of different views how most suitably to choose, follow, and use mass communications.

In a sociological sense, we would be justified in speaking of audience roles for at least two reasons:

> if it was established that people do relate to [mass media] communication in ways that are shaped by the expectations of others in their more immediate or remote environments or if communicators and audience members were found to be linked in a network of mutually shared expectations [Blumler, 1973].

Introspection, observation, and evidence strongly support the first line of justification. Women (in general) not only do not follow sports reports; they are not supposed to. In some social circles, one would be considered quite eccentric if seen perusing certain newspapers or journals. In some groups there is more support for round-the-clock television viewing and for seeing TV viewing's main purpose as one of gaining after-work relief and refreshment than in others. Thus social influences not only generate needs for media fulfillment, they also transmit ideas about such matters as the following:

- those gratifications that may suitably be satisfied in media use
- appropriate frequencies and manners of indulgence in media activity
- forms of content to be preferred and avoided
- how to tune in to certain media materials, or what one should expect to get out of them

This is because most media habits are formed and performed in social circumstances. With exceptions, of course, for certain individuals (single-person householders), situations (housewives on their own at home all day; motorists tuned to their car radios and cassettes), or forms of content (pornography), little media consumption is utterly private and unobserved.

Logic and a certain amount of evidence also support the second line of justification for conceiving of audience roles—a tendency for the shape that communicators give to media materials to intimate appropriate ways of attending to them. When going to a movie, for example, we may put ourselves in the mood that it seems designed to cultivate. In political communication, Gurevitch and Blumler (1977) have drawn attention to many correspondences of role orientation between the originators and receivers of messages:

Party Spokespersons	*Audience Members*
gladiator	partisan
rational persuader	liberal citizen
information provider	monitor
actor performer	spectator

And Patterson (1980) seems to have detected signs that people exposed to horse-race styles of campaign journalism were more likely to follow an American election in something like a spectator role, expecting, perhaps, to be excited and to be told the score.

Mass media systems, then, could be said to have developed within them a number of predefined options for relating to the communication experience, which may be termed "audience roles." Some examples might include the roles of fan, expert, aficionado; of gatekeeper (passing on media information to others); of information-seeking monitor; of spectator; of horizon-widening seeker of experience; of active participant; of escapee; of explorer or pilot-at-the-controls (as among skilled users of the new store-and-search communication technologies, perhaps). These are informal and unwritten of course, but they are made available to the media public via normative clues from social life, from senders, and also from the exercise of personal choice.

In conclusion, four advantages for the uses and gratifications perspective of developing such a roles notion may be mentioned. First, it speaks to the issue of audience activity and passivity, so central to the perspective. More or less active orientations to media use undoubtedly would form a part of different audience roles. Second, it offers ways of linking audience orientations with communicator orientations in mass media systems (as in the examples given above). Third, what uses and gratifications researchers investigate about audience members would no longer be just an intervening factor, pursued in the service of *other* phenomena (explaining media exposure or effects), but a socially regulated phenomenon deserving of study in its own right. And fourth, what we investigate could no longer be regarded as a merely "mentalistic" entity. We would have finally done justice to the "social character of media gratifications."

NOTE

1. The research was conducted in collaboration with Professors Michael Gurevitch and Denis McQuail. The material presented in this section also draws on a report by Alison J. Ewbank.

Chapter 3

AN EXPECTANCY-VALUE APPROACH
TO MEDIA GRATIFICATIONS

Philip Palmgreen
J. D. Rayburn II

RESEARCH IN THE SOCIAL SCIENCES has demonstrated rather convincingly that much human behavior is shaped by our perceptions of behavioral outcomes—by *expectations* that have been acquired through experience, through communication with others, and via processes of inference and deduction. Those concerned with the uses audience members make of the media of mass communication have been cognizant of the important role played by such expectations concerning the characteristics of various media and nonmedia sources, and the gratifications potentially obtainable from such sources. Indeed, it is difficult to find a publication within the framework of the uses and gratifications tradition that does not employ the term "expectation" or some synonym. It is a key element in Katz et al.'s (1974) now classic seven-part précis of the uses and gratifications approach. It is also a central concept in all three approaches to uses and gratifications phenomena (functional, structural/cultural, and action/motivation) outlined by McQuail and Gurevitch (1974). A fundamental assumption of uses and gratifications models, that of an active audience, is in fact founded upon the even more basic precept that audience members do have perceptions of the gratifications available from various alternatives, and that they act upon these perceptions.

Unfortunately, consensus regarding the *importance* of the expectation concept has not inspired equal accord on the concept's *meaning*. A number of authors have treated expectancies as equivalent to gratifications sought (for example, Katz, Blumler, and Gurevitch, 1973). Peled and Katz (1974) adopt a normative approach in defining expectations as

61

audience demands concerning what the media should provide. In Mendelsohn's (1974: 307) scheme, expectations "refer to affective anticipations regarding the prospects of particular events occurring in conjunction with certain associated consequences." McLeod and Becker (1981: 74) have defined expectations as "rough probabilities of satisfaction assigned . . . to various behaviors."

As these various approaches illustrate, we do not know quite what to expect when an author uses the term "expectancy." A way out of the beckoning conceptual morass may be found if, in the spirit of eclecticism proposed by Blumler (1979), we reach out to a research tradition that has focused upon a similar concept, and that has arrived at some resolution of the thorny issues involved. In this particular case, a major and well-tested theory of social psychology—expectancy-value theory—holds the promise of substantial clarification, and is a fertile source of hypotheses about the relationship among beliefs, values, gratifications, and media behavior. While there are various theories under the expectancy-value label and they differ somewhat in their emphases (Atkinson, 1957; Fishbein, 1963; Fishbein and Ajzen, 1975; Rotter, 1954; Tolman, 1932; Vroom, 1964), all view behavior, behavioral intention, or attitudes (or all three) as a function of (1) *expectancy* (or belief—that is, the perceived probability that an object possesses a particular attribute or that a behavior will have a particular consequence; and (2) *evaluation*—that is, the degree of affect, positive or negative, toward an attribute or behavioral outcome. Expectancy-value theory thus not only provides an explicit conceptualization of expectancy in terms of perceived probabilities that certain media behaviors will have certain outcomes, but also states that we must take into account the *value* that an audience member attaches to those outcomes.

Given the historical importance of the expectancy concept in the uses and gratifications tradition, we should not be surprised to find elements of expectancy-value thinking appearing occasionally in the uses and gratifications literature, though not explicitly recognized as such. Indeed, Katz, Gurevitch, and Haas (1973), in their classic study of Israeli media use, measured not only need importance (similar to "value") but also respondent perceptions of gratifications to be obtained from different media sources ("expectancy"). These were not combined in any fashion, however, in the examination of consumption. Lundberg and Hultén (1968) provide an even earlier example of the use of a conceptualization similar to expectancy-value theory, though the authors again do not draw a connection. Respondents in their study rated the perceived importance of certain goals and the perceived instrumentality of the media in helping them achieve these goals. A multiplicative index of the two measures successfully predicted reported media use.

An explicit merger of uses and gratifications and expectancy-value conceptualizations did not occur until the early 1980s, with the work of Galloway and his colleagues (Blood and Galloway, 1983; Galloway and Meek, 1981), Van Leuven (1981), and ourselves (Palmgreen and Rayburn, 1982, 1984; Rayburn and Palmgreen, 1983, 1984). Van Leuven's (1981) model of media and message selection is based on Vroom's (1964) expectancy-value theory of worker motivation. Galloway and his colleagues have also drawn upon Vroom and a worker motivation study by Hackman and Porter (1968).

Our own work is based upon Fishbein's expectancy-value theory (Fishbein, 1963; Fishbein and Ajzen, 1975). Fishbein's theory is the most prominent and well-specified of the various expectancy-value theories, and its information-processing assumptions are compatible with those of the uses and gratifications perspective. Drawing upon Fishbein's models of attitude and behavioral intention, we have postulated that gratifications sought from media experience are a function of both the beliefs (expectations) that audience members hold about media sources and the affective evaluations they attach to media attributes. Expressed formally:

$$GS_i = b_i e_i \qquad [1]$$

where

GS_i = the ith gratification sought from some media object, X (some medium, program, content type, etc.);

b_i = the belief (subjective probability) that X possesses some attribute or that a behavior related to X will have a particular outcome; and

e_i = the affective evaluation of the particular attribute or outcome.

This model implies that a particular gratification will not be sought from X if X is perceived not to possess the related attribute *or* if the attribute is very negatively evaluated. If the attribute is both strongly believed to be a component of X and is evaluated very positively, then relatively strong seeking of the appropriate gratification is predicted, with more moderate levels of seeking associated with more moderate levels of b_i or e_i.

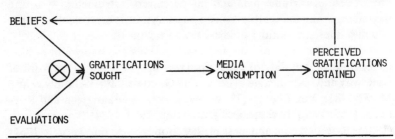

Figure 3.1   Expectancy-Value Model of GS and GO

A parallel formulation that predicts a generalized orientation to seek various gratifications from a particular source is as follows:

$$\sum_{i=1}^{n} GS_i = \sum_{i=1}^{n} b_i e_i \qquad [2]$$

Both models received support in a study of television news (Palmgreen and Rayburn, 1982). Correlations between each of fourteen gratifications sought and their respective belief-evaluation products ranged from .26 to .74. These correlations remained substantial and significant after the introduction of a control for gratifications obtained, indicating that expectations about the characteristics of television news and evaluations of these characteristics are important antecedents of motives to seek associated gratifications.[1] This finding has been replicated recently by Babrow and Swanson (1984).

A MODEL OF GRATIFICATION PROCESSES

Further analysis of the data in the 1982 study that included measures of media consumption and gratifications obtained supports the model in Figure 3.1. The model is a process one that posits that the products of beliefs (expectations) and evaluations influence the seeking of gratifications, which in turn influence media consumption. Such consumption results in the perception of certain gratifications obtained, which then feed back to reinforce or alter an individual's perceptions of the gratification-related attributes of a particular newspaper, program, program genre, or other media consumed. For example, if a person values "information about current issues and events" positively and believes (expects) that television news possesses such information, he or she will be motivated to seek such information from television news. Assuming that television news is available to the audience member (and that no better alternatives are perceived), exposure to television news should result. If the individual obtains the expected information, then this outcome (GO) will feed back to reinforce the initial belief about this program attribute. If he or she obtains information at a lower or higher level than expected, then his or her associated belief should be altered, with consequent change in motivation to seek information about current issues from television news.

The model postulates that *evaluations,* on the other hand, are not affected by perceptions of gratifications obtained; that is, we should not find that the more a gratification is perceived to be obtained, the more positively evaluated is the associated media attribute. Evaluations are viewed instead as relatively stable elements that are the product of an individual's needs and value system.

Fishbein and Ajzen's (1975) model for predicting behavioral intentions also includes a subjective norm component. This component takes into account a person's beliefs that significant others feel he or she should not perform a certain behavior, as well as the person's motivation to comply with the wishes of these other persons. Although the model in Figure 3.1 does not incorporate such a component, its inclusion might take into account certain important social aspects of consumption decisions. Such an expanded model would, in effect, contrast motivations for media use (GS) with social motivations to conform to the wishes of others.

The influence of such social factors was illustrated in a study of public television viewing (Palmgreen and Rayburn, 1979), in which, among those respondents who usually deferred viewing decisions to other household members, public television viewing was predicted best by the viewing behavior of the decision maker, while the influence of gratifications sought and obtained was minimized. For decision makers themselves, gratifications played a significant role in predicting exposure. This distinction may help explain why Babrow and Swanson (1984), in the only gratification study to date that included a measure of subjective norm, found no relationship between this variable and intention to view television news. It may be that the influence of a motive to comply with the wishes of others would emerge only among those viewers who ordinarily leave many of their TV viewing decisions to others.

GRATIFICATIONS OBTAINED VERSUS BELIEF

We should note an important distinction between the concepts of "belief" (expectancy) and "gratification obtained," as we have employed them in our research. Earlier we defined belief as the subjective probability that a media object possesses some attribute, *or* that a behavior related to that object will have a certain outcome. In our research we have chosen to operationalize belief in the former sense; that is, as the subjective probability that a media *object* possesses a particular *attribute* in the *general* sense (as a defining characteristic of the object).

By comparison, a gratification obtained in the abstract sense is not a belief at all, but is some outcome (cognitive, affective, or behavioral) of media behavior. Nonetheless, a *perceived* gratification obtained is conceptualized and operationalized by most researchers as a *belief* that a media behavior has a given outcome (conforming to the second interpretation of belief described above). This belief, however, is *personal* in nature in that it represents the subjective probability that the media behavior provides the *respondent* with a particular gratification. Thus, in our model, "beliefs" and perceived gratifications obtained are both operationalized as expectancies, but with quite different referents. While our research has shown the two concepts to be related empirically, responses to items measuring belief and perceived GO may be quite different. For example, a nonviewer of television news may believe that much of the content of TV news is concerned with information about political affairs; that is, that political information is an attribute of television news. He or she therefore should endorse measures that tap this belief. On the other hand, since the person is not a regular TV news viewer, he or she is unlikely to endorse a perceived GO measure such as "TV news gives me information about political affairs."

Galloway and Meek (1981), Blood and Galloway (1983), and Babrow and Swanson (1984) do not make a similar distinction, but operationalize expectancy only in terms of perceived gratifications obtained (as the subjective probability that media behavior will have a particular outcome for the respondent). While either approach is consistent with the way in which Fishbein and other expectancy-value theorists have operationalized the expectancy concept, the distinction may help account for one apparent inconsistency between our findings (Palmgreen and Rayburn, 1982) and those of Galloway et al. (Blood and Galloway, 1983; Galloway and Meek, 1981). Our model predicts an indirect effect of the expectancy-value index on media exposure through GS. This prediction was supported, and no direct effect of the $b_i e_i$ index on television news exposure emerged with GS controlled. Galloway and his colleagues, however, have found direct effects of $b_i e_i$ indices (EV indices in their model) on subsequent exposure to television programs. Because the Galloway et al. measure taps perceived personal outcomes (GO) from media use, it may be a stronger direct predictor of exposure. Other differences, however, may also account for the discrepancy, including the fact that we have defined evaluation in terms of affect, whereas Galloway et al., define it as importance. In addition, our study employed a control for GS, while the Galloway studies did not. Further research is needed that examines the theoretical and measurement issues raised by the two approaches.

A TYPOLOGY OF MEDIA MOTIVATIONS

A few uses and gratifications studies (such as Becker, 1979; Blumler and McQuail, 1969; McLeod and Becker, 1974) have distinguished between "positive" gratifications (reasons for seeking media consumption) and "negative" gratifications or avoidances (reasons for avoiding media consumption). Becker (1979) found that avoidance motivations are empirically distinct from gratifications, and called for more conceptual attention to avoidance measures.

Taking an expectancy-value approach to uses and gratifications offers a fruitful way of conceptualizing both gratifications and avoidances, and gives insight into different kinds of motivation for media use. An examination of avoidance items employed in uses and gratifications studies reveals that the majority involve a negatively evaluated attribute (presumed to be gratification related) that the media object in question (for example, political content) is believed to possess. An example of such an item tapping avoidance of political content on television is the following: "Because I'm not interested in watching candidates I don't like" (Becker, 1979). Endorsement of such an item would indicate a negative evaluation of information about "candidates I don't like" along with the belief that political content on TV possesses such information. Such a situation would involve a case of true and classic avoidance of a disliked entity.

The remainder of avoidance items commonly employed usually involve a *positively* valued attribute that the media object is believed *not* to possess. Such an item for political TV is "Because I prefer to relax when watching television" (Becker, 1979). Endorsement of this type of item indicates a positive evaluation of "relaxing when watching television" in conjunction with the belief that political TV content is *not* relaxing. This would reflect not so much true avoidance of political TV as exposure to alternative TV content perceived to be more relaxing. We shall term this type of motive, then, "seeking of alternatives."

As Palmgreen (1984b) has shown, cross-tabulating *evaluation* of media attributes with *belief* in their possession yields a fourfold typolo-

| | | Evaluation of Attribute | |
		Negative	Positive
Belief in Possession of Attribute	No	Negative Approach	Seeking of Alternatives
	Yes	True Avoidance	Positive Approach

Figure 3.2 Expectancy-Value Typology of Media Motivations

gy of media motivations hypothesized to result from differing percep-
tions/evaluations of media attributes (see Figure 3.2). Positive evaluation of a media attribute, combined with belief that the media object has
this attribute, will give rise to a motive to seek the associated gratification from that particular source (Palmgreen and Rayburn, 1982). This
cell is termed *positive approach* and represents the type of motivation
uses and gratifications researchers have studied almost exclusively.
Belief in possession of a negatively valued attribute should lead, as
discussed, to *true avoidance,* while disbelief in possession of a positively
valued characteristic is associated with *seeking of alternatives.* Finally,
if an individual believes a communication source does *not* possess a
disliked attribute (for example, "At least it's not boring"), he or she may
be motivated to use the source, particularly if available alternatives are
perceived to have the negative characteristic (are "boring"). Since true
seeking of a positive gratification is not involved, we shall call this kind
of motivation "negative approach."

It may be argued, of course, that negative approach is merely the
mirror image of positive approach; that is, disbelief in the possession of
a negative attribute (such as "boring") implies belief in possession of the
corresponding positive attribute (such as "exciting"). In some cases this
may be true; however, it may be argued that "true avoidance" is also the
mirror opposite of positive approach or gratification seeking. A study
by Becker (1979), though, indicates that this is not the case. Gratifications and avoidances contributed separately to variance in political
effects. Any "mirror-image" hypothesis, therefore, needs empirical testing and additional theoretical scrutiny.

It seems apparent, though, that responses to conventional Likert-
type GS items may actually be influenced by a number of different
motives. For example, both positive and negative approach motivations
may result in a positive response to a GS item, while both true avoidance
and seeking of alternatives may lead to a negative response. Uses and
gratifications research might profit from the empirical investigation of

all four types of motives in Figure 3.2. Do media consumption patterns differ depending upon the type of motivation that predominates? Does including measures of all four types of motivation lead to increased ability to predict media consumption and associated effects? If so, which type of motivation is generally the strongest predictor?

Providing answers to these and many other questions raised from an expectancy-value perspective will require that researchers explore a greater range of media attributes along both the belief and evaluation dimensions than has been generally the case. As we noted earlier, most investigations have employed gratification measures of positively valued attributes that media objects are believed to possess, leading to an emphasis on "positive approach" motivations. Usually missing are attributes that are negatively valued by large numbers of respondents and attributes that the media object in question is not perceived (by many respondents) to have. Such practices not only restrict the range of motivations that may be explored, but tend to restrict variance in measures of belief, evaluation, and GS and GO. Such variance restriction may help explain why, in a recent study (Palmgreen and Rayburn, 1984), we found that introducing the respondent's affective evaluation of gratification-related attributes did not significantly improve the ability of gratification models to predict satisfaction with television news. Of the fourteen attributes of TV news employed in this study, only one ("dramatic") was evaluated below the neutral point of the seven-point evaluation scale. In retrospect, a greater range of the evaluative index might have increased its predictive utility. The techniques employed by researchers in the study of "avoidances" show promise for eliciting more items that tap the negative pole of the evaluative continuum.

BELIEF FORMATION

The expectancy-value approach postulates that beliefs about a source are the primary informational components determining the seeking of gratifications. These beliefs have many origins and derive from the sum of an individual's experiences (direct and indirect) with a particular media object (a medium, program, content type, newspaper, or the like). Fishbein and Ajzen (1975) distinguish among three kinds of belief: (1) descriptive (2) informational, and (3) inferential.

Descriptive beliefs result from direct observation of an object. Exposure to a particular medium, for example, will lead to the formation and modification of beliefs concerning attributes of the medium.

Informational beliefs are formed by accepting information from an outside source that links certain objects and attributes. We may acquire beliefs about a magazine through a friend who subscribes to that magazine, or we may obtain information through advertisments for the magazine. Collectively, informational beliefs may constitute a large proportion of our total media belief system, especially concerning media objects with which we have little direct personal experience.

Inferential beliefs are also beliefs about characteristics of objects not yet observed directly, or that are not observable directly. We often infer such beliefs on the basis of formal logic, personal theories of implicit personality (Wiggins, 1973), causal attributions (Kelley, 1973), and stereotyping. Such inferential processes also apply to media attributes and are the basis of many of the beliefs we have about media objects with which we have little direct experience. Here cultural and social stereotypes and norms play a major role in forming both individual and collective expectations about media objects. For example, we may develop beliefs about a new television drama about police, even though we have never viewed the program, simply because we have heard it is.a "police show," and consequently we expect it to possess certain attributes in varying degrees. These expectations (in conjuction with their associated evaluations) may lead us not to seek gratifications from that program (and to a decision not to view). This could explain why the audience for *Hill Street Blues*—a nonstereotypical television police drama—developed so slowly.

As Palmgreen (1984b) has observed, it is illuminating to reexamine from this perspective the criticism that responses to gratifications measures may reflect "only" cultural or social stereotypes or myths, rather than individual "actual" experience with media content. Yet these stereotypes and myths consist of beliefs about the mass media—beliefs that may constitute a very significant proportion of an individual's meaning system for a given medium, program, or channel. From the standpoint of the individual, these beliefs will influence media behavior, regardless of their source. The person, then, who responds principally in terms of stereotypes or other inferential beliefs regarding a source, is still yielding valuable information about his or her media perceptions. From the larger social or cultual perspective it is, of course, important to determine the types and sources of beliefs about mass media. The extent to which one's media beliefs are socially or culturally determined, or influenced by the media themselves, is one area in which a merger of cultural and gratifications studies could yield rich dividends.

STUDIES OF BELIEF ACQUISITION
AND CHANGE

An expectancy-value approach emphasizes the importance of under-standing processes of belief acquisition and change regarding the mass media. Longitudinal studies of such processes are needed. Such studies may help us understand how and why audiences develop for new televi-sion series or magazines, and why certain television programs, such as *Taxi,* or newspapers, such as the *Washington Star,* that once rode the crest of the wave of success have subsequently disappeared. The expec-tancy-value approach also provides a means for studying major techni-cal innovations such as cable television or interactive cable systems. With the advent of cable television has come varied and highly special-ized programming. The expectancy-value approach may be fruitful in accounting for the reasons networks such as CNN now have substantial followings when heretofore no programmer would have dared broad-cast 24-hour news.

Studies could also explore life-cycle and age-related changes in media use as a function of changes in the belief system. In all cases, longitudinal studies could shed light on the ways in which direct media exposure, inferential processes, and exposure to media and interpersonal sources of information interact to form those beliefs that are the cognitive basis of media consumption. At the same time, the acquisition and change of beliefs could be linked to gratifications sought, media consumption, perceptions of gratifications obtained, and media effects. Thus with this approach we could begin to build a more comprehensive model of medium and content selection processes.

A BROADER CANVAS

At first glance the expectancy-value approach to uses and gratifica-tions would appear to be primarily cognitive in its orientation. Certainly the approach is dominated by cognitive constructs and information-pro-cessing assumptions, and the few empirical studies that have appeared thus far in the uses and gratifications area have had a distinctly cognitive flavor (some might say aroma). Of course, most uses and gratifications researchers are quite comfortable with such a "mentalistic" framework, and we have attempted to point out here some of the advantages of adopting such a theoretical orientation. This orientation is, for the most part, consistent with the action-motivation perspective as described by McQuail and Gurevitch (1974). Expectancy-value formulations need not be constrained, however, by the boundaries of this particular perspective. On the contrary, the opportunity exists to sketch the dynamics of gratification processes on a broader social and cultural canvas, perhaps within the framework of the structural/cultural perspective (McQuail and Gurevitch, 1974). This opportunity stems from the very nature of the core concepts of expectancy-value theory—beliefs and value. While more narrowly focused cognitive and micro-level investigations can yield valuable knowledge, researchers should also seize the opportunity to forge stronger theoretical ties between *media* beliefs and evaluations, and the belief and value *systems* characterizing particular societies, cultures, and social groupings. Blumler, elsewhere in this volume, describes the social character of many media gratifications. Much of this character derives from the particular social and cultural roots that feed our perceptions and evaluations of our media milieu. An expectancy-value approach, pursued via social and cultural avenues, can help us discover these roots and map them into a broader and more socially relevant uses and gratfications theory.

NOTE

1. It can be argued that the importance of an attribute or consequence to an individual's value system should be taken into account in predicting seeking of gratifications. Fishbein and Ajzen (1975), however, report that including importance does not markedly improve, and may even attenuate, predictions of attitudes, because the information provided by importance measures is redundant with beliefs and evaluations. Similarly, we found that the inclusion of importance did not improve predictions of GS significantly (Palmgreen and Rayburn, 1982). Galloway and Meek (1981) and Blood and Galloway (1983), on the other hand, have defined *value* operationally in their E-V model in terms of the importance to the individual of the perceived gratification obtained, while we have followed Fishbein in defining value as affective evaluation. Since importance and affect are ordinarily highly correlated, this distinction may make little predictive difference, but it is a conceptual distinction worth noting.

Chapter 4

TRANSACTION AND
MEDIA GRATIFICATIONS RESEARCH

Lawrence A. Wenner

The key term developed in *Knowing and the Known* is *transaction.* If I have understood the authors correctly, the term *transaction* insists on seeing events in the context of complex circular processes, rather than limited, linear systems (an interactional point of view) or in isolation (self action). In an interactional system, knowers, knowing, and the known would be separate entities related to each other in rather simple, cause-and-effect style. . . . The transactional view of Dewey and Bentley is at once simpler and more complicated; the knower is seen "as a phase of cosmic process with all of his activities including his knowings and even his inquiries into his knowings as themselves knowns. The knowings are examined within the ranges of the known, and the knowns within the ranges of the knowing" [Maloney, 1955: 319; review of Dewey and Bentley, 1949].

The term "transaction" appears with some regularity in communication research. Most often it is used in a descriptive sense in conjunction with the more frequently appearing catchword "process." Hence there are *transactional processes,* or the more convincingly stated *transactional view (or perspective) of the communications process.* Certainly, if the word "process has taken on proportions of a "God-term" in the study of human communication (Fisher, 1978), "transaction" might well be said to be an "emerging God-term" or, at the very least, a "God-term in waiting."

AUTHOR'S NOTE: Partial funding for this project was provided through a Faculty Research Grant from Loyola Marymount University.

If there is more than a degree of facetiousness in this introduction, it is undoubtedly propelled by the ambiguity that surrounds the origins of the term "transaction" and its implications for communication research generally, and media gratifications research in particular. This can be seen even in Barnlund's (1970) argument for "A Transactional Model of Communication," which is generally conceded to be one of the more well-developed statements of the transactional view as it applies to communication. In the body of Barnlund's article, the term "transaction" appears only once. Here, it is seen in defining communication as "not a reaction to something, nor an interaction with something, but a transaction in which man invents and attributes meanings to realize his purposes" (p. 88). Barnlund builds his model upon the postulates that communication is dynamic, continuous, circular, unrepeatable, and complex. Certainly, all of these notions are well within a "consensus view" of transaction. However, it is the origins of that view and their link to these notions that are not stressed, and it is just these things that may have the greatest implications for media gratifications research.

In an age of increasing specialization, it is not an uncommon occurrence to find competent researchers who have admittedly sketchy backgrounds in the broad philosophy that pertains to the social sciences and has strong implications for communication studies. Thus the blanks that Barnlund leaves to be filled regarding the origins of transaction may contribute to an inadequate understanding of the distinctions such as those Littlejohn (1983) makes among behavioristic, transmissional, interactional, and transactional perspectives in communication.

Whatever its origins, a situation exists in which such distinctions, particularly those between interactional and transactional views, are often blurred. Of course, some of this can be attributed to the employment of "multiple perspectives," a useful strategy that is very often appropriate to certain research formulations (Fisher, 1978), including gratifications research. However, it is more likely that a situation remains, such as Bauer (1973: 143) has suggested, such that "while lip service is often given to the proposition that the communication process is a transactional one in which communicator and audience play equally active roles, this notion has little effective impact on the organized research or systematic writing that is done." Certainly, for the most part, this has been the case in media gratifications research, where much attention has focused upon gratifications derived from media, but where comparatively little attention has been given to content characteristics apart from mere exposure to them. Although this is beginning to change, the bulk of gratifications research demonstrates little sensitivity to the implications of the transaction between content and gratifications.

Ironically, this is in spite of the more well-developed models of the media gratifications process (Katz et al., 1974; Palmgreen, 1984b; Palmgreen et al., Chapter 1, this volume; Rosengren 1974) embracing the transactional view, although they are not stated explicitly in such terms. More recently, we have seen the development of "working models," some actually called "transactional" (McLeod and Becker, 1974, 1981; Wenner, 1982, 1983a, 1984) and others not recognized as such (Palmgreen and Rayburn, 1982; Palmgreen et al., 1981: Rayburn and Palmgreen, 1984), that address effects questions from a gratifications perspective.

In pursuit of further development of this type, an attempt is made in this chapter to clarify the notion of transaction within a media gratifications framework. To do so, it is necessary to trace the origins of the term and its development by John Dewey, its applicability to the theory of perception via transactional psychology, its appearance in communication research, and its employment in "working models" of the gratifications process. Such clarification is aimed at pinpointing issues in the development of a transactional model that will facilitate the merger of gratifications and effects research.

JOHN DEWEY'S NOTION OF TRANSACTION

John Dewey's considerable impact on the fields of philosophy, psychology, art, education, and linguistics has netted sizable contributions to the field of communication (Belman, 1977). In his last major work, *Knowing and the Known,* with Arthur Bentley, Dewey develops "transaction" as a reactive term that has more primitive conceptualization in his earlier work (Dewey, 1930, 1938). Dewey and Bentley (1949) trace the origins of "transaction" to Maxwell (1877), who coined the term upon development of Faraday's observation that the workings of electricity "could not be held within the condenser box nor confined to conducting wire" (p. 106). However, the actual origins of the term may predate this considerably, as Toynbee (1952) has reference to the usage of "transactionalism" by the Greek historian Polybius (201-120 B.C.) in ways Cantril et al. (1961) see as consistent with Dewey.

As mentioned earlier, Maloney (1955), in a review of Dewey and Bentley's *Knowing and the Known,* sees "transaction" as the key term developed in the collection of essays. However, the work is of more general applicability to media gratifications research because of its concern for "a search for firm names" to combat what is defined as "the terminological problem." Dewey and Bentley's (1949: xii) "diagnosis of linguistic disease not only in the general epistemological field, where everyone would anticipate it, but also in the specialized logical field, which ought to be reasonably immune" should come as some comfort to gratifications researchers who have been attacked with some regularity for being afflicted with what appears to be a relatively common malady. Nonetheless, Dewey and Bentley's work should continue to trigger worthwhile reflection upon remedies for a festering sore that continues to ail gratifications research, along with most other social science areas.

Understanding Dewey's thinking about transaction, however, requires making connections well beyond the specification of terminological definitions and, as such, the limited treatment here does not do justice to the richness of thought a more thorough reading would yield. Amplifying Maloney's (1955) hesitancy in synopsizing the pragmatics of transactionalism referred to at the beginning of this chapter, philosopher and Dewey scholar Donald Piatt (1955: 305) reflects that "so revolutionary is Dewey's thinking, so recalcitrant our language, that I feel I need first to live with people, share their living experience, before I can explain his ideas to them." Nevertheless, the fundamental concepts in Dewey's notion of transaction revolve around distinguishing transaction from the earlier terms of self-action and interaction. Basic to these concepts is an ontological view of man as actively creating meaning within the context of a system, and a related epistemological view of scientific inquiry that stresses holism and process, no matter the intent or focus of such inquiry.

CONCEPTS IN TRANSACTION

Given their concern for teminological problems, it is probably best largely to defer, as Cantril et al. (1961) have, to Dewey and Bentley's own words to describe the transactional approach. Perhaps most central is that Dewey and Bentley (1949: 53) "proceed upon the postulate that *knowings* are always and everywhere inseparable from *the knowns*—that the two are twin aspects of common fact." This focus on *common facts* has led Dewey and Bentley and others to see the transactional approach as one having to do with *common sense*. Toch and MacLean (1962: 58) suggest that "common sense assumes that it is the 'user' of the perceptual process who is active, while perception itself is simply being manipulated," although Cantril (1950: 69) poses that, contradistinctive of scientific inquiry, "in common sense we usually are quite unaware of the assumptions on which our decisions are made." The awareness of assumptions issue is yet to be resolved, but it can safely be said that uses and gratifications research is founded on similar "commonsense" grounds, with gratifications always and everywhere inseparable from both the person perceiving them and the media object from which they are derived.

As can be seen above, the transactional approach shares with gratifications research a view of activity, which, stress Dewey and Bentley (1949: 52), "sees man-in-action, not as something radically set over against an environing world, nor yet as something merely acting 'in' a world, but action *of* and *in* the world in which the man belongs as an integral constituent." Here, action or activity is used "as a most general characterization for events where the durational process is being stressed" (Dewey and Bentley, 1949: 68). Moreover, in gratifications research, such "duractivity," as Levy and Windahl (1984) have called it, has traditionally been stressed in examining gratifications from "active" exposure. Referencing "duractivity" along a time dimension with a process view of activity consistent with transactionalism, Levy and Windahl (1984; see also their work in this volume) recently have suggested "preactivity" and "postactivity" as terms for complementary notions that might be seen as the pieces of bread that get put together as one builds a sandwich, which mixes "duractivity" with "gratifications" as the main ingredients of the filling.

Building on these ideas of activity, Dewey and Bentley (1949) distinguish the transactional approach from two others that they see as dominant in the development of science. First, *self-action* is seen as an "antique view" in that "things are viewed as acting under their own powers." Second, there is *interaction,* derivative of classical mechanics, "where thing is balanced against thing in causal interconnection." These concepts contrast with *transaction* "where systems of description and naming are employed to deal with aspects and phases of action, without final attribution to 'elements' or other presumptively detachable or independent 'entities,' 'essences,' or 'realities,' and without isolation of presumptively detachable 'relations' from such detachable 'elements' " (p. 108).

This can be seen in more concrete terms by returning to the sandwich analogy posed earlier in gratifications terms. Gratifications sought and obtained can be seen to "transact" in much the same way as the American sandwich favorite of peanut butter and jelly. One must be added first, but the net concoction requires experiencing more than either peanut butter or jelly alone, or even as they would be consumed in succession. While either peanut butter or jelly may be added first as filling to the sandwich, gratifications sought must always be added in this recipe for media activity before gratifications obtained enters the mixture. In either the sandwich or gratifications case, the net experience is the degree of satisfaction, and this depends on how the mixture or "transaction" digests in ways that are referenced by what was expected, deemed important, and what and when experiences follow consumption. Taking the analogy further, this all exists in a system in which need states dictate "hunger," and choices are made given what is available in the cupboard or refrigerator. And, of couse, consuming media is much like food in that what is available in the cupboard is limited by social factors as well as one's dietary preferences. From Dewey's point of view, *self-action* takes little notice of such "real" limitations on actions, and *interaction* tends to look at discrete elements working against each other within a system, rather than how the mixture of those elements combine to define a system and structure changes within it.

Ironically, as Dewey and Bentley (1949: 132) have pointed out, the interactional perspective "entered psychological inquiry just about the time it was being removed from basic position by the physical sciences from which it was copied." Influenced heavily by psychology, early communication inquiries largely followed suit. The interactional perspective is still influential today, although it can be seen clearly in the Fisher (1978) and Littlejohn (1983) analyses of perspectives, that interactional communication approaches are decidedly more circular and process oriented. Still, one must move on to the more pragmatic transactional perspective to see the stress on activity, sharing, and systems that has been influenced, in part, by Dewey and Bentley's ideas.

TRANSACTION AND TRANSACTIONAL PSYCHOLOGY

Dewey and Bentley's development of the transactional view served as an indictment that incited self-examination in a wide variety of fields (Hayakawa, 1955). The reworking of perceptual psychology along these lines reveals substantial parallels to the development of gratifications research as a response to limitations evident in the effects tradition that guided early communication research.

Central to the changes in the perceptual field that were propelled by transactional psychology was the view that "the world *as we experience it* is the product of perception, not the cause of it" and, thus, this form of "the study of perception takes the active perceiving individual as its proper point of departure." This is a considerable break from the "stimulus determination" view of perception, which reasoned from *object* to *organism*, asking "what is done *by* the environment *to* the organism while perceiving," rather than being "concerned with what is done *by* the organism"(Ittelson and Cantril, 1954: 5). The transposition evident here, is, of course, strikingly similar to that involved in shifting from "what media do to people" in the effects orientation to "what people do with media" in the gratifications paradigm.

Although influenced philosophically by Dewey and Bentley's observations, transactional psychology took form when these ideas were applied to a series of experimental demonstrations instigated by Adelbert Ames and his colleagues at the Hanover Institute for Associated Research (see Ittelson, 1961; Kilpatrick, 1961). Much of this research was aimed at understanding the *processes* behind attempts at attaining accurate visual perceptions of "ambiguous" and "distorted" objects. While Kilpatrick (1961: 56) admits that many of these experimental demonstrations are "concerned with quite simple, static, monocular situations," the focus on perceptual *process* led to the development of concepts and terms that may be applied to the study of more complex social perceptions, including those of the media. In particular, the work of Cantril and Ittelson (Cantril, 1950; Cantril et al., 1961; Hastorf and Cantril, 1954; Ittelson, 1961; Ittelson and Cantril, 1954; Kilpatrick and Cantril, 1961) suggests that many of these concepts have ready applicability to media gratifications research.

CONCEPTS FROM TRANSACTIONAL PSYCHOLOGY

Ittelson and Cantril (1954) suggest that three characteristics of perception deserve special attention in transactional psychology. Briefly stated, these characteristics involve *transactions,* the unique *personal behavioral center* of the individual, and the *externalization process* through which the individual "creates for himself his own psychological environment which he believes exists independent of experience" (p. 2).

Transactions

Given the influence of Dewey and Bentley (1949), it is not surprising that the first of these characteristics suggests that perception "can only be studied in terms of the *transactions* in which they can be observed" because "neither a perception nor object-as-perceived exists independent of the total life situation of which both perception and object are a part," and thus, "it is meaningless to speak of either as existing apart from the situation in which it is encountered" (Ittelson and Cantril, 1954: 2-3). Certainly, similar things have long been implied about the role of gratifications in media behavior. Here, it could well be argued that situations involving media audience behavior can be studied only in terms of *gratification transactions* as they are experienced by members of the audience. And just as it is meaningless to study perception apart from object, it may well be equally meaningless to study gratification apart from media content, or to think of either as existing apart from the situation in which they are encountered.

Personal Behavioral Center

The *personal behavioral center* is defined by a combination of *experiences* and *needs,* while taking into account the individual's unique position in *space* and *time* (Ittelson and Cantril, 1954). Discussed in more detail below, experiences and needs are basic to most uses and gratifications formulations. This is less true of space and time, although space, thought of as the situational context of media exposure, is being considered in some of the more recent gratifications research (Levy and Windahl, 1984; see also Levy and Windahl, this volume; Lull, 1980a, 1980b; Wenner, 1983a, 1984). Accounting for position in time requires longitudinal designs, and it is rare to find even related cohort analysis (Cutler and Danowski, 1980), although Rayburn and Palmgreen (1983) have made strides in addressing the issue of time as it related to the reporting of gratifications.

In transactional psychology, *experiences* are related to *significance,* which, when stabilized, form patterns of unconscious *assumptions* that serve, with other things, to guide the perceptual process. Significance, from this point of view, is used as it is defined by Whitehead (1925: 12). "Significance is the relatedness of things. To say that significance is experience, is to affirm that perceptual knowledge is nothing else than an apprehension of the relatedness of things." When viewed as the apprehension of significance, perception "is the product of the continual recording of the relatedness of things as defined by action" which, as a process, has the psychological consequences of bringing about changes in significance (Ittelson, 1961: 347). Nonetheless, because the concept of change is relative, and accentuated by frameworks referencing certain space and time limitations, some significances remain stable and endure because of the relative effectiveness of action, and thus become "prognostic directives for action" (Ittelson, 1961: 347). In a gratifications framework, this can be seen when an effectively obtained gratification relates back and stabilizes future gratification seeking of the same variety in similar contexts.

Such stable significances or experiences that come about through effective action are at the foundation of *assumptions*. These assumptions, as Ittelson (1961: 347) suggests, "May be conceptualized variously as *relatively stable ways of reacting*, as *patterns of probable significance*, as *value systems*, or as *concepts as to the nature of the objective world* which have been constructed through active participation in living, and may be considered as 'weighted averages' of past experiences" (emphasis added). What is most striking about the various conceptualizations that Ittelson sees as embracing assumptions is the surprisingly analogous way these relate to current conceptualizations of the gratifications process. For instance, if one looks at the expectancy-value model expanded upon in this volume by Palmgreen and Rayburn (Chapter 3), and posed elsewhere (Palmgreen and Rayburn, 1982; Rayburn and Palmgreen, 1984), the adaptation made of Fishbein's (1963; Fishbein and Ajzen, 1975) attitude model contains four variables that directly parallel Ittelson's notion of assumptions in the perceptual process. Taking the expectancy-value part of the Palmgreen and Rayburn model, *beliefs* or expectations can easily mean *concepts as to the nature of the objective world*, while *evaluations* can be seen clearly as derivative of *value systems*. In the gratifications portion of the model, *gratifications sought* can be thought of easily as the *relatively stable ways of reacting* to the media content which is to be apprehended, while *gratifications obtained* can be viewed as the *patterns of probably significances* that result from specific instances of consumption.

The point of the foregoing discussion is not that expectancy-value theory should be discarded in favor of a transactional approach, but rather that expectancy-value approaches directly address a small portion of the broad concerns that can be seen from the transactional view, and thus in a more limited way can be considered "transactional." Indeed, if one examines gratifications phenomena from both points of view, it will likely be seen that gratifications walk a narrow, but blurred line between attitudes and perceptions. Regardless, looking for similarities, rather than differences, will likely aid theoretical development concerning media gratifications.

In this spirit, the Palmgreen and Rayburn notion of *beliefs* can also be seen to dovetail into the transactional notion of *certainty*, which holds together *assumptions* by bringing *predictive reliability* to perceptions. Here, Ittelson and Cantril (1954: 30) suggest that every "action is based on the belief that highly probable events are certain events," and thus, "we act 'as if' we were dealing with certainty." In transactional psychology, the probability issue also enters into *evaluative significances,* which are linked to maximizing the seeking of *goals* that have a "greater probability of providing us with the value satisfactions we seek out of life" (Ittelson and Cantril, 1954: 22).

Seeking to maximize the probability of achieving *goals* is, of course, evidence of the *purposive behavior* that is a central tenet of both transactional psychology and media gratifications research. Again, the language used in perception is strikingly similar to that used in gratifications research. Ittelson and Cantril (1954: 12-13) point out that "we are constantly pursuing a number of purposes simultaneously," but with a basic priority of "experiencing some satisfaction or avoiding some dissatisfaction."

Externalization Process

However, common sense, transactional psychology, and the media gratifications paradigm recognize that people do not always get what they want. Even with good purposes, things can go awry. Assumptions can be ill-founded. Evaluations may err. People may also receive or perceive things that are unexpectedly useful or pleasing. In transactional psychology, these issues are not overlooked, but addressed through an examination of the *externalization* process mentioned earlier.

Long basic to the study of perception (Allport, 1955), and especially important in Gestalt psychology (Koffka, 1935; Kohler, 1947), the concern with the externalization process is aimed at an understanding of how accurate perceptual correspondence comes about between objective and apparent properties of objects. This focus, also referred to as the study of *constancies* or *veridicality,* is of basic importance because our comfortableness with and confidence in our perceptual "matches" to the world, to a large extent, make effective action possible. In simple terms, confident of our perception of a chair, we sit on it. However, in social perception, "objects" are markedly more complex, and certainly less concrete or stable. To handle this, Ittelson (1961: 350) suggests defining "constancy behavior as the attempt of the individual to create and maintain a world which deviates as little as possible from the world which he has experienced in the past." While this may seem a decidely homeostatic notion, it is recognized, as has been suggested earlier, that much can get in the way of such successful correspondence.

From the view of transactional psychology, those things that get in the way of constancy are called "hitches." According to Ittelson and Cantril (1954: 28), *hitches* arise "if we do not experience a significance which we expected to experience." However, because actions without hitches do not reveal anything new to us about the world, it is those "unsuccessful hitches" that "provide the occasions for increasing the scope and adequacy of our assumptions." Thus hitches are neither "functional" nor "dysfunctional" in any sense, rather, as is pointed out by Cantril et al. (1961: 8), "we run into hitches in everyday life because of our inadequate understanding of the conditions giving rise to a phenomenon, and our ability to act effectively for a purpose becomes inadequate." In media gratifications research, the concept of hitches should go a long way toward clarifying why a gratification sought is very often not a gratification obtained. In fact, unless one were to have some "perfect" predictive understanding of the media world, as well as associated "perfect" predictive abilities about it, such a situation of "perfect" correspondence would be unlikely to come about.

This tendency of hitches to get in the way of perfect correspondence between what is expected and what is attained, both in perception and gratifications puts, from the transactional perspective, considerable focus on *change*. In stable situations, change is unlikely because, in a sense, it is unnecessary. Here, our assumptions are met in the course of action, thus making action effective. In terms of media behavior, a gratification sought is obtained. However, once the situation changes as *hitches* come into play, stable assumptions do not provide the best foundations upon which to base action, and thus the preservation of such assumptions (or constancy) will not serve the individual in a changed world. The individual's "assumptive world" must be reformulated and stabilized, resulting in new constancies that lead to effective action in situations that exist in that changed world. Thus as Ittelson (1961: 351) has pointed out, "change is the midwife at the birth of constancy."

Since it is unlikely that all our assumptions are met in very many of our experiences with media, there is a strong need to understand the processes by which our assumptive worlds are revised. This should be of special interest in the study of exposure to and gratification from new media experiences. New forms of media such as those made available by cable or satellite distribution, "new" programs or specials on television, revised newspaper or television news show formats may be some of the more obvious situations that call for substantial revision of assumptions. Hitches, too, can come about within the context of exposure. Incidental exposure may frequently bring to bear faulty assumptions. When one's exposure is determined by others as is the case when we watch a friend's favorite television program, and knowing more about the friend than the program being viewed, our assumptions are ill-prepared for that exposure. Hitches may arise during "shared" media exposure as social interactions during exposure raise doubts about one's initial assumptions. The implications here for gratifications research are great, and thus it is easy to understand why the idea of transaction was proposed in the study of communication.

TRANSACTION IN COMMUNICATION RESEARCH

Transactional ideas, of course, are seen frequently in communication research, although most often they are not recognized explicitly as such, and their origins have not been traced in a fashion analogous to what has been attempted in the preceding discussions. As has been mentioned, the notion of homeostasis, so prominent a feature of Heider's (1946) concept of balance, Newcomb's (1953) ideas about interpersonal symmetry, Osgood's and Tannenbaum's (1955) principle of congruity, Festinger's (1957) theory of cognitive dissonance, and other influential treatments about the balancing of one's cognitive perceptions has parallel in transactional psychology. In mass communication, all that underlies the gratifications tradition (see Katz et al., 1974) has implicit ties to transactionalism. In particular, the work of the mid- to late 1950s, starting perhaps with Freidson's (1954) reconsideration of the concepts of the mass audience and capped by Klapper's (1960) thorough review of the state of mass communication research, calls attention to the limitations of effects inquiry and poses "active audience" alternatives to it. Nonetheless, references to transactionalism are few and far between in the communication literature.

The most explicit of the references to transactionalism in communication have come about when transactional psychologists, in some instances teamed with communication researchers, have examined phenomena in the communications situation. In a good overview of the possibilities, here, Toch and MacLean (1962: 67) stress that "perceptual communalities" (constancies) bring about the "universally shared meanings" which "are the *simplest* means of communication because they require little translation from one person's frame of reference into another." However, as has been mentioned earlier, Toch and MacLean (1962) recognize that "perceptual divergence" is more likely with events which, as they become more complex, tend to be perceived differently by different people.

The implications of this for mass communications research are demonstrated from a transactional point of view in Hastorf and Cantril's (1954) case study of Princeton and Dartmouth students "seeing" a markedly different football game between their teams when viewing the same "objectified" film version of it. In this study, which is similar in many respects to Lang's and Lang's (1953) famous study of differential viewpoints on the MacArthur Day parade, Hastorf and Cantril (1954: 133) conclude that "there is no such 'thing' as a 'game' existing 'out there' in its own right which people merely 'observe.' The 'game' 'exists' for a person and is experienced by him only in so far as certain happenings have significances in terms of his purpose." Perhaps more important than these ideas that reinforce the now familiar transactional view, is Hastorf and Cantril's (1954: 133) contention that "the rules of football game, like laws, rituals, customs, and mores, are registered and pre-served forms of sequential significances enabling people to share the significances of occurrences." Insofar as much media content is highly formulaic, it might be fruitful to take some notice of the rules by which certain media events are played, in addition to examining the mere exposure when evaluating a more broadly defined "media consump-tion" as it relates to gratification behavior. Certainly, there is a wealth of research on communication rules that might guide initial inquiries (Shimanoff, 1980).

Transactionalism, however, in mass communication research came to be associated with other more fundamental, but, in a sense, simpler concerns. Confronted, as many were, by the plethora of evidence con-cerning the relatively limited effects of the media, Bauer (1963: 36) suggests that "we view communications as a transactional process in which both the audience and communicator take important initiative." Seemingly more influenced by Davison's (1959) focus on needs related to action and Klapper's (1960) "phenomenistic" approach than on spell-ing out the lineage of transaction, Bauer's (1964: 319) now famous conception of the "obstinate audience" poses a "model that *ought* to be inferred from the data of research." As he sees it, the "argument for using the transactional model for *scientific* purposes is that it opens the door more fully to exploring the intention and behavior to members of the audience and encourages inquiry into the influence of the audience on the communicator by specifically treating the process as a two-way passage" (p. 327).

It is interesting to note that Bauer's model, while concerned with such "two-way passages," remains more focused on paths of influence rather than on the broader view of transaction which stresses the processes by which meaning is derived. This broader view is seen in Barnlund's (1970) general communication model mentioned earlier, and in Mortenson's (1974) application of it to social conflict. Even with such a focus, these models do not adapt particularly well to the media-audience relation-ship. Rather, the distinctions that are made between public and private cues work well in characterizing intrapersonal and interpersonal communication processes, but are more difficult to separate in the media-audience experience, which adds yet another level of complexity to the basic schema. Perhaps because of this, transactional approaches to media gratifications research have leaned more heavily on Bauer's (1964b) view of the active audience.

TRANSACTION IN MEDIA GRATIFICATIONS RESEARCH

The development of the concept of transaction in media gratifications research can be seen to run parallel to the increasingly sophisticated attempts at integrating gratifications with the study of media effects. Put simply, this stems from the idea that gratifications mediate effects much like assumptions mediate how an object is perceived. Conceptual development has been stimulated by the empirical testing of four "working" models, all of which have been guided by hierarchical notions of the role gratifications play in mediating effects. For the sake of simplicity, these models are called, in order of increasing complexity: (1) the *exposure-gratification model,* (2) the *mixed background-gratification* model, (3) the *ordered background-gratification* model, and (4) the *ordered background-gratification sought and obtained* model. The conceptual elements of these models will be stressed with the aim of developing a transactional model that will adapt easily to "working" research situations.

McLeod and Becker (1974) are clearly responsible for the development of the first explicitly-stated transactional model in their aim to test the validity of gratification measures in effects analysis. In a very basic sense, McLeod and Becker (1974: 141) look to the transactional model as a "reasonable synthesis of the hypodermic and limited effect models, in which the exposure characteristics of the message *combine with* the orientations of the audience member in producing an effect." They find strong evidence (reinforced by Becker, 1976) for an "additive" hierarchical *exposure-gratification* model. Political gratification and avoidance measures add much to media exposure measures in explanations of political effects including issue accuracy, probability of voting, campaign interest and activity, and political convention and advertisement viewing on television.

In the same article, McLeod and Becker (1974) also test a more sophisticated *mixed background-gratification* model. Here, even after partialing out the combined influence of education, political, and media exposure variables, they find that gratification measures explain significant amounts of additional variance in a wide variety of political effects. Using a similar strategy of mixing independent variables into a cluster, but without partialing out gratification measures by themselves, Palmgreen and Rayburn (1979) and Palmgreen et al. (1981) found that gratification discrepancy measures are often more important than demographic and exposure measures in explaining public television-viewing and network news program choice.

The *ordered background-gratification* model identifies a hierarchy among independent variables left unspecified in the *mixed background-gratification* model. While hierarchical ordering of the variables differs in the various studies, what remains constant is that gratifications sought measures are added late in the predictive equations after controlling for a variety of influences thought to be causally prior to them. For instance, McLeod et al. (1979) enter demographic, political, and mass media exposure measures prior to measures of gratifications sought and followed by interpersonal discussion measures in their predictive equation. Even when entered this late, the gratification measures, as a block, account for significant amounts of added variance in explanations of partisan program exposure and campaign news exposure. Becker et al. (1979) use a different order, entering demographic, communication exposure, and political measures prior to their consideration of gratification influences. Even so, the gratification measures add significantly to explanations of Presidential debate exposure.

The *ordered background-gratification sought and obtained* model has developed in recognition of the more recent research pointing to meaningful differences between gratifications sought and obtained (McLeod et al., 1982; Palmgreen et al., 1981; Wenner, 1982). The basic model that has been tested to date (Wenner, 1982, 1983a, 1984) relies on a more complex hierarchical ordering. The strategy has been to enter demographic and habitual media exposure measures in order prior to gratifications sought. This is followed by a group of variables tapping the context of exposure that should mediate gratifications obtained, which are the last variables entered in the predictive equation. Such a model has proven effective in predicting dependency on and exposure to television news programs (Wenner, 1982, 1983a) as well as a variety of political effects (Wenner, 1984). Typically, both gratifications sought and obtained are significant in the equations. This is particularly intriguing when differential seeking and obtaining lead to an outcome. For instance, it can be seen when high surveillance-seeking pairs with obtaining high entertainment to characterize dependency on news programs. Development of the context of viewing variables along the lines that

Levy and Windahl (1984) outline for "duractivity" holds special promise in understanding such transactions.

It can also be seen that some of the recent development of expectancy-value theory suggests important possibilities for this more complex background model. In posing a hierarchical model to predict gratifications obtained, Rayburn and Palmgreen (1984) order belief, evaluation, the belief × evaluation product, gratifications sought, and then media consumption. They report strong results for such a model, although they leave media consumption out of their analysis because of inadequate measurement. This is because Rayburn and Palmgreen (1984: 559) do not see media consumption in the same sense as habitual media exposure; rather it is seen in terms of "the meaning assigned by the respondent to content, structural, or contextual elements." Their definition is directly in line with a transactional view, and their concept of "media consumption" reinforces the importance of thinking in terms of transaction when examining the gratification sought and obtained relationship.

A TRANSACTIONAL MODEL

What should be evident is that much in the development of transactional models in media gratifications research has been guided by the notion of hierarchy. Although the hierarchies differ in degree of specificity and ordering, many basic trends are evident. *General background* elements suggested by demographic variables tend to be entered first. *General foreground* elements having to do with the "effect" in question tend to be entered next. For instance, when studying political effects, political dispositions tend to define the general foreground. Habitual media exposure patterns, which form the *media reference background,* tend to be entered next. The stable *beliefs* and *evaluations* that arise from such habitual exposure patterns also frame the media reference background. Finally, the gratifications sought followed by those gratifications actually obtained tend to define the *media reference foreground,* which is typically entered last in predictive formulations. Current thinking suggests that *contextual* and *structural* elements of consuming media content mediate the gratification sought and obtained transaction, and may be at the heart of the media reference foreground. The summation of such a hierarchical ordering forms the bases of both the general

(Figure 4.1) and specified (Figure 4.2) transactional models that are discussed in more detail below.

The fact that transactional models have been guided by the concept of hierarchy is completely consistent with Dewey's pragmatic perspective. The heart of this perspective as it applies to communication may be seen in Dewey's (1946) dialogue with Morris (1946) about signs. Fisher (1978) suggests that concerns such as these about the pragmatics of meaning or the "symbol-to-user relationship" become clearer when viewed in conjunction with systems theory (von Bertalanffy, 1968; Boulding, 1965; Kuhn, 1974). The principle of hierarchical organization is an axiomatic assumption of any systems approach (see Pattee, 1973). As Fisher (1978: 204-205) has pointed out, every system is part of "a larger system that encompasses it—a suprasystem—and there is also a smaller system (subsystem) included within it," and, perhaps more important in terms of communication, the "flow of information across the boundaries of the system suggests that the nature of the functional relationship between the system and its suprasystem affect to no small extent the structural-functional behaviors of the systems." It is this "information" transfer that proceeds upward and downward across systemic boundaries that is critical to understanding the system (Ozbekhan, 1971).

The general transactional model, as conceptualized in Figure 4.1, attempts to describe the broad systemic relationships that guide media consumption and their effects for the individual and society. The model is a most general one that sacrifices specificity for a conceptual understanding of process. For instance, there is a severe jump from the highest order suprasystem—*society*—which entails all others, to its most immediate subsystem of the *general background* of the individual. Society, of which the structure of the media is recognized to be a part, could easily give way to a considerable hierarchy of subsystems involving groupings within society before subsuming the individual's general background. Similar things can be said of jumps between other systems. However, what is most important is that the *general background* subsumes the *general foreground,* which subsumes the *media reference background,* which subsumes the *media reference foreground,* and all of these transact to bring about *effects,* which are changes within and among individuals, the media structure, and society. This, by definition, entails changes in any and all systemic relationships and demands that such transactions be viewed within the context of infinitely changing dynamics.

The specified transactional model, as conceptualized in Figure 4.2, attempts to draw out the elements of the more general model in a way

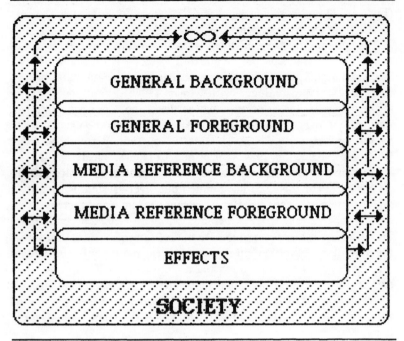

Figure 4.1   A General Transactional Model

that may be applied to research formulations. Still, even with additional specification, this is intended as a conceptual model. Much is recognized to exist that is not specified, and much could be added to the model to improve both its heuristic and practical value. As the specified model is subsumed by the general model, society is posed as a given. The "arrows" and "feedback" patterns featured in the general model are minimized, but certainly implied. The *general background* entails the social and psychological needs and values of the individual. In research practice, this has most often been tapped by demographic variables. However, as Rosengren's and Windahl's (1977) work with neuroticism and introversion/extroversion and Blumler's (Chapter 2, this volume) work with social characteristics suggest, there are other creative ways to assess such general background. The *general foreground* is cast largely in terms of *baseline effects dispositions.* This is in recognition that research problems need to be focused, and it is often unwieldly or unnecessary to include those less well-entrenched aspects of the individual that do not pertain to the area under investigation. Thus in political research, political dispositions may apply, while in developmental research a

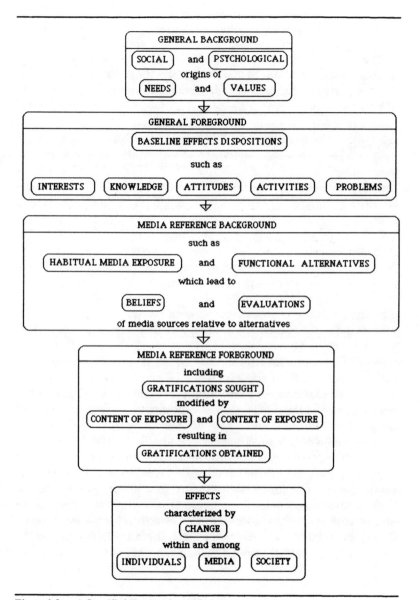

Figure 4.2   A Specified Transactional Model

completely different set of *interests, attitudes, activities, problems, knowledge,* and the like would be expected to apply.

The *media reference background* should include consideration of *habitual media exposure* patterns in association with the *functional alternatives* that exist and are available within the individual's repertoire of possible responses to the needs that take shape through the general background and foreground. Both media exposure patterns and experience with alternatives allow for *beliefs* and *evaluations* about media sources relative to the alternatives to be formed. It is especially important that both exposure and functional alternatives be tapped, as it is the combination of at least these experiences that allows for purposes to be adjusted adequately to form the assumptions that pertain to the situation.

In those instances where media are chosen over the available alternatives, the individual moves to the *media reference foreground,* where media-related *gratifications sought* come into the specific situation. In the effort to obtain the sought gratifications, *hitches* such as the *content* and *context* of exposure intervene. Very often it is difficult to form accurate assumptions about the *structural* elements that pertain to the content typically chosen from among limited alternatives, many of which are relatively unknown quantities. Similarly, it is often nearly impossible to control all the elements that exist in the *contextual* situation of exposure. These contextual hitches may be anticipated, such as deferring to someone else's television program choice, or may be unplanned, such as the interruption in exposure that a ringing telephone brings. Thus, for these and a host of other reasons, the *gratifications obtained* often do not directly reflect the gratifications that are sought.

The consequences of all of this, of course, can be looked at in any number of ways. Within the context of present "working" models, one would assume a focus in line with the general foreground and the baseline effects dispositions of interest. However, analysis need not be limited to such examinations. Patterns of cultural response certainly should emerge as those areas of the hierarchy between society and the individual's general background become more specified.

CONCLUDING COMMENTS

What is most important in this model, and the concept of transaction as it applies more broadly to media gratifications research, is the clear focus on dynamic *change,* not only within the individual, but *within and among individuals, media, and society.* The concept of transaction, if faithfully applied, provides the basis for a *transactional theory of media gratifications* that comes a long way indeed from the functional and tautological dilemmas that have hindered theoretical development in the past. It has been shown here that such a theory is grounded in a rich philosophical and theoretical heritage that is ultimately pragmatic, if nothing else. Such pragmatics are decidedly in keeping with the "common sense" reasoning that has contributed to the longevity of uses and gratifications research.

In applying the transactional view to future media gratifications research, it is important that a number of issues be addressed. A substantial need exists to differentiate gratification patterns in situations that have varying degrees of stability in assumptions. One of the more pressing issues of our time is how we adjust and revise our assumptions upon encountering the new forms of media that are constantly introduced by technological change and legitimized through our regulatory structures.

We should also ask whether stable assumptions need substantial revision as changes are implemented in longstanding media forms. For instance, when Dan Rather replaces Walter Cronkite on the *CBS Evening News,* it may be that the structural changes that accompany this signify markedly more than a mere change of anchormen. We need to investigate these "not-so-critical events" in terms of the changes in gratification patterns that parallel changes in cultural significances.

When stable assumptions break down, it seems clear that they are revised as a result of both structural and contextual factors. Thus it is crucial that we begin to look more rigorously at these elements that mediate the transaction between gratifications sought and obtained. In a sense, here we may begin to find the strongest evidence of the important media effects that hit at the core of defining our realities. How is it that we may come to the media situation seeking one thing but may come away content with obtaining quite another? What happens during exposure is clearly the key. Analysis of both content and context of exposure must be carried out within a gratifications framework if this framework is to be truly transactional.

Finally, it is important that we begin to study how the process of revising assumptions about media proceeds over time. In our longitudinal studies, we should be cautious not to assume that it is people who are merely changing and attribute this to media. Rather, it may be that it is the world that is changing, and we must realize, as Ittelson (1961: 351) has, that "as the world changes, so must we." The notion of transaction demands that we, as analysts of communication behavior, take notice of such things, or our "constancies" will lead to decidedly ineffective action.

Chapter 5

TOWARD A MERGER OF GRATIFICATIONS AND AGENDA-SETTING RESEARCH

Maxwell E. McCombs
David H. Weaver

IN THE EARLY 1970s, when agenda-setting was introduced by McCombs and Shaw (1972) as a media effect that seemed to override selective perception, many in the field of communication research paid little attention to the role of audience members' motivations to attend to various media messages. It seemed enough to show that agenda-setting was a powerful media effect after nearly 30 years of studies demonstrating the limited ability of mass media to change attitudes or candidate preferences (Berelson et al., 1954; Katz and Lazarsfeld, 1955; Lazarsfeld et al., 1944; Trenaman and McQuail, 1961). Klapper (1960) concisely summarized the general finding of much of this earlier research in his now famous statement that "Mass communication ordinarily does not serve as a necessary and sufficient cause of audience effects, but rather functions among and through a nexus of mediating functions and influence."

Although the McCombs and Shaw (1972) original agenda-setting study was a reassertion of powerful media effects, it was not an assertion of universal, undifferentiated effects. In their original article, they noted it was possible that individual differences in the judgments of the voters were lost by lumping all of them together in the data analysis, and they pointed out that the correlations between voter and media agendas were not uniform across all media and all groups of voters. They also recommended that subsequent research on agenda-setting move from a broad societal level to the social psychological level, comparing individual concerns with individual use of mass media.

One year after the original study by McCombs and Shaw appeared, McCombs and Weaver (1973) began testing whether differing motives to seek political information resulted in differing agenda-setting effects. They looked at the relationships between *need for orientation* (a combined measure of interest in and uncertainty about politics) and frequency of media use and strength of agenda-setting effects. They found that increased need for orientation was correlated with increased media use for political information, which in turn was correlated with stronger aggregate agenda-setting effects (McCombs and Weaver, 1973; Weaver, 1977a). In this study, they were moving from a linear effects model of agenda-setting to a more two-sided model in which audience motives and uses interacted with media content to produce differing effects. They were beginning to ask the gratifications question of what people do with media content in addition to asking the often repeated effects question of what media do to people, thus using the agenda-setting approach to try to bridge the gap between effects and gratifications research. Ultimately, agenda-setting's most important contribution to mass communication research may be as an integrating and bridging concept between distinct, and sometimes antagonistic, traditions.

THEORETICAL BACKGROUND

In terms of psychological theories of motivation, the idea of a need for orientation is derived primarily from cognitive utilitarian theories (McGuire, 1974), which provide an explanation for one of three basic media audience orientations (cognitive, diversion, and personal identity) identified by Blumler (1979) in his discussion of uses and gratifications research. As McGuire puts it, "these 'utilitarian theories' view the person as a problem solver who approaches any situation as an opportunity to acquire useful information or new skills for coping with life's challenges" (McGuire, 1974: 181).

Utilitarian theories of motivation also depict the individual as viewing the outside world, and communications from it, as a valuable source of relevant information. From this perspective, McGuire (1974) argues that mass communications offer a wide range of gratifications in the form of content that is perceived as instructive regarding how to live, how to manage, what is happening, and what it means. Such a view is consistent with the uses and gratifications approach to studying mass communication, which assumes that different audience members are oriented in different ways to mass media content, and that these different orientations are systematically related to different social circumstances and roles, different personality dispositions and capacities, different patterns of mass media use, and different media effects (Blumler, 1979).

Even though cognitive utilitarian theories of motivation are only one of 16 kinds of theories of cognitive and affective motivation identified by McGuire (1974), the utilitarian theories seem especially applicable to political information-seeking and media effects because these theories emphasize the role of information in problem solving. And political campaigns, with their demands for participation and allocation of power through voting decisions, are collective problem-solving activities. This is not to say that persons are oriented only in a cognitive utilitarian manner to political information in the mass media, but it is to argue that such an orientation is an important determinant of political information-seeking patterns from mass media and subsequent agenda-setting effects.

One of the earliest proponents of a utilitarian theory of motivation, E.C. Tolman (1932), argued that each person strives to "map" his world, to become familiar with his surroundings (both physical and cognitive) and to fill in enough detail to orient himself. From Tolman's concept of "cognitive mapping," from the writings of other utilitarian theorists, such as Berlyne (1960) and Jones and Gerard (1967), and from various information-seeking studies carried out by Atkin (1973), Chaffee and McLeod (1973), Donohew and Tipton (1973), Hawkins and Lanzetta (1965), and Westley and Barrow (1959), McCombs and Weaver (1973) defined political *need for orientation* in terms of two lower-order (less abstract) concepts: political relevance and political uncertainty.

Because the news media permeate nearly every aspect of American life and are readily available to most citizens, the third major factor suggested by these previous studies of information seeking (degree of effort required to receive the message) was considered a constant, although it can be argued that newspapers and other printed media require more physical and mental effort to use than do television and radio.

Earlier studies employing need for orientation defined three different levels of this cognitive information-seeking motive. Low relevance (regardless of degree of uncertainty) was assumed to result in a low need for orientation, high relevance and low uncertainty to result in a moderate need for orientation, and high relevance and high uncertainty to result in a high need for orientation. This reasoning was based on the assumption that high relevance is a necessary condition for pertinent uncertainty, but evidence from our 1976 year-long election study

Uncertainty

	Low	High
Low	Low Need for Orientation (Group III)	Moderate Need for Orientation (Group II)
Relevance		
High	Moderate Need for Orientation (Group II)	High Need for Orientation (Group I)

Figure 5.1   Revised Need for Orientation Typology

(Weaver et al., 1981) indicates the relationship is more reciprocal in nature than we first thought (Weaver, 1977b). This finding led to a modification of the original typology, as illustrated in Figure 5.1.

In this revised typology, high relevance and high uncertainty, combine to produce high need for orientation, as in the earlier version, but both high relevance and low uncertainty and low relevance and high uncertainty produce a moderate level of need for orientation. And finally, low relevance and low uncertainty result in a low need for orientation. There is still an argument to be made that the two moderate need for orientation conditions are different qualitatively, if not quantitatively. But to this point, no tests have been done to see if these moderate need for orientation conditions related differently to media use and media effects.

Although levels of relevance and uncertainty could be considered separate predictors of political information-seeking and media agenda-setting effects, there are theoretical and methodological advantages to combining both concepts into a single hypothetical construct labeled need for orientation. By combining uncertainty (the perceived existence of a gap or problem) with relevance (the perceived importance of the problem), one is tapping the major dimensions of many utilitarian theories of motivation in a single, fairly abstract construct that may be applied to a wide variety of settings. And methodologically, it is easier and more parsimonious to use only one variable to partition a sample to observe media use-media effects relationships, as is necessary when assessing aggregate agenda-setting effects.

PREVIOUS RESEARCH

Earlier studies (McCombs, 1967; McCombs and Weaver, 1973; Mueller, 1970; Weaver, 1977a, 1977b; Weaver et al., 1975; Westley and Barrow, 1959) have suggested that higher levels of need for orientation are associated with increased effectiveness of editorial endorsements in selected elections, with increased use of mass media for political information, and with increased aggregate agenda-setting effects of newspapers and, to a lesser extent, television news.

More recent agenda-setting studies have added to our knowledge of the relationship between the need for orientation motive and subsequent media effects. These studies have suggested it is important to distinguish between aggregate and individual-level agenda-setting effects and the nature of the political campaign being studied.

In our year-long study of the 1976 presidential election, using aggregate data, we found that although levels of motivation to follow the campaign had only minor effects on issue agendas during the spring and summer periods, those groups of voters with a high need for orientation had issue agendas in the fall that were substantially more similar to the newspaper and television agendas than did other voters (Weaver et al., 1981). In that study, motivation to follow the campaign was most important in the agenda-setting process near the end of the race when the need for information was greatest for the still-undecided voters. And after the election, voters with a high need for orientation were more likely than others to cite issues as more important than candidate images or political party in deciding for whom to vote.

In another study employing aggregate public opinion data, MacKuen and Coombs (1981) found that over a 17-year time period (1960-1977) those most interested in politics had group agendas most similar to the various media agendas, and that the dramatic character of events was more important in stimulating increased public concern than was the sheer frequency of coverage. Erbring et al. (1980), using individual level measures of issue salience from a 1974 U.S. election study, also found that increased uncertainty (weaker political party affiliation) and increased interest in public affairs were positively linked to increases in concern about government credibility.

Thus all the studies mentioned so far suggest that increased interest and uncertainty (high need for orientation) is correlated with increased media agenda-setting effects. But these studies are mostly set in highly prominent elections, and most of them employ aggregate, or group, measures of public agenda rather than individual measures of issue concerns.

In a study of potential voters in Madison, Wisconsin, which employed individual-level measures during the 1972 presidential election, McLeod et al. (1974) found *less* interested voters to show stronger agenda-setting effects than the more interested, but the more undecided younger voters showed stronger agenda-setting effects, suggesting that those with a moderate need for orientation (low interest and high uncertainty) are most affected. Likewise, in a study of West Germany voters using individual-level measures during the 1979 European Parliamentary Election campaign, Schoenbach and Weaver (1983) also found those with low interest and high uncertainty (a moderate level of need for orientation) were most influenced by media exposure regarding the salience of European issues. And Iyengar et al. (1983) found in two experiments with television news agendas using individual-level measures that more involved and attentive individuals were *less* affected by TV news agendas than were the less attentive.

These individual-level studies just cited suggest that we cannot always assume a positive relationship between need for orientation and media agenda-setting effects. There appear to be situations in which less interest (if not less uncertainty) is predictive of greater agenda-setting effects. Obviously, there is not a one-to-one relationship between the strength of the cognitive utilitarian motive of need for orientation and the strength of media agenda-setting effects. But there is no doubt from these various studies that levels of motivation of media audience members do influence the strength of media exposure-media effects relationships. It seems, though, that other variables must be taken into account, including the overall importance of the campaign or subject being studied, the personal experience of people with regard to the issues on the media agenda, and the degree of interpersonal discussion of these issues.

OTHER MOTIVES AND NEED FOR ORIENTATION

In addition to the considerations mentioned above, there is also the very real possibility that other kinds of motives besides cognitive utilitarian ones prompt members of the public to attend to print and broadcast news. Such motives could include those labeled *diversion* and *personal identity* by Blumler (1979) in his discussion of uses and gratifications research. Indeed, many researchers studying the uses and gratifications of media content have employed a wide range of motives in trying to account for patterns of media use and, to a lesser extent, media effects. This strategy of broadscale exploration of motives stands in contrast to the more in-depth approach of concentrating on a single kind of motive in the need for orientation studies mentioned above.

In order to address the question of whether there is an explanatory advantage in considering other kinds of motives (anticipated gratifications) in addition to need for orientation in trying to predict media uses and effects, Weaver (1980) treated different levels of need for orientation and different levels of other motives (cognitive, personal identity, and diversion) as contingent conditions within which the correlations between media use and media effects were analyzed.

When a general measure of cognitive motivation (need for orientation) was compared to a more specific cognitive gratification, the more general measure had greater influence as a contingent condition on the media use-media effects relationships than did the specific gratification measure. This finding was interpreted to support Blumler's (1979) proposal stating that we need to turn to basic audience orientations to predict and explain media influence processes, rather than adding still more measures of specific gratifications to our already long lists. Development of more general measures of motives would be more parsimonious from both a theoretical and methodological viewpoint, and such general measures might be more easily standardized across different studies to provide more comparable findings.

Construction of more general measures of diversion and personal identity motives might follow the reasoning used in constructing the need for orientation measure. That is, such measures might be *inferred* rather than directly ascertained. Instead of asking people directly if they use various media for entertainment or reinforcement, one might ask how often a person agreed with a particular kind of article or program, or how relaxed a person felt while using a specific medium or kind of media content. One might also try to identify the main dimensions of personal identity and diversion motives, as has been done for the cognitive motive of need for orientation, and then combine these dimensions into a single measure.

Such a strategy might not only produce more general measures of various motives, but might also avoid some of the social desirability problems associated with more specific gratification measures, as well as the methodological problems involved in trying to reduce specific gratification measures to consistent groups via factor or cluster analysis.

GRATIFICATIONS SOUGHT AND OBTAINED

While uses and gratifications research traditionally has emphasized the motives for media consumption, or, in other words, the gratifications sought from mass communication, there has been increased attention in the last decade to both a theoretical and empirical distinction between gratifications sought and gratifications actually obtained from this exposure. Recent evidence underscores the importance of examining both aspects of human experience with communication (Palmgreen, 1984b).

The concept of need for orientation as a theoretical explanation for agenda-setting effects clearly falls into the category of gratifications sought. People turn to the news media for orientation to the political environment (although the general nature of the NFO concept would allow the substitution of other environments as well). Within agenda-setting research no explicit attention has ever been paid to the extent that this need has actually been fulfilled by media exposure.

Explicit mapping of this consequence—or, effect, if you will—of media exposure would increase both the scope and precision of our theory. This would bring another mass communication subfield of long standing, knowledge acquisition, explicitly into the theoretical model.

Need for orientation as a conceptualization of gratifications sought may be sufficient to predict agenda-setting effects, but such a limited three-part model (NFO $\longrightarrow$ media exposure $\longrightarrow$ A-S effects) is far from the full picture of the mass communication process. Several aspects of this statement need to be noted. First, NFO as a conceptualization limited to gratifications sought may be sufficient to predict the appearance of agenda-setting effects. Obviously, a necessary condition for direct agenda-setting effects is exposure to the mass media. NFO may simply motivate people to attune themselves to the messages of the mass media, and agenda-setting effects often may occur as an inadvertant by-product of this exposure. McCombs and Shaw (1972) described agenda-setting in exactly these terms. It is quite possible that these agenda-setting effects may occur whether or not an individual's need for orientation is satisfied by exposure to the media. Of course, we will not know until the gratifications obtained from this exposure are actually measured and their relationship to agenda-setting outcomes analyzed.

Even in the absence of any systematic relationship between fulfillment of the need for orientation and agenda-setting effects, measurement of the gratifications obtained will enhance our understanding of subsequent media use patterns (and whether the opportunity for continuing and subsequent agenda-setting effects will be present in an individual's life). Consider the situations outlined in Figure 5.2. In the first instance, exposure to the media does not result in fulfillment of the need for orientation and, in frustration, this individual abandons any further use of this medium. While the presence or absence of any agenda-setting in the current situation is an as-yet unanswered question, clearly there will be no direct agenda-setting in the future. Of course, this scenario also raises the question of whether this frustrated individual now turns to other sources or just abandons the field altogether.

In the second instance outlined in Figure 5.2, the outcome of exposure is again negative. No gratification is obtained, but in this instance the individual does return to the media in a further effort to fulfill his or her need for orientation. Obviously, the opportunity for future, direct agenda-setting effects is present.

The final two instances deal with positive outcomes in terms of gratifications obtained. One depicts an individual who has little need for subsequent media exposure. The other illustrates the individual who continues to monitor the media, although it might be useful here to distinguish qualitatively between those individuals who continue to engage in active information seeking and those who engage only in casual surveillance of media content.

To recap, there are two questions to be considered here. First, is success or failure in fulfilling the need for orientation related to agenda-setting or is mere exposure sufficient? Second, is the typology of individuals outlined in Figure 5.2 anything more than an intellectual exercise?

This typology does seem to sort out key patterns in the media audience. For example, Weaver et al. (1981) found high levels of exposure to both newspapers and television news during March of the 1976 election year, a period when we might infer the presence of a high level of need for orientation. However, these levels of exposure were consistently lower for the remainder of the election year. This suggests that a considerable number of voters exhibited pattern C for the remainder of the election year. Once their need for orientation was gratified, they felt less need to keep up with the campaign. What distinguishes these voters from those in pattern D who continued to follow the campaign in the news media? Do these differences have

	Need Fulfilled	Agenda-setting	Subsequent Media Use	Agenda-setting
A.	NO	?	NO	no
B.	NO	?	YES	_yes_a
C.	YES	_yes_a	NO	no
D.	YES	_yes_a	YES	_yes_a

a. Conditional upon the various constraints outlined in the research literature.

Figure 5.2   Consequences of Media Exposure: A Typology

consequence for the agenda-setting effects that differed sharply across the months of 1976?

THE ACTIVE AUDIENCE

The preceding discussion moved forward from media exposure to consider gratifications obtained and their consequences. It is now time to backtrack and consider in more detail another area: how gratifications sought are translated into exposure to specific media and specific content.

Central to the uses and gratifications assumption of an active audience is the concept of *expectancy*, some set of audience beliefs about the various media of communications and their contents (see Chapter 3, this volume). What set of beliefs guides the selection of media used by individuals seeking to fulfill their need for orientation? In other words, which perceived attributes of newspapers and television in general, and which perceived attributes of the specific daily newspapers and television networks available to each individual, guide his or her pattern of exposure? These expectations about the news media guide decisions about where to turn in order to fulfill the need for orientation. Yet we know only a little about how these decisions are made.

The newspaper research literature suggests that general affect toward a particular daily and perceptions of its accuracy are important variables in these decisions (Cobbey, 1980). Public opinion research suggests that the perceived credibility of both newspapers and television are also important variables (McCombs and Washington, 1983). But none of this research has been integrated into the theoretical models of either uses and gratifcations or agenda-setting.

For the specific news messages selected in an attempt to fulfill the need for orientation, Graber's (1984) in-depth analysis of how voters process the news identifies the major criteria of story selection. Both personal relevance and societal importance are high on the list of criteria articulated by her panel of Illinois voters during the 1976 presidential campaign. Also appearing among the criteria are two concepts familiar to journalists, human interest and emotional appeal. Graber's pioneering work begins the complex task of sorting out attention to, learning from, and remembering of specific media messages. While we can speculate about how all this is linked to need for orientation, much territory remains to be mapped.

One portion of the theoretical territory involving specific media content has been mapped in the agenda-setting literature. In one of those rare cumulative instances of social science, the kinds of issues for which media attention does not result in agenda-setting effects have been specified. In the language of agenda-setting, *obtrusive* issues, such as inflation, are ones for which people can rely upon their own personal experience and observations and have little need to turn to the mass media for orientation. In contrast, *unobtrusive* issues, such as foreign affairs, are those for which people must rely upon vicarious media experience, rather than personal experience, to form their pictures of the world. Detailed analysis of voters' agendas during the 1976 U.S. presidential campaign (Weaver et al., 1981), and of public trends and media coverage across several decades (Winter and Eyal, 1981) have documented the agenda-setting effects of media coverage on unobtrusive issues and the lack of effects for obtrusive issues.

While early research and the illustrative descriptions here have classified issues as obtrusive or unobtrusive, in reality these terms are the anchors for a continuum on which each individual must locate each issue (Blood, 1981). Some issues, such as inflation and foreign affairs, have extreme modal values and little variance. But others, such as unemployment, have considerable variance and quite different modal positions on this continuum among different groups.

Conceptualizing issues as obtrusive/unobtrusive defines one dimension of people's perceptions of media content and how they respond to it. Renewed effort must be given to identifying other relevant dimensions of mass communication that govern the interactions of media effects and audience uses and gratifications.

LINKS TO THE SPIRAL OF SILENCE

The "spiral of silence" is a theory proposed by Elisabeth Noelle-Neumann (1984) to explain the shifting distributions of public opinion over time. According to this theory, most persons who perceive their position to be waning or in the minority reduce their overt support for their position in fear of isolation from the majority position in society. This reduction of overt support further strengthens perceptions of decline, leading to yet further reductions, a spiral of silence accounting for major shifts in public opinion, both actual and perceived.

Two concepts are important constants in this theory. One, the fear of social isolation as the motivating variable for the spiral of silence, is traced by Noelle-Neumann (1979) through several centuries of Western thought on public opinion. The other concept, that of a quasi-statistical sense, is presented as a psychological characteristic of humans that enables them to perceive and be sensitive to the shifting distributions of public opinion over time.

This concept of a quasi-statistical sense is related to the agenda-setting concept of a need for orientation. Both are assumed to be psychological characteristics of all individuals. The idea of a quasi-statistical sense asserts that individuals have a need to know their social environment and the distribution of social support for various positions. Put another way, the idea of a quasi-statistical sense suggests that individuals are sensitive to the levels of social support for their positions on political and public issues. The concept of need for orientation emphasizes that individuals will strive to map their environment, especially in a new or ambiguous situation. That is, need for orientation is a motivating variable in its own right, whereas Noelle-Neumann's theory links the quasi-statistical sense to a motivating variable, fear of isolation. Now at least in some instances people may simply be curious about what is going on around them in society and what are likely to be future trends. Fear of isolation is not always the motivating drive behind information-seeking behavior.

In any event, the concept of a need for orientation clearly implies individual differences in the level of this need (as well as individual differences in the level of need for orientation in regard to various

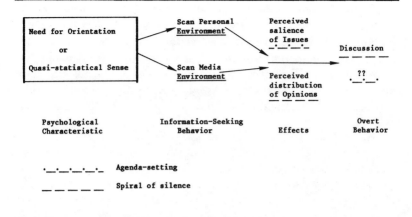

Figure 5.3   Agenda-Setting and the Spiral of Silence

objects of attention). Similar individual differences could be inputed to the quasi-statistical sense, although Noelle-Neumann tends to treat it as a constant in her theory of public opinion.

Emphasis on individual differences brings to the fore questions about variations in people's experiences with issues or other public topics and the question of under what circumstances people turn to the media to orient themselves. Both concepts, need for orientation and quasi-statistical sense, assert that people turn to the media and to interpersonal sources for information about their environment. Under what circumstances do people prefer one or the other source? What conditions predict the selection of various sources of orientation?

While both concepts predict subsequent information-seeking behavior, their origins in different theoretical traditions lead them to emphasize quite different effects of this information seeking. As Figure 5.3 outlines, agenda-setting emphasizes shifts in the perceived salience of issues while the spiral of silence emphasizes perceived distributions of opinions as the outcome of information seeking.

While the spiral of silence is quite explicit in its treatment of subsequent overt behavior, agenda-setting research to date has explored these behavioral outcomes in a more casual and cursory manner. Joint consideration of the two theoretical traditions and their sets of concepts promises to enhance our understanding of mass communication, both in terms of the uses and gratifications that bring people into the media audience, and in terms of the effects that result, especially in the areas of political communication and public opinion.

Continuing exploration and development of the agenda-setting role of the mass media promises to bring a number of research concerns, ranging from communicator behavior to audience transactions with the media, into a common theoretical framework. In addition, continued examination will further the merger of our field's research traditions into a more coherent paradigm. Agenda-setting can be a fruitful bridge between the effects tradition and the uses and gratifications tradition.

Chapter 6

THE CONCEPT OF AUDIENCE ACTIVITY

Mark R. Levy
Sven Windahl

ONE OF THE LONGEST-LIVED CONTROVERSIES in the short history of communication research centers on the nature of the mass media audience. Is that audience an active or a passive participant in the communication process? How does this active or passive orientation arise? And what are its consequences for mass communication, especially most communication effects?

Some scholars, particularly those influenced by the notion of mass society and/or critical theory (see, for example, Noelle-Neumann, 1973; Swingewood, 1977), see the audience as overwhelmingly passive, manipulated and dominated from above, with the mass media acting as a powerful agent of ideological control. Others (for example, Gans, 1980; Barwise et al., 1982) believe the audience is essentially passive, but ground that judgment in less overtly ideological explanations.

By contrast, the limited effects tradition (Klapper, 1960; Bauer, 1964b) offers the image of an audience that resists media influence in an active, obstinate way. Two other perspectives that depict individuals as actively processing and creating meanings from mass media messages are constructivism (Delia, 1977; Swanson, 1979b) and sense-making (Dervin, 1981). Finally, economic models of audience behavior (see, for example, Owen et al., 1974) also assume that media use is essentially active.

Audience activity is, of course, central to the uses and gratifications tradition (Katz et al., 1974). Indeed, the assumption of audience activity

AUTHORS' NOTE: We would like to thank Michael Gurevitch, Jay Blumler, Karl Erik Rosengren, Phil Palmgreen, and Jim Webster for sharing their insights with us.

represents a major difference between the uses and gratifications approach and traditional effects theories, and also places uses and gratifications research at odds with most critical studies.

As commonly understood by gratifications researchers, the term "audience activity" postulates a voluntaristic and selective orientation by audiences toward the communication process. In brief, it suggests that media use is motivated by needs and goals that are defined by audience members themselves, and that active participation in the communication process may facilitate, limit, or otherwise influence the gratifications and effects associated with exposure (Lin, 1977). Current thinking (Levy, 1978a; Blumler, 1979; Levy and Windahl, 1984) also suggests that audience activity is best conceptualized as a variable construct, with audiences exhibiting varying kinds and degrees of activity.

Within the uses and gratifications tradition, there is some evidence to support the notion of an active audience. Studies have shown, for example, that audience members can differentiate between and among channels on the basis of gratifications sought and/or obtained (Katz et al., 1973; Lometti et al., 1977; A. Rubin and R. Rubin, 1982b; Barwise et al., 1982) and that audience motivations affect the active assignment of meanings to messages (Garramone, 1983).

Despite its centrality to mass communication theory, however, the notion of audience activity has received little conceptual development or direct study (Windahl, 1981). Previous reports (Blumler, 1979; Katz, 1979; Levy and Windahl, 1984) have dealt with the principal criticisms that have been raised concerning use of the activity concept in gratifications research. In an attempt to move beyond the sterile aspects of that debate, this chapter will first consider several different approaches to understanding audience behavior and examine how each deals with audience activity. Next, we will discuss two different strategies for identifying types of audience activity, and we will conclude with some thoughts about the linkages among activity, media gratifications, and communication effects.

ORIGINS OF AUDIENCE ACTIVITY: THREE APPROACHES

It has often been argued (Blumler, 1979; Windahl, 1981) that the uses and gratifications approach is not one theory, but rather an umbrella for a rather diverse set of theories and models. Given this diversity in underlying assumptions, explanatory frameworks, and research methods, we would expect to find considerable variety in approaches to audience activity. One potentially fruitful way to explore this issue is to consider how some common theoretical perspectives on audience behavior deal with the question of audience activity.

McQuail and Gurevitch (1974) identify three such perspectives: the functional, which has a "needs-gratifications" focus; the structural-cultural, which emphasizes the social regulation of both media content and exposure behaviors; and the action/motivation, which stresses the individual as purposive actor.

At first thought, it is tempting to conclude that the action/motivation approach postulates the most active audience, with the functional and structural-cultural perspectives implying a much more highly determined and hence much less active audience member. Certainly the image of the individual under the action/motivation perspective is one of substantial autonomy, an almost boundless freedom to engage in the so-called projected act (Schutz, 1972). By contrast, functional explanations would seem to argue that psychological and social factors determine individual needs, motives, and media-related gratifications (Swanson, 1979b), thus undermining audience voluntarism. Similarly, the structural-cultural approach emphasizes a materialistic and/or cultural determinism that its proponents (see, for example, Elliott, 1974; Hall, 1977) contend severely limits choice and activity.

On reflection, however, this simple rank ordering in terms of activity becomes more problematic. Indeed, we would suggest that each of the three perspectives allows for varying kinds and amounts of audience activity. Following the action/motivation approach, for example, an individual may freely seek out media exposure in order, say, to "kill time," and he or she may freely interpret the messages received as trivial or uninvolving. Such a person, as our discussion of activity types that follows will make clear, ought not be considered an especially active audience member. With regard to the functional approach, while it is true that psychological and social factors may influence individual needs, motives, and behaviors, there is no theoretical or empirical basis to conclude that such factors are completely or even substantially deterministic. To use a statistical turn of phrase, much less than half the variance in audience activity can be explained in terms of its social psychological antecedents (McLeod and Becker, 1981). Finally, with regard to the structural-cultural perspective, we contend that position in social structure is as likely to make individuals active toward media use as it is to make them passive, and that the activity of individuals can vary enormously both within and among social classes. After all, even those scholars who argue from a position of materialistic determinism (Hall, 1980; Parkin, 1972) allow for audience activity in the sense of negotiated and oppositional "readings" of hegemonic messages.

In summary, then, all major approaches to the study of audiences contain assumptions, either implicit or explicit, about activity. In the next section, we will examine in detail the theoretical parameters of that crucial concept.

A TYPOLOGY OF AUDIENCE ACTIVITY

Building on earlier work (Levy, 1983; Levy and Windahl, 1984), we will now develop a typology of audience activity. The typology is constructed from two orthogonal dimensions. The first—the *qualitative orientation* of audience members toward the communication process—has been given three nominal values: (1) selectivity, (2) involvement, and (3) utility. By "selectivity," we mean a process involving the nonrandom selection of one or more behavioral, perceptual, or cognitive media-related alternatives. We understand audience "involvement" to be, first, the degree to which an audience member perceives a connection between him or herself and mass media content; and, second, the degree to which the individual interacts psychologically with a medium or its messages (Rosengren and Windahl, 1972). By "utility" we mean that individuals use or anticipate using mass communications for manifold social and psychological purposes (see, for example, Atkin, 1973).

The second dimension that defines the typology of audience activity is *temporal* and asks whether audience activity occurs before, during, or after exposure (Blumler, 1979). How long before exposure is "before" and how long after is "after" remain unspecified in this current version of the typology. Future work must seek to clarify this point, since it has been suggested, for example, that seeking *exposure* to television per se may be a relatively passive behavior, but choosing which program to watch may reflect a more active decision (Barwise et al., 1982).

Cross-tabulating audience orientations with time results in a ninefold table, the cells of which represent various types of audience activity (see Figure 6.1). There is no reason, of course, to assume that our two dimensional typology is exhaustive. Indeed, later in this chapter we will discuss other possible variations in audience activity not directly subsumed in this initial typology. Rather, this typology is offered as a

COMMUNICATION SEQUENCE			
AUDIENCE ORIENTATION	Before Exposure	During Exposure	After Exposure
Selectivity	Selective exposure-seeking	Selective perception	Selective recall
Involvement	Anticipation of exposure	Attention Meaning creation Parasocial interaction Identification	Long-term identification Fantasizing
Utility	"Coin of exchange"	Using the gratifications obtained	Topic use Opinion leadership

Figure 6.1   A Typology of Audience Activity (with some examples)

heuristic device, the merit of which must be judged by its utility in clarifying and exemplifying the activity concept.

With the twin goals of explication and exemplification in mind, we will now examine each cell of the typology shown in Figure 6.1, starting with the type of activity (selectivity before exposure) that has been most widely discussed in the literature (see Katz et al., 1974, and the more than twenty studies cited in Palmgreen, 1984b).

Selectivity before exposure. Historically, the term "selective exposure-seeking" has had at least two interpretations. The first, oldest, and perhaps most problematic meaning (Sears and Freedman, 1967) denotes a psychological process that is fundamentally defensive, growing out of the individual's desire to avoid the dissonance that might arise from exposure to messages that conflict with preexisting attitudes, opinions, and the like. The classic political campaign studies (e.g., Lazarsfeld et al., 1944) typify this approach.

More recently, however, uses and gratifications investigators have applied a different interpretation to the term. In the uses and gratifications tradition, selectivity in exposure-seeking is said to reflect the individual's decision to be exposed, since, based on learned perceptions of the media and prior experiences with them, the individual has come to expect certain levels of gratification. Viewers of television news, for example, have been shown to plan exposure to newscasts deliberately because they believe watching TV news will help them gratify certain cognitive and affective needs (Levy, 1977a, 1978b).

We would argue that both the older and more recent interpretation of selective exposure are dealing with manifestations of audience activity. Attempting to regulate one's exposure to dissonant and nondissonant messages, whether successful or not, most certainly represents an active orientation to the communication experience. But we would also contend that selective exposure for gratificational ends, attempting as it does "to impress the media into the service of individual needs and values" (Katz, 1979: 75), suggests a more sweeping and more active quality to selectivity before exposure.

Selectivity during exposure. While previous applications of selectivity theory to uses and gratifications studies have largely been confined to the preexposure phase of the communications sequence, it is clear that the consumption of media messages is itself a selective behavior, involving a large number of choices (see, e.g., the importance of choice, Howard and Tipton, 1973). The principle of selective perception, in other words, suggests that audience members pay attention to certain messages or parts of messages, disregarding others. Studies of the Sunday newspaper readers, for example, have shown that two persons while reading the same newspaper have in fact consciously chosen to expose themselves to very different message sets (Bogart, 1981).

To the extent that selective perception during contact with mass media messages represents a conscious, motivated behavior, such an audience orientation should be judged to be relatively active. To the degree that selective perception is found to be a comparatively "automatic" or unconscious information-processing strategy, we would consider that to be an indicator of a less active orientation.

Selectivity after exposure. Selective recall is the most obvious example of postexposure selectivity, and suggests that individuals remember only a small fraction of the information to which they have been exposed. It has been found, for example, that approximately only one-third of the major news stories presented over a one-week period are remembered in any form by persons who claim to have been exposed to the news (Levy and Robinson, forthcoming.)

While selective recall has not traditionally been viewed as a type of audience activity, we would suggest that it ought to be included. An individual who, by whatever cognitive processes and for whatever gratificational ends, recalls larger amounts of media content must be considered a more active participant in the communication process than another person for whom media content "goes in one eye and out the other" (Gans, 1980). Indeed, the quintessential image of a passive audience member most certainly must be of a person who has absolutely no recall of the communication experience.

Involvement before exposure. Less oxymoronic than it first seems, the term "involvement before exposure" is meant to suggest that some level of anticipation may be associated with projected media use. When, for example, an individual says he or she is "looking forward to" seeing a particular television program, motion picture, or whatever, that individual may be thought of as engaging in a form of preexposure involvement. Another example of this preexposure activity might be daydreaming about or trying to guess what will happen in, say, the next episode on a TV drama series. While preexposure involvement might be a comparatively rare phenomenon, it is also possible that this type of activity may have important consequences for exposure patterns, particularly repeat viewing.

Involvement during exposure. Several very different types of activity occur during exposure to mass media messages. One way to understand them better is to consider at what levels of psychological consciousness the types of activity occur. Tagg (1981) suggests that music is received at three different levels of consciousness. His discussion may have implications for media use more generally. Following Tagg, we will examine the subconscious, preconscious, and structurally conscious levels. On the *subconscious* [...] measurable neurological responses o[...] al is unaware of the message and little[...] kes place. In the case of music, an exa[...] markets and elevators. An example f[...] playing of a television set as "backgro[...] 's no special attention to what is bein[...]

On the *preconscious* le[...] he presence of the stimulus and resp[...] ual is, by and large, unable to report verbally on what just happened in the music or what it "did" to him or her. As for mass media use, the preconscious level may be exemplified by the inability of many people to recall the details of, say, a TV newscast to which they have just been exposed. The *structurally conscious* level, by contrast, is one in which the music listener is aware of the stimuli, is capable of verbalizing what is happening *in* the music, and can express the kind of experience he or she has had with the music. Similarly, the structurally conscious mass media user is aware of the content, tries to provide it with meaning, and has a more or less clear understanding of the structure of the message. The structurally conscious mass media user is also able to link content to the exposure experience. Although affective responses may predominate at the preconscious level, responses at the level of structural consciousness may be more cognitive.

With regard to the types of activity that occur during mass media exposure, we would suggest that the truly attentive audience member is involved on the level of structural consciousness, and that the degree of involvement increases with attention. Attempting to provide content

Not in the domain of uses and gratifications

with meanings (see, for example, Delia, 1977; Dervin, 1981; Swanson, 1979b) represents an especially important aspect of audience activity. We assume meaning-making takes place primarily at the level of structural consciousness, but may on occasion be located on a preconscious level. Para-social interaction (Horton and Wohl, 1956; Levy, 1979) and the closely related notion of identification (Rosengren and Windahl, 1972) might be either preconscious or subconscious phenomena, suggesting relatively lower levels of audience involvement or activity. In short, by linking levels of psychological consciousness to types of audience activity, it may be possible to study more fruitfully the mechanisms by which active *and* passive audiences are affected by exposure.

Look at Pingree on Important point is not audience

Postexposure involvement. In principle, an individual's active involvement with mass media messages need not be confined solely to the moments of actual consumption, and may indeed continue long after direct contact with the messages has ceased (Rosengren et al., 1976). Children, for example, who take on the identity of a fictional superhero and carry that identification over into their play, we would contend, are engaged in a kind of postexposure involvement. Similarly, children or adults whose daydreams or fantasies are based in part on the content of mass media messages also fall into the category of the postexposure involved (McIlwraite and Schallow, 1983).

can generate gratifications out of almost any type of content Rosengren & Windahl p. 166

Utility before exposure. Even before mass media exposure occurs, it may offer intrapersonal and social utilities for the individual. We are thinking here primarily of a "coin of exchange" function (Windahl, 1981) in which upcoming media presentations provide the subject matter for socially integrating conversation. ("Hey, you gonna watch *the* game, tonight?"). Moreover, it is possible to conceive of a specialized form of opinion leadership in which leadership status is based on information and opinions about forthcoming media messages and in which leaders alert nonleaders to opportunities for potentially gratifying exposure.

Utility during exposure. During exposure, individuals may find social and psychological utilities arising from their interaction with the media. Many of the cognitive and affective gratifications obtained from media use are experienced in the situation of exposure.[1] The TV viewer who uses parts of program content in order to assure him- or herself that he or she is "right" in some opinion, attitude, stereotype, or other view is one example of a concurrent use. Indeed, the mass media are often used for making sense of reality. In a complex world, individuals may use what they have just read, heard, or seen to affirm their commonsense

parasocial interaction

view of the world or to justify a change in their perception of reality. This sense-making use may continue after exposure as well.

A related use occurs when what one learns about other people through media exposure is applied in one's own life and situation (see, for example, Herzog, 1944). Indeed, this comparing oneself with others use may be one of the principal reasons for the popularity of "human interest stories" in both the informational and entertainment media.

Yet another example of utility during exposure is that of the individual who makes a snide comment about a news item while viewing a television newscast. Such a person has seized the moment to express and thereby share some political or social sentiment (Levy, 1977a). In general, we would postulate that the more social and psychological utilities an individual experiences during exposure, the more that individual should be considered an active participant in the communication process.

Postexposure utility. Nearly all uses and gratifications studies have found postexposure utilities associated with media use. If an individual actually talks about things he or she has seen or read, actually reflects on or otherwise integrates information gained into psychological or social behaviors (for example, opinion leadership; see Levy, 1978d), then such an individual may be thought of as exhibiting postexposure activity.

INTERRELATIONS OF ACTIVITY TYPES

In the ninefold typology just outlined, we have postulated that selectivity, involvement, and utility are three aspects of the same concept, namely, audience activity. It would be appropriate therefore to ask how, if at all, these three orientations are interrelated, both across time and within the same phase of the communication sequence.

Based on our earlier work (Levy and Windahl, 1984), we would suggest that there is no theoretical or empirical basis for an a priori specification of either the diachronic or synchronic relationships among activity types. First, with regard to the across-time associations, one could imagine that audiences might be relatively consistent in their selectivity, involvement, and utility orientations to the communication process, a given medium, message genre, or communication setting. If this is so, then one would expect audience members to manifest approximately the same degree of activity at each stage of the communication sequence.

On the other hand, it could also be argued that audience activity will not be consistently high or low across time, even controlling for message systems, channels, and the like. Such a temporal inconsistency would not, however, suggest the absence of a theoretically meaningful association among selectivity, involvement, and utility. We have reported data about viewers of television news in Sweden that show a relatively strong correlation between selectivity in exposure seeking and post-exposure use, but no significant relationships between those pre- and postexposure activities and involvement during viewing. We interpret those findings to suggest that the needs that motivate TV news exposure and the uses to which that exposure are put can be met adequately by a comparatively low level of audience activity during exposure. In short, the audience member decides how active he or she wants to be or must be, and when.

As to activity within the same phase of the communication sequence, we would contend that the interrelations of types is also a matter for empirical investigation. However, certain kinds of associations among activity types might be logically expected. For example, an individual who is highly selective in exposure seeking may be actively anticipating his or her exposure—a linkage of two different orientations. Further, someone who is actively involved with, say, media personae during exposure, perhaps to the point of identification, may be experiencing gratifications of an immediate, intrapersonally useful sort. Finally, an individual who actively recalls some information gained during exposure may be doing so in order to use that information to satisfy the role demands of opinion leadership, and that, too, represents an important linkage across activity types.

Overall, we would urge operationalization of the extended typology given above so that the issue of activity-type interrelationships can be addressed empirically. One possible line of research might flow from extending the ninefold typology by combining two or more activity types. For example, preexposure selectivity and involvement during exposure might be considered as dichotomous variables, each with high and low values. Combining the two variables results in a new typology, the cells of which represent four subtypes of audience activity (see Figure 6.2).

As Figure 6.2 illustrates, *motivated gratification seeking* is clearly an especially active orientation. Individuals who fall into this high-selectivity, high-involvement cell may deliberately search for content and communications situations that they expect will yield strong immediate gratifications, and that they in fact experience as being gratifying.

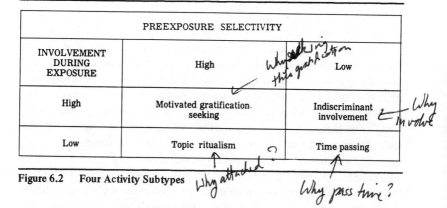

Figure 6.2 Four Activity Subtypes

[handwritten annotations: "Why seeking in this graph option", "Why Involve", "Why attached", "Why pass time?"]

Topic ritualism represents the consumption of media content in a habitual, relatively noninvolved fashion. Exposure may be highly valued as something "good" in its own right, or because of substantive message content. Still, the topic ritualist remains comparatively uninvolved with the communication situation, a potentially far less active member of the audience than the motivated gratification seeker.

Indiscriminant involvement is a theoretically interesting activity subtype that raises the possibility of audience members who actively process and relate to almost any type of media content. People who watch television rather than watching specific programs may exemplify this subtype. *(Lost in a book, extreme distraction)*

Time-passing is obviously indicative of a comparatively inactive orientation. We have in mind here the widespread stereotype of the "boob tube" audience, viewers who use that medium as an easily accessible and largely unfulfilling way to pass time. Whether such persons exist and to what extent they are truly passive vis-à-vis the communication experience remains unexamined. *Truly non-instrumental in terms of orientation, but just as highly motivated to take part.*

A CONTINGENCY PERSPECTIVE ON AUDIENCE ACTIVITY

Thus far, we have argued that audience activity is best treated as a variable construct, that people are more or less active in their roles as members of the mass media audience, and that the kinds and amounts of activity displayed are likely to vary across time in the communication sequence. In this section, we will suggest that activity is also contingent on a number of other factors and these factors can be grouped into individual, social, and media variables.

Turning first to individual-level factors, it is obvious that human beings differ from each other in potentially relevant ways such as sex, age, intelligence, personality, and place in the life cycle. And it is equally obvious that factors such as mood, levels of physical or mental fatigue, and availability of leisure time may vary both among individuals and within the same person at different points in time. Although virtually none of these individual differences has been studied from the focus of activity, we believe such research would find that these and other individual-level factors do influence activity. *activity is a reflection of need state*

Indeed, there is already some evidence to support our contention. It has been shown, for example, that both para-social interaction and identification vary with age (Levy, 1979; Rosengren and Windahl, 1972); that adolescents are especially active consumers of identity-related content (Brown, 1976); and that young children actively process TV messages (Anderson, 1979). Other limited studies have linked activity to personality types (Rosengren and Windahl, 1977; Gunter et al., 1983), to media dependency (Rubin and Windahl, 1980), to mood (Zillmann et al., 1980), and even to time of day of exposure (Gunter et al., 1984).

Individual-level factors aside, a number of social contingencies may also affect audience activity. Important links, for example, have been reported between social class and selectivity in media consumption (Piepe, 1975; Frank and Greenberg, 1980). Other social position variables (Blumler, 1979), such as marital status, work-force participation, social mobility, and measures of interaction potential (Rosengren and Windahl, 1972), could profitably be examined to determine how such items, first, generate media-oriented needs, and, second, condition the orientations of audiences toward the media. Finally, the social situation of media consumption may also affect audience activity, for, as has been reported (Webster and Wakshlag, 1983), selectivity is lower in group viewing of television than when an individual watches alone.

Media considerations, including differential availability, differences in message complexity and "style," and variations in the substantive content of messages, are also likely to affect audience activity (see, for example, Krull et al., 1977; Katz et al., 1977; Collins, 1979; Levy and Fink, 1984). Indeed, each of these media considerations may invite, require, or produce variations in the kinds and amounts of media consumed, in audience perceptions of media messages, in audience involvement with those media, and in audience gratifications.

To take but one brief example, one might compare the consequences for audience activity of an information-rich medium such as television with, say, radio. We suspect that the combination of TV picture and sound requires less active involvement, while radio "forces" the listener to visualize actively what he or she hears (Singer, 1980). Although surprisingly little work has focused on this area, we would suggest that media vary in the way they give their users a "full picture," and that message completeness has powerful consequences for audience activity.

AUDIENCE ACTIVITY, GRATIFICATIONS, AND EFFECTS

In earlier work (Levy and Windahl, 1984), we reported positive, significant correlations between measures of audience activity and indicators of gratifications sought and obtained. In the case of activity and gratifications sought, those findings suggest that, to the extent an individual expects media exposure to gratify certain social or psychological needs, he or she will more actively attempt to fulfill those expectations through the communication process. Thus gratifications sought or motives are seen to cause variations in activity. By contrast, the activity-gratifications-obtained linkages seem to imply a different causal direction. If, as we have shown, more active individuals experience higher levels of gratifications, then activity must be seen as a causal variable. Taken together, these findings provide an important empirical demonstration of the previously implicit and untested assumptions linking audience needs, motives, goal-directed activity, and gratifications.

What must be done now is a more thorough investigation of which types of activity are associated with which kinds of motives and gratifications. We would expect, for example, to find that preexposure activity is linked to cognitive, diversionary, and/or personal identity motives, depending on the entire range of contingent conditions discussed above. Activities during exposure, such as parasocial interaction and identification, might be linked to affective motivations and gratifications; while meaning-creation activity might be associated with cognitive motives and gratifications. Similarly, postexposure activities are most likely tied to interpersonal and social-utility gratifications.

Based on a better understanding of activity-gratifications relationships, it may then be possible to move closer toward the long-sought merger of gratifications studies and effects theory. We are all too painfully aware of manipulation by and through the mass media. And we recognize that narcotization is as likely an effect as mobilization. As

Activity is premised on motivation to meet needs
Satificing — Save effort — Not max m.2

members of society, we are, in Elliott's words, more spectators than partakers. Still, the mass communication experience is one in which the audience often is (or can be) quite active.

Indeed, there is already a fair-sized body of evidence linking audience gratifications to such effects as information gain, media dependency, perceptions of social reality, agenda-setting, and assorted political effects (Palmgreen, 1984b). Future research must ask whether more active audience members are more or less likely to be affected by their exposure. Do certain kinds of "positive" effects (such as information gain or vote guidance) increase with activity, while other "null" effects (reinforcement or social reality judgments, for example) also increase? Ultimately, understanding the activity-gratifications nexus holds great promise for increasing our knowledge about the role of mass communication in human life.

This is a long term effects question

NOTE

1. This is not meant to imply that utility during exposure is identical to gratifications obtained. Similarly, our earlier discussion of utility prior to exposure was not intended to suggest an isomorphism of gratifications sought and preexposure activity. Nor would we necessarily argue that the postexposure use of gratifications obtained during exposure is the same as the gratifications themselves. Activity in the form of utility and gratifications sought/obtained are closely related, but conceptually distinct constructs. Put somewhat crudely, gratifications sought are the motives for media consumption. Gratifications obtained have to do with either the rewards or the uses that emerge during or after exposure. Activity, on the other hand, deals with whether or not, or how much, gratifications are sought and obtained, that is, "used."

Chapter 7

STRUCTURAL FACTORS
IN GRATIFICATIONS RESEARCH

Lennart Weibull

IN THE EARLY 1940s, when Herta Herzog presented her studies of the soap opera listening habits of American housewives, there were probably very few who realized that the studies were to develop into a special branch of mass media research. At a time when audience research was primarily occupied with studying the effects of mass media content, Herzog (1942) was asking questions about audience interest in the media. Berelson's (1949) observations during the 1945 press strike in New York, Katz' and Lazarsfeld's (1955) launching of the two-step flow of information, and Klapper's (1960) classic summary all pointed in the same direction: the habits, interests, and needs of the audience affect the influence of the media. Bauer (1964a) spoke of the "obstinate audience" and Klapper (1963) exclaimed in a research review, "Viva los uses and gratifications studies!"

This is not the place for a general survey of the growth of the uses and gratifications tradition. This has been done by others, some within the covers of this volume. Most interesting in this context is that uses and gratifications research was developed primarily by psychologists and social psychologists. The questions were formulated accordingly, and were aimed at discovering how user characteristics were related to media consumption. As many critics have pointed out, the media and the media content were thereby pushed into the background. They were reduced primarily to a question of what the public experienced (see Chaney, 1972; Elliot, 1974; Windahl, 1981).

Given this background, the aim of this chapter is to raise some questions concerning the influence of the mass media structure on people's use of the media, or the extent to which media systems and media content affect the volume and direction of media consumption. This does not necessarily mean to give any support to what has been termed "the return of the concept of the powerful mass media" (Noelle-Neumann, 1973), but rather to demonstrate how the structure of the media can be included in an analysis of individual media use.

THE MEDIA FACTOR IN
USES AND GRATIFICATIONS RESEARCH

In early efforts, uses and gratifications researchers primarily stressed the needs and interests of the individual as a way of understanding media use. Subsequently, the perspective was broadened to cover needs and interests originating in the social environment of the individual (see Katz et al., 1974; Rosengren, 1974; Palmgreen, 1983). Even though the approach was broadened in this way, researchers still sought the answers to questions of media consumption in user analyses. In their review article, Katz et al. (1974: 21) took "the active audience" with "goal-directed" mass media use as the starting point. Furthermore, they assumed that the media in this context "compete" with other sources of need satisfaction, and that it should be possible, on the basis of analyses of audience experience, to derive the capacity of the media to satisfy different needs. Katz et al. (1974: 25) also discuss the role of the mass media in media use, stating that every medium offers "a unique combination of (a) characteristic contents . . . (b) typical attributes . . . e.g., print vs. broadcasting . . . (c) typical exposure situations." The main question for the uses and gratifications researcher then becomes "what combinations of attributes may render different media more or less adequate for the satisfaction of different needs." The problem that arises here is to what extent differences in access to media with given characteristics influence the character—extent and direction—of media use. Katz et al. only hint at the problem, saying that the question has received little attention (however, they refer to Lundberg and Hultén, 1968, as an exception).

A very common criticism of traditional uses and gratifications research has been that it produces only variations on different themes from psychological and sociological research. This has meant a lack of a mass communication perspective: The communicators and the media have normally been excluded from the paradigm (see Elliott, 1974; Nowak, 1979; Windahl, 1981). The significance of the media for media use was lost. Critics such as Elliott (1974) have called for investigations of ownership, control, and production processes within the media system, with the object of placing different media and their audiences in a mass communication context.

The fairness of this far-reaching criticism of uses and gratifications in this respect is open to discussion. Many of the studies carried out under the classical paradigm were primarily intended to throw light on what gratifications a given media structure offered compared with other sources of gratification (see Katz, Gurevitch, and Haas, 1973). A certain media system with certain inherent properties was taken as given, and the question asked was what use the individual made of this system and what needs he or she satisfied through media use. The result has been a detailed description of media gratifications. However, as soon as uses and gratifications research has any claim to or ambition of presenting an explanatory model of media use, we are back at square one. In an explanatory approach the problem of the influence of media structure arises again. With such an approach the mass media must be included as an important explanatory factor, alongside individual needs.

The objection discussed seems particularly relevant when one reads some of the representative overviews of uses and gratifications research (Klapper, 1963; Katz et al., 1974; McQuail, 1983; Palmgreen 1983). It then emerges quite clearly that the tradition has developed from a research approach into an explanatory model. Even so, questions concerning the role of media structure have received limited attention. Sven Windahl (1981: 176-177) is of the opinion that this is primarily because uses and gratifications researchers have limited their ambitions to a "model of the receiving process," and he calls for a broader perspective (see below). This is, however, most certainly not the only reason. It is clear from the discussion in McQuail and Gurevitch (1974) that even where there is some attempt at an explanation, the media factor has not really been taken into account. Another reason may be found in the great stress that the uses and gratifications approach has put upon the role of the active audience. It is significant that critics have often concentrated on this assumption. In this context there is a kind of ideological difference between those who have stressed the importance of structure and those who have underlined the independence of the individual. A parallel reading of the introductory sections of the two volumes *The Uses of Mass Communication* (Blumler and Katz, 1974) and *Massenkommunikationsforschung 2: Konsumtion* (Prokop, 1973a) is extremely fruitful for an understanding of the ways in which mass media consumption is perceived. The comparison demonstrates a great difference in basic approaches to society and the individual that were characteristic of the debate within social science research of the 1960s and 1970s: Uses and gratifications emerges as an expression of the liberal view of the media, and the critical approach to the media is associated with the collectivist view (see Rosengren, 1983; Siebert et al., 1956).

It would be inappropriate, however, to interpret in exclusively political and ideological terms the way uses and gratifications research stressed the individual as a free agent. It should rather be stressed that in the background there has also been a culural difference that has left its mark on discussions. A look through the critical contributions and those concerning structural questions shows that, to a striking extent, these studies come from European scholars (Prokop, 1973b; Elliot, 1974; Rosengren, 1974; McQuail and Gurevitch, 1974; Windahl, 1981). Given the direction mass communication research has traditionally taken in Europe, it has been natural to include questions of media structure and media systems. In Europe there were systematic attempts to relate media structure, media effect, and media use at a relatively early stage (for example, Maletzke, 1963), attempts that have received remarkably little attention in Anglo-Saxon research.[1]

A third explanation of the neglect of the media perspective can be sought in the fact that uses and gratifications research has, to a large extent, been a matter of TV research. Because television is comparatively homogeneous *within* most countries, researchers have not encountered any great variation in the media factor and, therefore, have not given it much attention. If the uses and gratifications tradition had originated in newspaper readership research, it is likely that the media factor would have received more attention from the beginning (see Weaver et al., 1977), since the variation among newspapers can be considerable among the various regions of one and the same country.

EXPLAINING THE BEHAVIOR OF THE MEDIA PUBLIC

Although the mass media system's influence on media use has not been given any particular attention in uses and gratifications research, it would be wrong to say it has not been touched upon at all. An increasing trend can be discerned toward an emphasis on structural factors, of which media structure is one. This tendency runs parallel with the gradual change of uses and gratifications into a broad explanatory model. In his paradigm, Karl Erik Rosengren (1974) stresses social structure as a factor that affects all links in the use process, including individual basic needs and media behavior. Media structure is here regarded as a part of the social structure. Rosengren comments that a comparative approach is required to test the structural factor.

The idea that light can be thrown on the significance of social structure through comparative studies appears in a number of empirical studies carried out at this time by Rosengren and Windahl (1973, 1977). In these studies media structure does not itself stand in the center, but its relevance is underlined because the studies concern media involvement in areas with different media situations. The need to combine individual and sociological variables is emphasized. One weakness, however, in Rosengren and Windahl's (1973, 1977) work is that the media factor receives minor emphasis. The media structure is made a part of the greater social structure, but the position held by the media structure is unclear. Questions concerning media involvement are relatively general. Other reports from the same group of Swedish researchers are more directly connected with media factors, particularly with media content (Nordlund, 1976; Hvitfelt, 1977; compare Nordlund, 1978). Particularly in Nordlund (1976: 146), differences in audience media interaction are related to the program policy of Swedish TV (for instance, differences in transmission times of different types of programs).

Most researchers, however, within the uses and gratifications tradition would seem to have hesitated before including media structure as an independent factor in their models. Karl Erik Rosengren (1974) is an exception, as he considers structural factors to be a type of framework around the use process. The most interesting aspect of his model is that it touches upon questions that have been included in effects research: What influence does content have on media exposure and thereby on attitudes among individuals? It is characteristic, therefore, that those who put forward a structure-oriented uses and gratifications model seek to integrate the two traditions of research. One good example is Windahl (1981: 176), who has proposed a "uses and effects model." His approach represents a fruitful development of Rosengren's (1974) "paradigm outlined." Pronounced emphasis on the "active" role of media structure has been added. It is no longer a question of "social structure, including the media structure," but of "communicators," who, on the basis of their own needs and interests produce messages and make media choices (p. 183). This process is contrasted with the use process of the receiver, in which media use is specified more clearly than it was in earlier models (see also Weibull, 1980a, 1980b). The entire interplay takes place within the framework of a given social structure, which is also affected by the relationship between communicator and receiver. The strength of Windahl's account is primarily his emphasis on

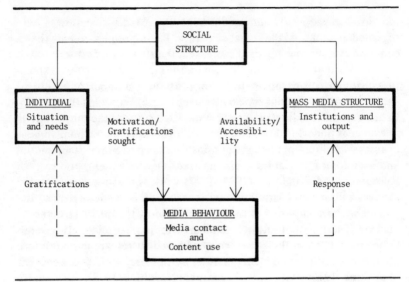

Figure 7.1   A Structural Model of Media Use

media use as a part of a *communication process*. This makes the model more "realistic" than previous ones in the uses and gratifications tradition. On the other hand, it must also be pointed out that there is very little in Windahl's model that Maletzke (1963) did not include in his. A weakness of Windahl's model is that the relations among the communicator, the media, and the media use are unspecified.[2]

A STRUCTURAL MODEL OF MEDIA USE

Given the previous discussion, a structural model of media behavior entails that individual characteristics, media characteristics, and structural factors must be defined as explanatory variables. Furthermore, the model demands that its own central dependent variable, *media behavior*, must be extremely precise. To avoid inconsistencies in terminology, I have chosen this more general term for what has up to this point been called "media use." A structural model of individual media behavior is presented in Figure 7.1.

A first step in discussing the structural model is to relate it to the uses and gratifications tradition. In its original form this tradition can be said to have concerned the relationship between individual needs and media behavior. The various steps in the user process, in which motivation or gratification sought is the connecting link, were elaborated during the 1970s. The development of uses and gratifications research can be described as an explication and specification of the relationship among the three factors that constitute the left-hand part of the model. There are two reasons for paying less attention here to the left-hand side of the figure. The first is that this is the main theme for most of the articles in this volume. The second is that the clarification of media characteristics does not necessitate such a discussion. On the contrary, the structural model represents, as the title suggests, an attempt at a general explanation, in which individual properties could be specified in ways other than those that have been common in the uses and gratifications tradition, such as media behavior as an information-seeking process or an act of playing (see Chaney, 1972; Weibull, 1983a). In the following section the interplay between individual and media properties will be examined.

MEDIA STRUCTURE AND MEDIA BEHAVIOR

What in the model is termed *media structure* in reality comprises a number of contributory factors at various levels. Media can be classified in a variety of ways. In his overview of mass communication theory, McQuail (1983: 19-32) devotes more than ten pages to discussing the basis of such classifications. In Germany, the discussions within the older *Zeitungswissenschaft* devoted a significant amount of attention to the question of what are the most significant features of a daily newspaper (for example, Dovifat, 1967).

In principle, most classifications of media structure have been based on the forms of production, distribution, and content. Media have been classified according to their technical form (electronic media versus printed media), dissemination ("universal media" versus specialized media), or content (news media versus entertainment media). This is, in principle, the same starting point as in Katz et al. (1974), in which, however, the receiver situation is also regarded as a media characteristic. The latter would seem dubious, especially if media are to be analyzed as an explanatory factor. A survey of the literature in this field suggests it is very difficult to find any generally accepted definition (see Strid and Weibull, 1983).

To understand the role of media structure in the individual's media behavior it is important, however, to make at least a distinction between the mass media as *institutions* and the *output* of mass media (see

TABLE 7.1
Media Structure

Level of Analysis	Institutions	Output
Quantitative	number of media available	volume of produced media content
Qualitative	type of media available	type of media content produced

McQuail, 1977; Asp, 1985). When talking about media as institutions, what is meant is the mass media as a kind of organizational structure, such as newspaper titles, radio channels, and TV companies. The institutional perspective thus includes the technical, political, and economic aspects of media structure. The "output" of the media refers to volume and character of media content. This includes, for example, program schedules for radio and TV, or content profiles of newspapers.

A more thorough elaboration of the mass media structure will show that there are quantitative and qualitative levels of analysis for both the institution and the output perspective. This can be summarized as in Table 7.1, which shows four main components in what in Figure 7.1 was labeled "mass media structure." When analyzing the role of media structure it seems important to consider which component is most relevant to an understanding of individual media behavior.

A final point about mass media structure must be raised. What has been specified in Table 7.1 can be described as the "structural" aspects of media structure. What is meant by this somewhat tautological phrase is that so far, we have focused upon the stable features of the mass media. In practice there is also a dynamic aspect of the media factor: Not all media are available each day and there is a daily difference in actual media output. These dynamic features of media structure will be discussed more thoroughly in a later section.

The relationship between media structure and the individual user is a matter of *availability* or *accessibility* (see Chaney, 1972), which corresponds in Figure 7.1 to motivation or gratifications sought as expressions of the relationship of individuals to media use. This brings us to the second component in the structural model to be elaborated upon: *media behavior*. To some, this term might call to mind a certain research tradition, but it is used here only as a label, and must be specified. The elaboration of media behavior should be discussed against the background of media structure as a question of both institutions and output. One way of expressing this from the individual's point of view is to say that he or she makes two choices. The first is the choice of media, the second the choice of media content. The choice of media entails a choice among the media institutions, and the choice of content entails a choice within media output. The choice of media as institutions expresses what in commercial research is termed "exposure." For reasons to which I shall return, in my opinion it is better to describe this choice among media as an expression of *contact* with a medium, partly because this says nothing about what the reader, listener, or viewer is exposed to within the medium. In a corresponding way the choice of the content is a question of how the medium is *used*. This conclusion may seem to be trivial and to contribute relatively little to previous studies (for example, Windahl, 1981), but the important point is that use presupposes contact, which in turn is influenced by the existing media structure. At the same time, it is quite obvious that there is a clear connecion between these two aspects of media behavior. For example, it is quite reasonable that an individual make use of a medium on the ground of its content. This does not mean, however, that only the preferred content of the media is used.

Furthermore, it is interesting to note that the connection between media choice and content choice varies from medium to medium. For the daily press and television, which have often been shown to satisfy a number of very different functions (see Lundberg and Hultén, 1968, for an overview), the gap is greater than, say, for specialized weeklies. In the latter case the distance between the two choices is probably so small that one could travesty Marshall McLuhan (1964) and declare that "the medium is the content."

From an operational point of view, it is both reasonable and important to make clear that both media contact and content use have quantitative and qualitative levels. This leads to a simple summary (see Table 7.2) of what has been labeled "media behavior," which corresponds to the one for media structure shown in Table 7.1. Table 7.2 shows four types of media behavior. "Media consumption" expresses the extent of media contact. "Media preference" focuses on which media are the receiver's main media or in which he or she has the greatest confidence. "Use volume" refers to how much is used in the medium (or media) chosen. "Use profile" refers to how the user combines various types of media content.

This typology makes no claim to be a final solution to the problem of how to analyze the individual's media behavior. What it does attempt to show, however, is that it is possible to develop what I shall call realistic media use measurements. By "realistic" measurements I mean variables that give a realistic picture of how the media public make use of the

TABLE 7.2
Media Behavior Level

Level of Analysis	Media contact	Content use
Quantitative	media consumption	use volume
Qualitative	media preference	use profile

existing media structure. This is the first step toward being able to measure the influence of media structure on media use.

SOCIAL STRUCTURE, MEDIA STRUCTURE, AND MEDIA BEHAVIOR

Before we go on to throw some empirical light on the influence of media structure on media behavior, there are two more relationships that should be mentioned briefly. The most important of these is represented in Figure 7.1 as an arrow between social structure and media structure. As has previously been mentioned, media have usually been treated as parts of the social structure. What are the implications of the distinction made here and how do social structure and media structure relate to each other? As has been shown in the preceding section, media structure includes both the institutions and the output through which various communicators try to transmit their messages. Maletzke (1963: 76-77) observes that there is a permanent media structure that contains a number of communications processes, resulting in a given content. In this way communicators, or rather the larger groups of actors and groups who wish to communicate via the media, must be seen as parts of the social structure (see Windahl, 1981).

This means that the term "social structure" refers to the whole of society—partly the reality on which the media are based, and partly the interests wishing to influence the media content. In this respect, there is reason to refer to news research, particularly the area of research that is usually labeled "gatekeeper studies" (see Lewin, 1947; White 1964; Rosengren 1974). This research tradition treats the relationship between social structure and media content. There are a number of interesting links between this tradition and uses and gratifications research, not the least of which is the meaning of social structure as an integrating element in the relationship between individual needs and media content. There seem to be reasons to believe that when the social structure is homogeneous, either constitutionally or as a result of exterior pressures, individual needs and media content appear to exhibit the same profile, which in turn means a greater interest in the media output (see Janowitz, 1981).

The conclusion to be drawn from this discussion is not that the media should be regarded merely as technical channels. On the contrary, one of the assumptions of gatekeeper research is that the media, considering policy, resources, background of editors, audience, and social structure determine the selection of media output (see Olsson and Weibull, 1973). The question of interest in this connection is how media organizations view their public. This is one of the classic questions in media research: do media wish to influence their public or do they seek to adapt themselves to the tastes of their public? It would seem reasonable to assume that commercially-based media in the West wish to suit the taste of their audience, so as to offer their advertisers a large auditorium (see McQuail, 1983). With reference to the relationship between media structure and social structure, it seems reasonable to claim that media companies desire media use whereas communicators desire media effects. This distinction is very important for the understanding of the relationship between uses and gratifications research and effects research.

The discussion of the media as a link between the social structure and the public points out another relationship in Figure 7.1—that from media behavior to media structure. This represents what in communications models is usually termed "feedback." The arrow "response" covers the user reactions to the media, which in turn can influence the media output. This relationship is much discussed in the context of modern mass media technology (see McQuail, 1983: 168-171). The extent of response possibilities varies according to the conditions of the media institutions. With modern developments in media technology, however, this sort of two-way communication is, in the long term expected to be ascribed greater significance in the understanding of media behavior.

USES, GRATIFICATIONS, AND MEDIA STRUCTURE: EMPIRICAL EXAMPLES

Let us now relate this discussion of media structure and behavior to the uses and gratifications tradition through exemplifying analyses of the influence of the media structure. Starting with the uses and gratifications approach, we assume that the origin of behavior is to be found in the individual or in the individual's relationship to the social structure (see Rosengren, 1974; McQuail and Gurevitch, 1974; Palmgreen, 1983). In this context the media structure—the media institutions and media output—can function either as *reinforcement* or as *constraint* in the relationship to gratifications sought. The media can facilitate or restrict the possibility for a user to "satisfy his needs."

The role of the media will be illustrated here with examples based on the four aspects of media behavior distinguished in the typology outlined above. The empirical data are drawn primarily from Swedish mass communications research.

MEDIA CONSUMPTION

What governs the regular use of a medium? As far as the daily press is concerned, most Swedish studies show that the proportion of regular newspaper readers is high. About 80 percent of the Swedish general public can be classified as daily readers of morning newspapers. Two factors that distinguish somewhat between various user groups are social situation, (particularly the level of stability in personal circumstances and the level of social integration) and, to some extent, social status (for example, education). The significance of the latter factor, however, is limited. A third factor positively related to daily readership is declared political interest (see Weibull, 1983b). The results shown here can generally be interpreted as support for Berelson's (1949) and Kimball's (1959) explanations of why people maintain their interest in daily newspapers. At the same time, however, the proportion of daily morning newspaper readers in Sweden has been shown to be over 15 percentage-points higher than in the U.S. The gap is more or less the same between Sweden and most countries on the European continent. The question, then, becomes whether individual needs per se are higher in Sweden, or if the Swedish press has given its readers a higher level of reinforcement than the press in other countries (see a corresponding discussion of TV in Sweden and the United States in Asp and Miller, 1980).

Evidently it is not possible to present a final answer to this question here. We can only outline some possibilities for analysis. We may illustrate the approach by studying the situation *within* Sweden. The question is whether there is any regional variation in readership related to the types of newspapers available in a specific area. We find very little such variation in Sweden (Weibull, 1983a)—but one area shows a

TABLE 7.3

Consumption of Daily Morning Papers in Areas with Different
Newspaper Situations, with Control for Social Situation and
Interest in Local News Events, Sweden, 1984 (in percentages)

| | Metropolitan Area | | | | Countryside Area | | | |
| | Low Social Stability | | High Social Stability | | Low Social Stability | | High Social Stability | |
	No Local Interest	Local Interest	No Local Interest	Local Interest	No Local Interest	Local Interest	No Local Interest	Local Interest
% Reading Newspaper Daily	42	67	70	69	69	71	74	86
n	39	136	147	532	22	105	105	696

SOURCE: Unpublished data from the Newspaper Research Programme at the Unit
for Mass Communication, University of Göteborg.
NOTES: Indicator of social stability is the number of household members. A one-
person household indicates low stability; more than one person indicates high stability. Interest in local news events is based on a dichotomy of a five point scale on interest in various local issues. Scale values 4 and 5 are treated as local interest, others
as no local interest.

deviation in the form of lower figures for morning newspaper reading:
the metropolitan area of Stockholm, where the proportion of readers is
at the "American level." We may now rephrase our question: what are
the reasons for this deviation—is it the situation or the motivation of
individuals, or is it the mass media structure? From studies of the
Swedish media public we know that social stability and interest in local
events is somewhat lower in the Stockholm metropolitan area than they
are in the countryside. This is often referred to as a typical feature of a
metropolitan area. At the same time, the media structure differs, above
all in its local news coverage, which is not as extensive in Stockholm
newspapers as it is in the countryside daily press. To determine the role
of the local situation we have to analyze daily newspaper readership in
both area types, controlling for social stability and interest in local
events. Such an attempt is made in Table 7.3.

A simple analysis of the percentage differences in the table shows that
there are effects of interest in local events and social stability on newspaper readership. In both the metropolitan area and the countryside,
newspaper readership is more closely associated with social stability
than with interest in local events. From a geographical point of view,
this means that readership seems to be related to the individual's social
habits. If we now introduce the area factor, however, we observe that the
percentage of effects of both individual factors are higher in the metro-

politan area than in the countryside. There seem to be more constraints on the reading of a newspaper in the metropolitan area than in the countryside area. The next problem is to determine the character of the area effect—is it related to the media structure or are there some other effects of social structure, not connected with social stability and interest in local events? Unfortunately it is not possible to decide that in this analysis.

The analysis presented here serves as an example. The introduction of structural factors has proved very fruitful for the understanding of the relationship between individual motivation and mass media use. There are indications that this may be an effect of media structure, but the need for more control has also been pointed out. Returning to the first question about international deviations in newspaper readership, the example suggests some ideas for a research strategy. It is evident that such comparisons would need to include studies of the newspaper structure of each country. As the Swedish example shows, area comparisons are not sufficient in themselves, since social structure cannot then be distinguished from media structure.

MEDIA PREFERENCE

Clearly, the weakness in the first example is the lack of any detailed content analysis of the daily papers read by different individuals. This problem is taken into account in our second example, which is intended to show why certain readers like to have a daily newspaper containing a political line with which they sympathize. The problem should be regarded against the background of the Swedish daily press, the majority of which comprises daily papers with clear party political profiles (see Hadenius, 1983; Weibull, 1983c). This makes it relatively easy to classify readers of daily papers by the party affiliation of the newspaper they read.

To limit the question somewhat we have chosen to concentrate on the reading of socialist versus nonsocialist press. The problem, therefore, is this: to what extent is reading an expression of a clear party interest profile and to what extent is media structure of importance for the level of readership? Our first observation is that there is an obvious connection between party sympathy and choice of party newspaper. The socialist press is read by 62 percent of the socialist sympathizers, but by only 15 percent of the nonsocialists. The nonsocialist press, which dominates the newspaper circulation in Sweden, reaches 93 percent of the nonso-cialist sympathizers, but only 15 percent of the socialists. If we pick out the politically interested party sympathizers the difference between the groups increases. This clearly indicates that reading of party press is closely connected with the reader's own political orientation (see Wei-bull, 1983c, for more empirical data).

Let us now include the media factor. If we restrict ourselves to the subscribed newspapers, we find a wide dispersion in the availability of local papers and different politically oriented papers within Sweden. About two-thirds of social democrats live in areas in which they have a party press of their own, while one-third live in areas in which they have not. It can be shown that the proportion of social democratic readers of social democratic morning press is 44 percent in areas where at least one social democratic newspaper is published; in areas with no social demo-cratic press, the corresponding proportion is 24 percent. The trend is the same for the sympathizers of all parties. How, then, does the interest factor relate to the media factor? Table 7.4, which shows the morning paper choice of social democratic sympathizers with control for political interest and area, provides a basis for assessment.

In Table 7.4 we can see to what extent social democrats read their own press in situations of different availability. We can observe the effect of the local newspaper structure, which is to be seen in all groups. At the same time, however, we find that the interest factor plays an even more important role. If we choose to take out the extreme groups of daily readers we can see that interest has twice as much importance, measured in percent difference, as the availability of a local party newspaper. The interesting thing is, however, that almost the entire structural effect is to be found among those with low or moderate interest in politics. Another way of expressing this is to say that the effect of political interest is greater where no local social democratic paper is available; here a higher level of motivation is necessary to read a social democratic paper (for further discussion, see Weibull, 1983c).

In connection with the earlier discussion of the influence of media structure, it can be said that the availability of social democratic press functions as a reinforcement for semi-interested social democrats. Judg-ing from other studies and the example in the preceding section, it seems possible to generalize that the influence of structure can be found primarily among those persons with lower levels of individual motiva-tion. For persons with clear preferences and high levels of motivation, the structural factor plays a less important role.

TABLE 7.4
Newspaper Readership Among Social Democratic Sympathizers, by Availability of Local Social Democratic Newspaper and Interest in Politics, Sweden, 1979 (in percentages)

Newspaper Reading	Regions with Social Democratic Press				Regions without Social Democratic Press			
	Interest in Politics				Interest in Politics			
	High	Middle	Low	All	High	Middle	Low	All
At least one newspaper daily	89	83	75	86	73	84	77	79
At least one Social Democratic newspaper once a week	59	50	33	44	55	28	12	25
At least one Social Democratic newspaper daily	52	43	27	37	42	19	7	16
n	130	338	376	844	33	109	115	257

SOURCE: Weibull (1983c).

USE VOLUME

What affects the extent of people's consumption of a certain medium? The general tendency in uses and gratifications seems to have been to explain the time set aside for media use in terms of demographics and lifestyle. As a rule, strong correlations can be found (see Kline, 1971, 1974). The same pattern can be found in the Swedish data. The time devoted to media use increases among those who have a high level of interest in the content of a medium and among those who have more time available (see Weibull, 1983a, 1984).

Once again we must ask our standard question: What relevance does the extent of the media output have in this context? It appears that this question has rarely been discussed. It is sometimes almost incredible how, for example, the increase of TV viewing over a given period can be discussed without including a measure of the growth of transmission time (see Peterson, 1981). In the same way, seasonal variations in Swedish TV viewing, almost twice as much in winter as in summer, have often been described without taking into account that there is a similar variation in transmission times (see Wachtmeister, 1972). This has led to the assumption that the need for, or interest in, television is different in summer and winter. This would seem to be quite a reasonable assumption, but it is doubtful whether it can be accepted without control for the media structure.

The basic data on Swedish newspaper readership is somewhat better as a basis for judgment. Analyses of average reading time have been undertaken for different newspapers with control for available reading time among the readership. The results that have emerged (see Weibull, 1983a: 218-220) suggest that the volume of a morning paper—the amount of editorial content—influences the reading time. Metropolitan papers are read for a longer period than provincial ones, about 35 minutes as compared to 25 minutes. The pattern remains the same after control for the social structure: metropolitan press is read for a longer period of time regardless of whether it is read in the city or in the provinces. The differences in reading time between the voluminous metropolitan papers and the thinner provincial papers is still there after control for available time, measured here by means of the age factor (see Cutler and Danowski, 1980).

This analysis also shows that the individual's situation and needs have a greater effect on the length of reading time than has the volume of the newspaper being read. A Swedish pensioner has an average reading time of somewhat more than 40 minutes a day, which is about 15 minutes longer than that of a middle-aged person. At the same time, the effect of metropolitan compared with provincial press is just ten minutes. It seems possible that the influence of newspaper size is greater when more time is available. The implications of such an assumption are extremely interesting in an international comparison. The longer television viewing time among children in the United States compared with Sweden, for example, can then be explained in this way. An increase of TV viewing among children and pensioners has been predicted if more TV channels become available at new times in Sweden (Hemanus and Østbye, 1979). Among people in the active ages the effect will probably be small and, given that personal circumstances are the limiting factor, the effect of the output volume is slight.

USE PROFILE

How the use profile of an individual is influenced by the existing media structure is perhaps the most interesting question, but also the most difficult one to answer. As has been mentioned in the discussion of the content factor, reliable conclusions demand clear measurements of media content, both concerning the type of content available and how the different types are presented in different media. It is, of course, possible to achieve a certain amount of knowledge through comparative studies of preferences for the output of different media, as Edelstein (1982) proposes and Weaver and de Bock (1980) have shown. The obvious weakness of these studies however, is, that it is not known whether the observed differences should be classified as an effect of social structure or media structure. The similarities in the functions of TV, for example, that Weaver and de Bock compare between the U.S. and Holland *could* depend on extensive similarities in output, because Holland uses a large proportion of material produced in the U.S. (Varis, 1974), rather than on cultural similarities.

Another example from Swedish television research gives an additional angle on the same problem. In the days when Sweden had only one TV channel—before 1969—it was shown that the main news program at 7:30 p.m. was the program that had the highest audience figures. The general public also said they got important news from TV. The interpretation of this was that a central function of TV was to supply news. When a two channel system was to be introduced in Sweden, there was a belief that news and entertainment could be sent at the same time, and that a large audience would still follow the news program. In the new situation, however, a large proportion of viewers chose not to watch the news. This error in predicting the use profile obviously arose because consideration had not been taken of the fact that the news had been transmitted during prime time without any competition. The change of TV program schedule revealed the mistake. Later studies have also shown that what is sent during prime time has very little effect on total viewing: it is normally watched anyway, since it is the home situation that is the deciding factor (see Berg and Höijer, 1972a).

The interesting thing about this observation is not so much that the home situation determines viewing, but that both transmission time and program content, as well as channel alternative must therefore be taken into consideration in an assessment of the audience's content profile. Berg and Höijer (1972b) have also made an analysis of this sort. Not surprisingly, they found, among other things, that entertainment is normally the most popular TV content, but they proved at the same time that if there is a choice between a national and an imported entertainment program the national one is chosen. If this observation is put in the context of the earlier discussion of motivation and interest in relation to output, the consequence of what has been said here is that a very high motivation is necessary to "find" programs at unusual transmission times. The same tendency has been shown for West Germany by Holzer (1973).

Swedish analyses of daily newspaper reading have shown a positive relation between the reading profile of the public and the content profile the papers normally have (Weibull, 1983a: 261-264). This conclusion, however, rests on less secure foundations, since social structure and media structure have not been fully separated. It could be, for example that the greater interest for national and international questions in the metropolitan areas depends primarily on the social structure in the area. In the same way, the interest shown for local news in the countryside could depend on the social structure of these areas. A study of the differences within various provincial areas (Reimer, 1984) shows that it is probably the social structure rather than the media content that is the decisive factor: the smaller the area of residence, the greater is the interest in local news among readers of the same paper.

The examples that have been discussed here have intended to illustrate the role media structure may play in relation to the individual's needs, interests, and social situation, as these factors are normally analyzed in the uses and gratifications tradition. It has been shown that if any conclusions about the needs of the individual are to be drawn, the structural factor is, as a rule, a necessary element of the analysis. Examples have shown that if the situation in which a certain conclusion is valid is not specified, it is easy to produce misinterpretations. Another observation is that mass media structure can influence the media consumption of different individuals in different ways. The most important trend is that individuals with less defined objectives in their media use are influenced primarily by the media output. A third observation is of a more methodological character. The examples have shown that it is always very difficult to distinguish between the influence of social structure and the influence of media structure.

MEDIA BEHAVIOR:
MEDIA HABITS AND MEDIA EXPOSURE

Most uses and gratifications studies ask questions about the *general* use of the media, regardless of whether the use is of the media or of the content. Questions are asked concerning what type of TV program is usually watched, how often daily papers are usually read, or how much time is usually devoted to magazines. Research on methodology has shown us that this sort of average question expresses more the individual's inclination to do something rather than what he or she actually does. In most cases, however, we do not need to worry about this, since we can count on a reasonably strong relationship between inclination and action anyway. It is quite probable that this problem may also play a very minor role for the analysis of relationships between individual needs and media behavior.

This is, however, not entirely sure. Commercial research studies, for which the estimation of levels of media consumption and media preference are extremely important, usually include both "frequency" and "recency" measurements (Henry, 1982). "Frequency" corresponds to how often one usually does something. "Recency" concerns what an individual actually has done within a certain period of time, for instance, yesterday or last week. If we take this distinction as our point of departure, it seems fruitful to our analysis of media use to distinguish between *media habits* and *media exposure*. Media habits represent the individual's inclination to a certain media choice or to a certain content. Media exposure represents the actual media or content choice at a given point in time.

If we look back at the structural model as presented in Figure 7.1, it is seen to be mostly a model of media habits. As has been pointed out in the discussion, the model aims to explain how media are used (for instance, how the structural character of society and mass media affect the individual's motivation for media use). The stress on the structural factors probably means that what we mainly explain is habitual behavior. Given this, it is important to add a more dynamic perspective: what affects media exposure at a given point of time? Media exposure is, of course, determined by media habits developed over time, or "media orientation," but also by those media and media contents that are available just then, as well as by the current social situation. This leads to a further development of the model that is presented in Figure 7.2.

The advantage of the model in Figure 7.2 over that in Figure 7.1 is that it gives us a better understanding of the stability of the individual's media behavior. One can get an idea of how this may be influenced by incidental changes in media content and social situation. This model is, therefore, much more realistic, since it is necessary to consider the influence of media structure: The actual content of the media is, in fact, different every day, even if the general content profile is probably the same.

Figure 7.2 shows that the lower part of the expanded model of media behavior is a mirror image of the upper part. The lower part represents, in principle, the situation of the individual, media exposure, and media output within the framework of what has been called the "social situation" as it is at a given point in time. The minor deviations in terminology between the upper and lower parts are intended to underline the fact that the lower part refers to the situation at a certain point in time—in reality, a certain day or a certain week.

This model has been tested in studies of daily reading (Weibull, 1983a: chaps. 8, 12) from the point of view of both media contact and media use. As expected, the figures for media exposure on a given day are higher than the figures for regular reading. It emerged that the individual's daily exposure is determined by the situation. The result is hardly surprising: Journeys, illness, and similar events change the conditions for reading. What is more interesting is that those who miss a day's reading are those who already had a low level of motivation as far as habits are concerned. For those with strong habits and high inclination to read daily papers, the daily situation is less significant. The newspaper output on a given day has no significance beyond the trivial fact that the number of readers sinks on days when local newspapers are not distributed—but only a little among those with an interest in newspaper reading, since they find alternative newspapers.

The individual's media orientation is also a good predictor of content exposure. The interesting thing here is that the daily situation of the individual means less for specific than for general content types. For

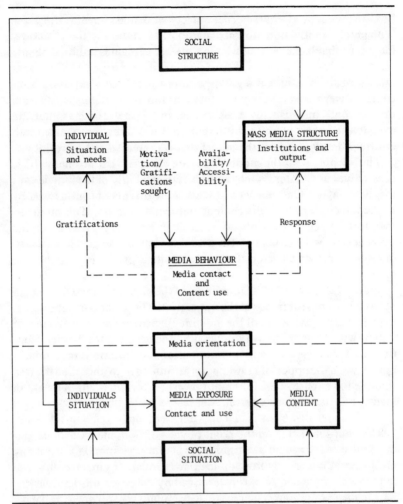

Figure 7.2   A Structural Model of Media Use: Relations Between Habits and Media Exposure

example, someone who is interested in sports news reads the sports pages even if he has only a limited amount of time at his disposal. Someone who is not interested in sports does not read this content even if he has plenty of time for newspaper reading. Comic strips show a similar pattern. General information, national news, foreign news, or letters to the editor, for example, are to a very large extent influenced by daily situation. Exposure to this latter material is also much more influenced by the newspaper's editorial presentation and layout than is, for example, the reading of the sports pages (Weibull, 1983a).

These results support the empirical observations made previously. When an individual is highly motivated to obtain specific gratifications, he or she is less affected by the media structure, regardless of whether it concerns the general output or one day's content. Individuals with less interest in media or media content seem to be more influenced by specific contents or by content composition. It is also important to note that this pattern can be found within one individual: He or she may be interested in some types of content but not in others. There are, however, also some indications that the general framework of layout and content profile in traditional newspapers influences the actual reading, even among highly motivated readers (Reimer, 1985): The newspaper creates some sort of "reading environment." This interplay between media orientation and media content for one day's exposure seems to be a fruitful area for further research.

CONCLUDING NOTE

In this chapter the intention has been to bring to light some of the possible effects of media structure on the individual's media use as analyzed by the uses and gratifications tradition. My thesis is that the more the uses and gratifications approach claims to offer an explanation of the way in which people use the media, the greater becomes the demand that clearly specified media characteristics must be included as a complement to the model. I have proposed a model in which media structure is treated as an independent explanatory factor. In the outline of the model there is a distinction between media as institutions and media output. The former includes media as production units; the latter, the content they produce. These two aspects of media structure must be kept apart, since they influence media consumption in different ways. Furthermore, I have proposed a special scheme for the way in which media use should be regarded and measured. With the help of examples drawn mainly from Swedish research, it has been shown how media structure can be included in uses and gratifications research, and I have also discussed some general observations based on Swedish data. The most important one has been the relatively strong influence of media structure on media use among those who have unclear goals in their media behavior.

Many of the results given here should be regarded as preliminary. Continued research will most certainly lead to modifications of the model specified here. There are, however, some conclusions of strategic value to future research that may be drawn. The first concerns an improved methodology for the measurement of media use, involving more realistic measurements of both media use habits and media exposure. In the future there will be an increasing need for empirical information on both aspects of use within one and the same research approach. Apart from calling attention to this, an obvious conclusion is that media structure factors must be integrated more frequently in uses and gratifications research. In practice this involves the application of a careful research strategy whose aim is also to ensure variations of the media structure variable.

The best way to achieve the desired variation in the media structure factor would be *comparative studies* between different regions, between different countries, and between different points in time. Trends in the uses and gratifications tradition toward more macro-orientated comparative studies are to be greeted with great satisfaction. This applies to studies such as those by Rosengren and Windahl (1977), and Weaver and de Bock (1980). As Edelstein (1982) maintains, however, there is room for many more comparative studies. This could be done, for example, by duplicating older studies with the object of studying changes over a period of time. There is a great deal of material waiting to be developed.

It should also be noted that measurements of media structures do not need to be carried out simultaneously with measurements of media use. Media structure data is normally available even after a considerable amount of time. The latter is particularly important when studying the influence of the media factor over a period of time. A number of other approaches in related areas suggest that historical development studies could be a productive area of research (see Weibull, 1984).

Another important point: In the macro-oriented comparisons that have been carried out, no distinction has normally been made between social structure and media structure. As long as this is not done, there is no possibility of discerning which of these factors explains regional, national, or time differences. Such an approach places great demands on the design of comparative studies. In the uses and gratifications approach it would appear necessary to return to what was the methodological origin of effects research: experimental, or at least quasi-experimental studies (see Zillmann's chapter in this volume). Advantage should be taken of all possible opportunities for natural experiments in the field. One alternative would be to study the use of the same program output in different cultures. This has been done, for example, with the American TV series *All in the Family* (Vidmar and Rokeach, 1974) and the miniseries *Holocaust* (Rundfunk und Fernsehen, 1980). Such approaches provide an opportunity for isolating the influence of social structure. Another alternative would be to study countries that are socially similar, but that have media systems that differ from one another. The opportunities for doing this have hitherto been limited. The differing models governing the development of new media technology in the United States and Europe would seem, however, to open the way for such an approach.

NOTES

1. Maletzke (1963) is not mentioned in the references of the review article of uses and gratifications by Blumler and Katz (1974). It is perhaps even more surprising, however, that there is no mention in McQuail (1983).

2. Here I shall not discuss Windahl's proposals for a new terminology. In my opinion the terms proposed create more problems than they eliminate, particularly the term "conseffects."

Chapter 8

GRATIFICATIONS RESEARCH
AND MEDIA THEORY:
Many Models or One?

Denis McQuail

THE PROBLEM

This chapter had origins other than the invitation to participate in updating the state of the art of media gratifications research. One of these was a prior interest in charting the divisions and conflicts of mass communication research as whole and another was a wish to review a position taken some time ago about the scope for alternatives to the functionalist model in uses and gratifications research (McQuail and Gurevitch, 1974). In the course of pursuing the first of these preoccupations, I had been led by Rosengren (1983) to consider an overview of sociological paradigms applied by Burrell and Morgan (1979) to the field of organizational sociology. Like Rosengren, I found this relevant and stimulating and have been unavoidably influenced by the work of these three predecessors in reaching a revised view of the state and location of theory for gratification research. Their work is especially relevant to the task of finding and evaluating alternatives to functionalism.

One major difference between the present enterprise and the work referred to is that they were dealing with much wider fields of inquiry, with much more variety and potential for divergence than is the case with uses and gratifications research. The latter is constrained by its problematic definition to deal ultimately with one rather limited and possibly minor aspect of individual human behavior, however potentially wide ranging are the issues of culture and society that lie over the horizon of research attention. There is thus a question of level of discussion to be faced. There are many pressing strategic and operational choices facing researchers that have been ignored here in favor of a rather global treatment of what may seem to be problems no longer on the agenda of debate. It must therefore be said that this chapter deals more with context of gratification theory than with urgent issues within the field itself.

The starting point is thus a simple observation that gratification research is a reality of practice within a contested theoretical environment. It appears to meet a recurring need of students of mass media processes, sometimes of mass communicators themselves, and, from time to time, even of those members of audiences who are curious about their own attachment to media and look to news of the motives of others for solutions to the puzzle. Viewed this way, the business of trying to find out what people are getting from their media experience and what their motives are seems a straightforward matter, requiring no more theoretical justification, attack, or defense than does the counting of audience numbers and the description of audience composition. In fact, this kind of research has, for some time, been a far from peaceful pragmatic activity, but, instead been a focus for debate and controversy (for example, Elliott, 1974; Swanson, 1977). It would be naive to be surprised at the incidence of controversy surrounding any academic enterprise that claims to be taken seriously, but there is something surprising in the depth of division and the seemingly all-or-nothing character of some criticism. This has not only focused on the interpretation of evidence, which happens with all research, but has challenged the central tenets of theory and method, and even the desirability of such research.

There are several fairly superficial explanations at hand for the nature and degree of the controversy. First, the period of renewed development of the research tradition, between the late 1960s and late 1970s, was a time of polarization in the social sciences and especially in sociology, between, on the one hand, traditional approaches, based mainly on structural functionalism, on positivist, empirical, quantitative methods and, on the other hand, neo-marxist or radical-critical modes of social science, which were often more qualitative and interpretative in method. Secondly, there was a much older interdisciplinary dispute between sociology and psychology over the relative validity of collective and individual explanations of social phenomena. Third, there was another, also older, issue of debate between critics of the established media order and the labeled or self-confessed agents of media management and commercial exploitation. Mass communication has often been implicated in moral and political criticism of the social order and in a time of line-drawing and confrontation it is not so surprising that the research approach should have been placed on one or the other side of the growing divide. Nor is it altogether surprising that it was regarded as on the less progressive side—as traditional, functionalist, positivist, and as more suitable for delivering tools to media management and manipulators than knowledge for its own sake or for liberation and reform. Moreover, it was regarded as unduly psychologistic by sociologists, as insensitive to cultural meaning within a growing school of cultural studies (such as Carey and Kreiling, 1974), and to psychologists it must have seemed insufficiently behavioristic. On a number of these points, the approach was avowedly "guilty," because its practitioners extolled the virtues of empiricism, methodological individualism, cultural relativism, and theoretical eclecticism, and many of their formulations were either openly or implicitly functionalist. Even so, few, if any, of the researchers concerned saw themselves as wishing to increase the manipulative power of media managers and most regarded their work as a contribution to knowledge that could also serve change and democratic purpose.

It is likely that calmer waters have been reached, a time when the potential of this kind of audience research for reaching an understanding of media processes and serving critical as well as "administrative" purposes is more widely recognized. To the extent that this is true, it may not seem particularly fruitful to fish in the stagnant waters of old debate. However, before the matter is considered closed as an episode in intellectual history, it is worth trying to clarify the nature of the theoretical conflict in which the research approach found itself and could still do so again. The explanations offered above are vague, broad, and seem to imply that uses and gratifications research was a more or less innocent victim of the politicization of social science or of interdisciplinary feuding among sociology, cultural studies, and psychology. There is more to it than that, and a theoretical ambiguity, or worse, continues to lie in the heart of uses and gratifications research that must be laid bare and consciously resolved one way or the other. One of the charges made against gratifications research was that it was "atheoretical," and one of the defenses offered was that it was theoretically eclectic—borrowing from and contributing to different theoretical standpoints. There is some truth to both claims, yet both are misleading in their implication that research can be conducted without some implicit theory. Both are also unsatisfactory in that they gloss over the nature of alternatives and ignore the underlying theory of the "pragmatic" approach.

As has already been noted, if there is a consistency of underlying theory, it has seemed, more often than not, to be functionalist (Katz, 1979). Yet I have (with Gurevitch, 1974) tried to show, in effective (though unclaimed) support for the eclecticism position, that there were at least two alternative frameworks within which much the same phenomena could be studied. One of these was labeled "structural-cultural" and indicated an interpretation of media choice and response in terms of given constraints of media availability, socially patterned habits of use, and socially distributed meaning systems for interpreting the experience. Another framework, labeled "action-motivation," proposed a model of individual freedom to choose, use, respond to, and interpret media content in variable and unpredictable ways according to a self-chosen view of the world and personal plans and intentions. Both suggested, for different reasons, that media use and the meaning given to it might only be contingently and not functionally related to social circumstances and to the chosen applications and actual effects of the media experience.

These other options were presented as more or less ready-made, complete alternatives to functionalism, which could be harnessed directly to uses and gratifications research. On reflection, it now seems to be a somewhat arbitrary and unexplicated choice, more in keeping with the spirit of eclecticism than with theoretical consistency. While not withdrawing the suggestion that the alternatives exist more or less as described, this chapter is more concerned with locating the various options of theory for gratifications research in a nexus of choices and oppositions that shape the field of media research more generally.

CONFLICTS OF MEDIA THEORY

As already pointed out, the debate specifically about gratifications research reflected other, more fundamental, divisions of theory about society, media, and scientific method. These can be treated at varying levels of science and society in general, of all communication research, or only in relation to uses and gratification research. The choice made here is for the second of these levels, with an eye on the more general debate, bearing in mind the need to say something about uses and gratifications research in particular. Thus a small number of divisions or dimensions of theoretical perspective are chosen for discussion and are related to each other. The work of Burrell and Morgan (1979) referred to is an excellent source for treating the most general level and their framework merits a brief summary. They suggest that the field of sociology (and, in particular, organizational sociology) has been structured by two major dimensions which, when plotted against each other, locate four main paradigms. Their vertical dimension is (top-down) the "sociology of radical change" versus the "sociology of regulation," corresponding with conflict and consensus models of society, respectively. The horizontal dimension (left to right) separates "subjective" from "objective" views of the world and modes of inquiry. This latter dimension corresponds with several other fundamental oppositions in the social sciences—nominalism versus realism; anti-positivism versus positivism; and voluntarism versus determinism; ideographic versus nomothetic methodologies. The four paradigms are: top left, radical humanism; top right, radical structuralism; bottom left, interpretative schools of sociology; bottom right, functionalism. Rosengren (1983) used much the same scheme to discuss choices of paradigms in communication research, paying particular attention to the dominant paradigm, that of functionalism. According to his interpretation, the dissident paradigms (the three that are not dominant) have contained the most fruitful ideas, but are deficient in the means for testing them, while the reverse has been true of functionalism. His preference was for the harnessing of the power of the dominant paradigm (especially by multivariate analysis) to the task of testing the ideas raised elsewhere in the theoretical space. With these summary but very rich materials in mind we turn to the choice of dimensions appropriate to mapping out the field of media theory. There are several possibilities, but four in particular seem to deserve attention. Although these are described using terms appropriate to media theory, it is not difficult to see the broad correspondence between the chosen dimensions and those just described. Nevertheless, the correspondence is far from exact and it has seemed more difficult to establish clear and distinct paradigms for research in communication.

MEDIA-CENTERED VERSUS SOCIETY-CENTERED THEORY

The basic choice is between a view of technology and message as prime mover in social change and a view of both as so dependent on society, its structure, and distribution of power, that communication phenomena have to be regarded as effects rather than causes of change. In its more extreme form, the "media primacy" view has found expression in the work of Innis (1951) and McLuhan (1964), but there are many who see a partial explanation of social developments in the typical forms and contents of media, from newspapers to television (such as Gouldner, 1976), and there are a good many heralds of future change who place great store in the capacities of new media technologies for interaction, storage, and ready access, against the older, center-peripheral mass distribution forms of media.

The use of a single dimension under this label is complicated by the existence of another kind of media-centered theory in which most attention is paid to typical, recurring, and systematically shaped content as a determinant of outlook, beliefs, and interpretations of the world on the part of mass audience members. Prominent here is the "cultivation" theory of Gerbner (1969), but a good deal of other theory accords with this model, including that relating to socialization and "cultural imperialism." The counterview of societal determination, as found, for instance, in Murdock and Golding, (1978) sees production, distribution, and use of media content as shaped by more fundamental social and economic forces, so that society is a more appropriate starting point for research than the media themselves. The dimension named also draws attention to another major issue of dispute in media theory over the degree of media power. The issue is between those who see media as very powerful (such as Noelle-Neumann, 1973) and those who see effects as the outcome of conditions affecting choice and response of the audience so that effects are likely to be filtered and variable according to the circumstances of individual and group life.

This summary presentation of alternatives is especially relevant to gratifications research because of the association of this tradition with the last-named view of media effects as dependent on their audiences. Presented this way, it appears to be a society-centered version of media theory, with society viewed not as a collective structure but as a nexus of relationships between individuals and groups. At the least, it must be admitted that the dimension sketched is very "impure" and does not lend itself to unambiguous or consistent uses.

It may be that a distinction between collective and individual approaches would help resolve some ambiguities, but only at the cost of a too-great differentiation of positions for clarity. Beyond that, some of the ambiguities may be resolved partly by reference to one or more of the other dimensions yet to be named.

CENTRIFUGAL VERSUS
CENTRIPETAL TENDENCIES

This dimension represents a contrast of values and empirical predictions as between the notions of change, freedom, diversity, and fragmentation (centrifugal tendencies) on the one hand, and those of order, control, unity, and cohesion (centripetal tendencies) on the other. For theory formulation, much depends on whether one takes a positive or negative view of the concepts named. The centripetal effect can be seen (as in some versions of mass society theory) as pathological—the creation, through monopolistic, homogeneous, and powerful media of a conformist and obedient society or in a beneficial light as a contribution to an integrated community or society. For instance, Janowitz (1981) has interpreted major tendencies in modern media content and practice as having caused a loss of personal and social control of the kind and degree necessary for an ordered democratic society. The centrifugal effect also has its dark and light side—on the one hand leading to greater freedom, individualism, diversity, and modernity and, on the other, to isolation, anonymity, privatization, and vulnerability to manipulation. In general, mass media seem to have a more or less equal potential for both tendencies (Carey, 1969; McCormack, 1961), which are, in any case to be found occurring simultaneously in most societies.

Again it is apparent that we are not dealing with a single, simple dimension and it will help to clarify its meaning by building-in the variable of value-judgment that has been described. Thus at one pole we can put together a negative view of centripetal tendencies as leading to excessive control and manipulative power, and a negative view of centrifugal tendencies as leading to isolation and alienation (and thus facilitating control from above). At the other pole, we can locate a positive view of the centripetal effect as leading to a desirable degree of order and integration and a positive view of centrifugal tendencies in the light of freedom, diversity, and change. The evaluative dimension so formed parallels the next conflict to be described.

DOMINANCE VERSUS PLURALISM

The terms to label this opposition (rather than dimension) are chosen from a range of possibilities, none of them very satisfactory. Nevertheless they point to the clear division between theories of (mainly) Marxist standpoints and those of liberal-pluralist perspectives (Gurevitch et al., 1982; McQuail, 1983). The opposition is important not only for helping to classify different positions, but also because it takes care of the main source of political-ideological variation and valuation, which cannot be merely wished away. Its main contribution here is to separate versions of media and media research that stress either the dominant, monopolistic, integrated, and class-aligned nature of the main mass media or, on the other hand, a view of media as being organizationally and ideologically diverse, catering to freely expressed demands and requirements of many individuals, groups and, interests in an ever-changing mosaic. The opposition is also between "critical" research and what may be regarded as "neutral-objective" research in the traditional mode of the social sciences, which lends itself more to purposes of management. In practice, this latter mode has often been structural-functionalist in concept, concerned with the problem of order and with explaining how societies persist, adapt, and manage tension.

It is obvious that this opposition corresponds closely to that between conflict and consensus, and radical change and integration (Burrell and Morgan, 1979). The weakness of treating all these oppositions as coinciding in one dimension, with a single label at either end, is readily apparent. Among critical theorists there are some for whom pluralism is a value that is simply unattainable under reigning conditions of either hegemonic capitalism or bureaucratic socialism, and others for whom media hegemony is inevitable, but must be conquered and replaced by a new hegemony directed to radical change. Among pluralists, there are those who see pluralism as a threatened value to be defended or fought for against tendencies in the system, as well as those who believe the present system in Western society already delivers the best possibility for pluralism.

CULTURE VERSUS SCIENCE

Again the reference is to another complex set of differentiations of substance, spirit, and method, which is poorly summarized by the terms chosen. However, no other terms seem to serve as well. Broadly speaking, according to a cultural view, mass media constitute a set of practices and texts that are produced, published, stored, enjoyed, and used in specific contexts of ideas, values, and experiences. Communication, in the first instance, refers to the ways of storing and experiencing certain texts that are available and rich in meaning, as well as connected intimately with other aspects of life. The scientific view of communication treats it more as a means to an end, as instrumental rather than expressive, as open to quantification as to amount, direction, reach, and effectiveness. In this respect, it is materialist rather than idealist, objective rather than subjective in mode. Cultural theory is likely to be associated with ritualistic, expressive, content (Carey, 1975) and likely to require methods that are interpretative and qualitative, intensive rather than extensive. By contrast, scientific theory and method are concerned with information, with causes and effects, and call for positivistic and behavioral methods. As described, it may seem that the two modes are alternatives for different purposes, but there is a fundamental difference that makes them difficult to reconcile and is particularly relevant to work on audience uses of mass communication. From the cultural position one should take the text as starting point and possible source of needs and interpretations of media experience, while from the scientific position, one would begin with behavior and assume needs for media to have an external, independent, origin.

INTERRELATING THE DIMENSIONS

As will have been apparent in the course of the foregoing descriptions, these four oppositions are not easy to relate to one another in any simple way in two-dimensional space and there is really no unique or best way of relating them. Yet some ordering is needed to make sense, or clarity, of the diversity. There is a case for a solution very similar to that of Burrell and Morgan (1979), giving precedence to the dominance-pluralism opposition because it accounts for most of the ideological variation and to the culture-science dimension because it accounts for most of the scientific variation—differences about communication and methods. The centripetal-centrifugal dimension (reformulated as suggested—by giving positive or negative valence to the poles) can be thought of as "shadowing" that of dominance-pluralism, so that its negative view of control and social fragmentation is close to the dominance pole. The media-society dimension is least easy to place, but probably best also viewed as a "shadow" of the culture-science division. The justification for this is that in its emphasis on media form and content as determinant, it veers toward the cultural pole and to a certain kind of idealism, rather than materialism. The main difficulty

	Culture	Science
Dominance	I Cultural- Critical	II Critical- Structural
Pluralism	IV Subjective- Functional	III Objective- Functional

Figure 8.1: Options of Media Theory

with this solution emerges with some theories of powerful mass media that emphasize the effects of recurring and systematic patterns of meaning in media content and also collective social forces. Such theories are sometimes open to testing by way of empirical, positivistic, methods (Noelle-Neumann, 1973; Gerbner, 1969). They are at the same time both media-centered and society-centered and also both subjective or cultural and objective or scientific. Despite this, as well as other ambiguities that have been mentioned, an attempt is made in Figure 8.1 to combine the various dimensions and oppositions into a single framework, in which the choice between dominance and pluralism and that between culture and science are cross-classified. It can be kept in mind that, associated with the first of these divisions is a split between a negative and a positive version of the centrifugal-centripetal opposition and with the second, a media-centered and a society-centered option. It is also important to remember that all these oppositions are more likely to be dimensions rather than dichotomies.

LOCATING THEORETICAL PERSPECTIVES
FOR GRATIFICATIONS RESEARCH

It is tempting to follow the example of Burrell and Morgan and attach paradigm labels for communication research to each of the four cells. One possible version is given in Figure 8.1, in terms of four kinds of theory. However, more important is to try and locate the main theoretical positions in the uses and gratifications research tradition and this will be attempted in Figure 8.2. Within the space so mapped out, we can locate several different things: theories of media use, actual

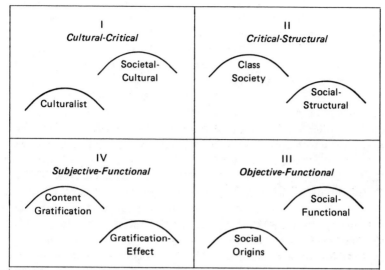

Figure 8.2: Variants of Theory for Gratifications Research

examples of research, and alternative views about how audiences are related to media. The locations chosen are bound to be approximate, based on a large measure of generalization and typification. This applies especially to placing *within* a cell, since some locations will be central, others peripheral. Because the uses approach has tended to converge on a common set of assumptions and methods, it is not surprising to find that potential entries are unevenly distributed. Most models and research examples are located in the two lower cells of Figure 8.1 and alternative approaches and critical perspectives are located above. However, it is important to represent the variant (or opposed) formulations, as well as those most established and tested.

Adopting a clockwise sequence, in cell I (cultural-critical theory), the emphasis is on culture and the message itself as a source of expectation, interpretation, and effect. Toward the upper right, the emphasis veers toward ideas of determinism and audience dependency. There are two main positions to be identified. One is a distinctly *culturalist* view, in which attention centers on the built-in meanings of texts as a starting point for the analysis of audience response. The cultural product as a whole, especially in its ritual or expressive aspects, is the main object of analysis. It is assumed that many gratifications are built into content in expectation of certain kinds of use and that needs associated with media originate in media themselves. This theoretical position could indicate gratification research, especially, as a source of evidence about the meaning of media content and media experience for audiences of varying cultural backgrounds and about some of the connections within

the cultural system. However, one central assumption of much gratifications research—that content means what the receiver takes, or wants,
it to mean would be in conflict with the culturalist position.

The second variant indicated within the quadrant approaches the
critical pole and can be labeled as *societal-cultural,* bringing together
several different possible versions of the media-audience relationship
and ways of examining it. One is a Marxist or neo-Marxist view of mass
media as offering a hegemonic culture, as a product of a "consciousness
industry," which functions to help maintain a particular social class
order, by diverting the underclass from awareness of problems (and
solutions) and into temporary and superficial pleasures. Various
theories of mass culture, including those of Frankfurt School adherents
(Jay, 1973), offer a view of mass media as a concealed ideology and
audience attraction as the manipulated outcome of the capitalist system
of work and leisure. Media content, in this view, is either completely
anodyne or oriented to fantasy. The lack of choice or change restricts
genuine freedom to choose or use media for aims other than those
intended by the suppliers. From a position of this kind, uses and
gratifications research can do little more than, at best, report back the
programmed responses of dependent mass audiences. At worst, it may
seem to provide confirmation that people like and even need what they
are given. There are, however, possibilities for less total and more
testable propositions about the use of media culture as compensation
for social deprivations of different kinds. There is also scope for research
into subcultural uses of media and varying choices or deviant interpretations shaped by relationship to the dominant social order. Such
critical research, although disclaiming an affinity with gratifications
research according to the dominant paradigm, has been carried out,
often in relation to music and concerning youth or ethnic minorities (for
example, Murdock and Phelps, 1973; Hall and Jefferson, 1975;
Hebdige, 1979). Research of this kind has a subjective as well as a critical
identification, not only because it pays a good deal of attention to
messages and ways of decoding them, but because it favors intensive,
qualitative, interpretative, and ethnographic approaches. The concepts
of culture itself and of taste are likely to be objects of investigation,
rather more so than the individuals who belong to subcultures.

In cell II (critical-structural theory) belong more materialist social
structural versions of media use, with the emphasis still on determinism,
but of a material rather than idealist kind. Thus society is first mover,
offering a mechanism of material production and distribution of
cultural products, and also providing a set of social norms and life-
chances, which (in combination) may provide an explanation of

patterns of media use. It is useful to distinguish a critical *class-society* version from a more neutral *social-structural* view. The former shares some of the elements that have already been described, but is more explicit about the political-economic forces that underlie cultural production, distribution, and choice. The second version records correspondences between media use and position in a social structure, without offering a single overarching explanation and interpretation of media use patterns. The two are thus not inconsistent but contain different versions of cause and effect, and of the possibilities for change.

The second, more neutral, version is not unlike that labeled "structural-cultural" by McQuail and Gurevitch (1974). It tends to undermine, or bypass, the notion that the overall pattern of media use is the outcome of a large number of individual, voluntary, acts of choice of media to help solve some personally experienced problem, meet some need, or provide some personally chosen satisfaction. Its tendency is toward the view that we choose what is most accessible (in the widest sense) in our social milieu and most in accordance with reigning conventions, habits, and norms of that milieu. Choice as well as the meaning of what is chosen are interpreted according to socially distributed norms. A short summary view would be that media-related needs derive not from content, but from society. Both the more critical and more neutral versions make use of positivistic methods, especially the more neutral versions since they lack any grand theory and depend on the interpretation of empirical evidence about correspondences between cultural patterns and social position.

In entering the third cell, we also enter the territory that is well populated with actual examples of research. Here belong those formulations and here we find the research that places the most weight on society and social experience as sources of individual needs, which may be then satisfied by media. These needs are especially likely to concern order, integration, and maintaining or forming social relationships. The term "social-functionalist," in its most common meaning in sociology, serves fairly well as a general descriptive label for the kind of uses and gratifications research that belongs here. A good example is the extensive inquiry of Katz et al. (1973) into the needs satisfied by different media (and other sources) for connecting Israelis with friends, family, tradition, culture, and the national society. The underlying proposition of this research was that membership in social groupings involves strongly felt needs to belong and that the media constitute one mechanism for fulfilling these needs. The research was both strongly society centered and integration oriented, but also committed to the empirical (positivist) method, and also more collective than individualist in tendency. A key aspect of this theoretical position (the social-functionalist) is that the needs for which media provide some fulfillment do not originate in the media, or in the individual, but in the more fundamental and enduring requirements of a social system.

Another variant kind of research that belongs in this cell, closer to the lower vertical pole, is that directed at finding relations between media use and social circumstances—sometimes referred to as research on the *social origins* of media use (for example, McQuail et al., 1972; Blumler, 1979). This differs from the variant just described in that it has a much lower emphasis on integration and order, and a greater emphasis is placed on diversity of media gratifications and the variety of conditions associated with expectations from media. There are many limited and specific uses and gratifications studies to which much the same comments would apply, united by little more than the assumptions that social experience does precede and help shape orientations to, and expectations of media and that people play a large part themselves in the interaction with media.

Cell IV, also rich in examples of research, returns us to a sphere where content itself, and the specific uses or satisfactions built into cultural and information products, take on more importance, but where the starting point for research is less likely to be postulated *social* needs than the perception by individuals of needs and solutions in content for these needs. There is a negotiation between diverse possibilities on the "offer" side and diverse, individually varying and changing expectations and applications on the "demand" side—that of the audience member. The term media-person interaction coined by McQuail et al. (1972) sums up important aspects of this relationship. Many of the first generation of media gratification studies from the 1940s belong here—on soap operas, quizzes, and radio music, as well as later research on gratifications derived from television news, newspapers, and political communication. The more child-oriented research on children and television of recent years (Brown, 1976; Noble, 1975) can also be cited, although the probable location in cell IV would be closer to the right-hand corner.

The option described by McQuail and Gurevitch (1974) as action-motivation, with its emphasis on variability, selectivity, voluntarism, open-ended activity, and personal assessment of satisfaction, which would also belong here, although it is not easy to exemplify in the stated theory of actual research. Within the space of the cell it is possible to make a broad distinction between those variants that are more culturalist (media centered) and those that are more functionalist. The former emphasize the content itself and the expressive (noninstrumental) aspects of media experience—emotional release, pleasure, fulfillment, fantasy, and others (McQuail, 1984). They include some studies that derive ideas about appeals of content from the content itself, and their methods are more interpretative than statistical and extensive. The second variant includes studies that are more empirical/statistical and lean more towards the investigation of social influences on media choice, informational content, and the part played by gratifications in the effect process. The separation from functionalist research is not absolute, but the emphasis in cell IV is on more voluntaristic and open-ended processes. The two variants are not easily labeled, but the terms *content-gratification* and *gratification-effect* summarize a number of the key differences. In Figure 8.2, the variants described are given an approximate location in the cells that were identified and labeled in Figure 8.1. (The arcs are intended to mark off the approximate area of location.)

THE TASKS OF GRATIFICATIONS RESEARCH AND THE OPTIONS OF THEORY

This approximate mapping of the field of theory, research, and critical perspective helps us to take further some of the questions raised at the outset. It suggests that, despite the attempt to identify a dominant paradigm on the basis of certain agreed assumptions and precepts of methods (Katz et al., 1974), it will not be easy to contain inquiry within a single theoretical framework. There are several sources of strain: between critical social analysis and accounting for order; between deterministic and voluntaristic views of social behavior; and between culturalist and materialist tendencies of method and interpretation. Viewed this way, the approach is not *a*theoretical, but *multi*theoretical and it is not surprising that the choice of theory is often shaped by influences and factors that do not seem directly related to the central problems and tasks of the research field. In order to take the discussion one step further, we need to consider briefly what these tasks are. They can be summarized as sets of questions under five headings, as follows:

- *Media gratifications—their nature and substance*: What are gratifications or similar concepts of satisfaction, use, motive, and so on? How should they be differentiated and labeled? What gratification goes with what content? How is their expression distributed in a given population? How are separate gratifications interrelated?

- *Gratification and media use*: How do expectations relate to kind and amount of media use? Do they predict use? Are they consistent with use? Is choice active, guided by expectations in advance? How are expectations related to eventual satisfactions, by way of media use?

- *Social origins and media gratifications*: Do expressed gratifications vary with social background and current circumstances? What processes underlie patterns of interrelationship—for instance, escape, compensation, adjustment, or chance?

- *Gratifications and effects.* Do gratifications predict measured effects on behavior, on learning or change in opinions, attitudes, or the like? What kinds of gratification go with what kinds of content, with what kinds of effect? What are the associated conditions of the gratification-effect relationship?

- *The sequence—originations-motivations-media use-satisfactions-consequences/effects*: Can such sequences be empirically discovered or alternative orderings of the same elements? What is the relative importance of different steps and the nature of relationships between them?

While all these questions have been asked at some time or another, the yield of answers is very unevenly distributed (Palmgreen, 1984b). The main point at issue is whether there is any clear relationship between the tasks as formulated and the theoretical options described. Do some questions go more with one variant of theory than another, and have some options of theory been more successful than others in generating or helping to design research? Or should we expect adherents of all theoretical positions to develop ways of answering all questions? Inevitably, there is a variation of emphasis in the options of theory that makes them more appropriate for handling some tasks rather than others. Questions about the nature and distribution of media gratifications should receive attention in all theory, but in practice they have been explored almost exclusively in the subjective-functional variants, and elsewhere they have been taken largely as conceptual and empirical givens. The precise connections between gratifications and media use have also received almost no attention from theories in the two upper cells of Figure 8.2, because, from a culturalist point of view, there is little interest in behavior and, from a structuralist point of view, subjective ideas about media use are redundant, mentalistic or epiphenomenal, and certainly not causal. This latter assumption does at least seem to garner some support from the findings of those who have tried to investigate the relationship (such as Kippax and Murray, 1980; Lichtenstein and Rosenfeld, 1983). The options as described, however, do not seem very helpful on important aspects of this problem, for instance the nature of audience activity (Levy, 1983) or the relationships among advance expectation, media use, and subsequent satisfaction (Palmgreen, 1984b).

The third set of questions (social origins) has a larger place in the theoretical space and almost all theories can lead to some proposition about the relation between some kinds of social position or circumstance and media preferences and tastes, even if empirical testing has largely been left to functional theorists. However, the confirmation of any strong set of hypotheses connecting social origins and media use remains more an aspiration than an achievement.

The last two sets of questions or tasks—concerning the relation between quality of media use and the consequences of that experience and, secondly, the systematic interrelating of all stages, from social origins to effects—have so far largely defied clear theoretical statement and evaded empirical demonstration. In general, on this whole matter of the relationship between the tasks of the field, which can be specified for research, and the theoretical options described, there seem to be some very large gaps and discontinuities, with theories often very selective in what they attend to and empirically either very patchy or simply missing in relation to important components of theory (especially with respect to societal-cultural and class-society variants).

CONCLUSIONS

This brief and possibly arguable commentary on a large body of research and theory leads to a number of observations about the theoretical status and future prospects of gratifications research. First, much past research is scattered over a framework of not very compatible theoretical positions. Second, the validity of some alternative theories has not been put to empirical test. Third, all the options described are deficient with respect to one or more of the main tasks of the field. Fourth, certain questions—such as those about audience activity and the basic processes of experiencing media may not really figure in the theoretical space as mapped out.

A number of models of the whole gratification-media use process have been formulated, as if these theoretical problems and divisions could be bypassed, if not ignored (for example, Rosengren, 1974, Palmgreen, 1984b). Rosengren (1983) has gone on to suggest that modern developments of multivariate analysis allow one to investigate the interrelations between elements specified by such models—personal circumstances, gratifications sought, media choices, norms and evaluations of media content, and satisfactions and consequences, as well as time-order of occurrence—without theoretical presuppositions of a kind that uniquely belong to any location in the above map. Theory would play some part, however, in the choice of variables, in operationalization, and in the interpretation of results. This true eclecticism has already been put into practice in the Swedish Media Panel studies (Hedinnson, 1981; Roe, 1983b; Johnsson-Smaragdi, 1983) with interesting results. It is both a tempting and challenging choice, when one considers the inadequacy and inconsistency of theory as described.

Burrell and Morgan (1979), whose work contributed to this discussion as well as to Rosengren's (1983) major statement, offered a different solution for their field of research interest. Their argument was that each of the four paradigms (named above) "needs to be developed in its own terms." They advocate a form of "isolationism," so that each paradigm can be "true to itself." They state,

> Contrary to widely held belief that synthesis and mediation between paradigms is what is required, we argue that the real need is for paradigmatic closure. In order to avoid emasculation and incorporation within the functionalist problematic, the paradigms need to provide a basis for their self-preservation by developing on their own account. . . . For those who wish to leave the functionalist orthodoxy behind, many avenues offer themselves for exploration [Burrell and Morgan, 1979: 397-398].

While it is true that Rosengren is far from advocating a functionalist hegemony, he is advocating the methodology of the dominant (functionalist) paradigm as the only way to answer questions rather than simply raising them (as seems to be the case with several of the alternative theory options) or offering ready-made, self-fulfilling answers.

We are thus faced with a similar choice to that posed by Burrell and Morgan: synthesis or separate development? In our field as well, there are a number of avenues for exploration as alternatives to eclecticism. The exploration engaged in here does not yield an obvious answer, but leads the author to a number of tentative conclusions. One is that empiricism of the kind advocated and practiced by Rosengren may result in constructions built on rather unstable foundations, because the results can be assembled in theoretically diverse ways. But equally, those who hold rather global theories (of a critical or class-structural variety) about the control exerted through and by the media, are not absolved from the empirical testing of the nature and degree of dependence on media culture and information by their audiences. Third, the general Burrell and Morgan option of theoretical "apartheid" seems unlikely to lead to much that is new, interesting, or relevant to the changing media situation. Fourth, at least one alternative option—the critical-cultural variant—perhaps does need to develop separately because of its roots in the humanities. Finally, what the field may need most is to develop more of its own theory to solve its own particular problems of concept and method.

PART III

PERSPECTIVES ON KEY RESEARCH AREAS

Chapter 9

THE NATURE OF
NEWS GRATIFICATIONS

Lawrence A. Wenner

HOW DO PEOPLE USE NEWS? This question has obvious significance for two types of communication researchers. For researchers with
a *scientific* view (see McQuail, this volume), this has much to do with
empirical questions about information and how people are influenced
by and make decisions according to their interpretations of the news.
For researchers with a *cultural* view, how people use news is a sign of
culture to be interpreted by means of intensive analysis.

In 1949, Wilbur Schramm began his article "The Nature of News" by
suggesting an answer that is seemingly satisfactory from both views.
Undoubtedly influenced by Lippmann (1922), Schramm (1949: 259)
posed that "news exists in the minds of men." However, Schramm did
not leave it at that. Rather, he speculated and provided evidence concerning the motives for and rewards of news consumption. Influenced
by Freud (1934), Schramm saw news consumption as guided by either
reality motives, which have delayed rewards, or *pleasure* motives, which
have immediate rewards. However, as Schramm observed, real life news
consumption takes place amidst the countervailing pulls of at least these
two motives, rather than being propelled exclusively by any one motive.
Thus even with the apparent neatness of his construct, Schramm had
begun the opening of an extremely messy can of worms.

AUTHOR'S NOTE: Partial support for this project was made possible through a
University Research Grant from Loyola Marymount University. I would like to
acknowledge the helpful comments and suggestions made during the preparation of the
manuscript by Dr. Mark R. Levy of the College of Journalism at the University of
Maryland.

171

For a few years after Schramm's analysis, some research activity about news consumption took place (Kay, 1954; Turner, 1958; Westley and Barrow, 1959), but apart from Stephenson's (1964, 1967) explication of the play aspects of news reading, very little theoretical development was aimed at understanding the dynamics of news gratifications. With the revival of gratifications research in the late 60s and early 70s, research specifically focusing on news gratifications began to appear. However, much of this research (Becker, 1976, 1979; Becker et al., 1979; McLeod and Becker, 1974, 1979; McLeod et al., 1979; Wenner, 1977, 1983b) had a political focus inspired by Blumler and McQuail's (1969) landmark study *Television in Politics: Its Uses and Influences*. Although much news is of a political nature, much, and perhaps most, is not. And even political news can be gratifying in explicitly nonpolitical ways (Wenner, 1983b).

Much recent news gratifications research has tended to focus on television news, although some studies have been reported which examine gratifications from newspapers (Becker, 1979), and many others have involved the concept of newspaper use (Weaver and Buddenbaum, 1980). Research on television news gratifications has centered on the audience for regularly scheduled newscasts, and much of this research has as its focus the audience for one of the three American nightly network newscasts (Davis and Woodall, 1982; Gantz, 1978; Levy, 1983; Palmgreen et al., 1980, 1981; Wenner, 1982, 1983a, 1984). Occasionally, studies have appeared that examine other types of television news programming, ranging from news interview programs (Levy, 1978c), to morning news programs (Rayburn and Palmgreen, 1981; Rayburn et al., in press), and news magazine programs such as *60 Minutes* (Rubin, 1981b; Wenner, 1982, 1983a, 1984).

While much of this research has ties with specific theoretical notions, a good deal of it has stemmed from a basic interest in the variety and structure of media news gratifications and that which may be linked to them. Although valuable, this research has been hindered by the lack of a broad-based theoretical structure from which to examine the nature of media news gratifications. This chapter is an attempt to formulate such a structure. The approach has been most influenced by two seminal studies in the media gratifications literature. Since similarities, rather than differences, are the key to understanding in any literature review, the Katz, Gurevitch, and Haas (1973) notion of a "functional circumplex" has been adapted in the structuring of similarities among media news gratifications into a conceptual map. Similarly, if a literature review is to have any lasting value, some sense of theoretical meaning must be derived from it. Here, McGuire's (1974) suggestions are followed about relating his 16-fold matrix of motivations for media gratifications to research findings. The McGuire matrix is used to clarify theoretical relationships and make sense of the mapping based on similarities among media news gratifications.

THE CONTENT-PROCESS DISTINCTION

Getting a good picture of the shape and form of media news gratifications is not easy. The schemas that have been used to conceptualize news gratifications differ substantially. Some consider two gratifications (Schramm, 1949; Swanson, 1976), while others visualize four (McQuail et al., 1972), five (Palmgreen et al., 1980, 1981), or more (Levy, 1978b; Wenner, 1983b) kinds of news gratifications. Sometimes subsets within gratification categories are used (McQuail et al., 1972; Wenner, 1983b), and these tend to make the "gratifications web" for news seem even more unwieldly.

However, more often than not, recent schemas for news gratifications can be traced to either the fourfold typology of surveillance, correlation, social transmission, and entertainment suggested by Lasswell (1948) and refined by Wright (1960), or an alternate typology developed by McQuail et al. (1972) that embraces many of the same notions in its division of surveillance, personal identity, personal relationships, and diversion gratifications.

While the conceptualization presented here owes much to these formulations, its basic structure is derived from a more fundamental distinction that has appeared with remarkable regularity in the study of news and communication. In gratifications parlance, this distinction can be summarized as one between content and process gratifications. Cutler and Danowski (1980: 269-270) define *content gratifications* as those "derived from the use of mediated messages for their direct, substantive, intrinsic value for the receiver" while *process gratifications* are "derived from the use of mediated messages for extrinsic values that do not bear a direct link to particular substantive characteristics of the messages: the individual receives gratifications only or mainly from being involved in the process of communication behavior, rather than the message content." Characterizing content gratifications are message uses to gain knowledge, increase or reduce uncertainty in personal and social situations, or support existing predispositions. Process gratifications are characterized by consumption activities that take place apart

STUDY	CONTENT ⬚⬚⬚	PROCESS ⬚⬚⬚	FOCUS OF STUDY ⬚⬚⬚
Dewey (1925)	instrumental	consummatory	communication
Freud (1934)	reality principle	pleasure principle	mental functioning
Schramm (1949)	delayed reward	immediate reward	news consumption
Key (1954)	conscious	unconscious	news reading cathexes
	ego involving	non-ego involving	
	personal identification	entertainment	
Szasz (1957)	communication pain	communication pleasure	communication
Stephenson (1964, 1967)	objective work	subjective play	news reading
	non-ego involving	ego involving	
	call for action	no call for action	
Carey (1975, 1977)	transmission	ritual	communication
Wenner (1977), Levy (1977a)	cognitive	affective	TV news gratification
Cutler and Danowski (1980)	substantive	non-substantive	gratification.
	intrinsic	extrinsic	

Figure 9.1   Theoretical Linkages to Cutler and Danowski's (1980) Distinction Between Content and Process Gratifications

from content per se, and include a myriad of "escape" uses, stimulation uses that often involve engagement in "entertainment," and uses combatting social isolation through connections with mediated culture and its actors.

The content-process distinction encapsulates and can be seen as derivative of similar dichotomies made by others (see Figure 9.1). Perhaps its best known link would be with Schramm's (1949) delayed and immediate reward theory of news consumption, which has origins in Freud's (1934) reality and pleasure principles. Other links include Stephenson's (1964, 1967) development of a play theory of mass communication based on the work of Szasz (1957), Carey's (1975, 1977) cultural approach, which contrasts transmission and ritual views of communication in line with the instrumental-consummatory distinction made by Dewey (1925), and the division between cognitive and affective modes made by many and that can be seen with special reference to television news gratifications in the work of Wenner (1977) and Levy (1977a). Although the concerns and boundaries of each of the distinctions shown in Figure 9.1 vary to some degree (even to the point of disagreement, such as the contrasting views of Stephenson (1964) and Kay (1954) as to the role of ego-involvement in news consumption), there are far fewer differences than similarities, and these are reducible to the fundamental difference in approach illustrated by content and process gratifications.

A MEDIA NEWS GRATIFICATIONS MAP

Content and process gratifications form the principal axes of the map of news gratifications presented in Figure 9.2. Each axis is anchored by orientational (or self-referent) and social (or other-referent) poles. This referential scheme is a simplification of that used by Katz, Gurevitch, and Haas (1973) and others. The net result of axes with these poles is that four areas with common boundaries may be charted. Orientational and social gratifications are the two areas which comprise media news content gratifications. *Orientational gratifications* are message uses for information that provide for the reference and reassurance of self in relation to society. *Social gratifications* are message uses that link information about society derived from news to the individual's inter-personal network.

News process gratifications are also divided into two areas—para-social and para-orientational—which coexist on the same level with and provide substitution for the content gratifications that are normatively deemed valuable for their substance. *Para-social gratifications,* derivative of Horton's and Wohl's (1956) notion of para-social interaction, are process uses that provide for personal identity and reference through ritualized social relationships with media "actors" who coexist with news content. "Actors" can be television newscasters, newspaper columnists, as well as the people who are the subject of news reports. *Para-orientational gratifications* are process uses that ritualistically *reorient* news content through play activity that tends to reinforce predispositions by using expressive strategies that are often aimed at tension reduction or ego defense. Here "play activity," while framed implicitly with reference to content, often needs few *specific* content cues to stimulate gratification; in no sense is its goal merely information gain (Stephenson, 1964, 1967), and rather often the goal combats such gain in aiming at reinforcement or avoidance of a perceived information overload.

From the *scientific* view (see McQuail, this volume), the content gratification axis could represent a larger "transmission path" through

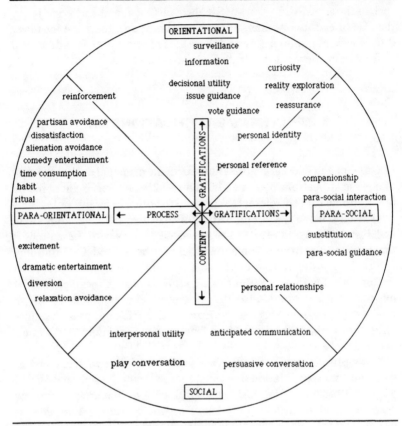

Figure 9.2   Media News Gratifications Map

which information flows and agendas are set. For instance, in the "flow" of personal influence, one might look to orientation (first step) to social dispensation (second step). From the *cultural* view, the process gratification axis likely represents *anything but* a "path." Instead, it might well be conceived of as "playground" of extrinsic gratifications which, when studied as ritualistic media activity, help make cultural assessments possible. The *transactional* view taken here (see Wenner in Chapter 4) is an amalgam of the scientific and cultural views. Here, *content* gratifications must be *processed*, and it is not possible for *process* gratifications to be formed without some reference to the *content* characteristics that provide information for orientation.

ORIENTATIONAL GRATIFICATIONS

To describe this set of gratifications with a cognitive bent, "orienta-tional" was chosen over other terms, such as "surveillance," because of its greater breadth and more clearly defined theoretical development. The term's origins are evident in the utilization framework seen in Tolman's (1932, 1948) molar view of purposive behavior and "cognitive mapping." Developed in communication in the Westley and MacLean (1957) model, and by Westley and Barrow (1959), the concept is evident in many later information-seeking studies (Atkin, 1973; Chaffee and McLeod, 1973; Donohew and Tipton, 1973). McCombs and Weaver (1973) defined the political *need for orientation* in terms of political relevance and uncertainty, and the concept has remained central to agenda-setting research (see McCombs and Weaver, this volume). Implicit in their definition, and adopted here in a context broader than merely political communication, is the idea that information cannot be useful only for information's sake. Rather, the utility of information emerges when it is referenced to the individual, thus providing the needed orientation of self to society.

A number of conceptual problems surround "surveillance." In the way it has been defined in much media news gratifications research, there are inconsistencies and troublesome ambiguities due to a lack of specificity in its operationalization. As Wenner (1983b) has pointed out, operationalizations of surveillance often only begin to scratch the surface of the news consumer's underlying needs for news, tapping instead a vague and socially acceptable notion of how news *should* be used. Many of the varied definitions of surveillance fail to get at the heart of the matter; they do not specify *why* the individual feels the need to do such things as "keep up with the main issues of the day." Certainly, one could expect an individual to "keep up with the main issues of the day" for a variety of reasons, including helping to facilitate decisions, locating (or relocating) oneself on the political spectrum, increasing one's self-esteem, or providing information that could be used in conversation. There may be a good chance that social pressure upon respondents to report using news in societally acceptable ways, when combined with an ambiguity as to the *why* of surveillance, may have contributed to an overestimation by media scholars of the importance of surveillance gratifications relative to other gratifications derived from media news consumption.

Nonetheless, questions about surveillance and other orientational gratifications are important ones that are most pertinent to how media are used in the political decision-making process (see McLeod and Becker, 1981). Indeed, much evidence suggests that orientational gratifications are linked to exposure to, attention to, and dependency on a wide variety of television programming that contains political information (Becker, 1976; Levy, 1978d; McLeod et al., 1979; McLeod and Becker, 1974; Wenner, 1983a, 1983b, 1984). In addition, orientational gratifications have positive ties to such things as political interest, political efficacy, political knowledge, public affairs opinion leadership, the correct recall of news items, and the likelihood of voting (Gantz, 1978; Levy, 1978d; McLeod et al., 1977; McLeod and Becker, 1974; Wenner, 1983b, 1984).

As a subset of orientational gratifications, *surveillance* and *information* are placed as similar concepts near the top and center of the map, representing a passively initiated, but utilitarian, motive directed at cognitive orientation. *Curiosity* (Blumler, 1979), another similar general term, has been defined operationally by more active initiation with a personal identity component to it. *Surveillance* and *information* have been characterized as having empirical ties with para-social gratifications (Davis and Woodall, 1982; Levy, 1978b; Palmgreen, et al., 1980, Rayburn and Palmgreen, 1981) and social gratifications (Becker, 1979; Levy, 1978b; Palmgreen et al., 1980). More limited evidence suggests that a combination of information and entertainment gratifications is indicative of affinity for television news magazine programs (Rubin, 1981).

More specific orientational gratifications involving *decisional utility* and political subparts of it, such as *vote guidance* and *issue guidance* tend to merge in factor analysis with the broader-based concept of surveillance (Becker, 1979; Levy and Windahl, 1984; Palmgreen et al., 1980; Wenner, 1983b). Both vote guidance, concerning candidate choices, and issue guidance have empirical ties to para-social gratifications; the para-social relationship emerges with candidates in vote guidance, and with reporters in issue guidance (Wenner, 1983b).

Para-social elements can also be seen in findings about *curiosity* (Blumler, 1979) and *reassurance* gratifications (Levy, 1978b), both of which have conceptual ties to *surveillance*. The *reality exploration* and *personal reference* components of the Leeds *personal identity* category (Blumler, 1979; McQuail et al., 1972) may be viewed as degrees of emphatic information acquisition gratifications that conceptually sandwich the notion of *reassurance* (Levy, 1978b). In total, the evidence suggests that many kinds of orientational gratifications involve para-social relationships.

PARA-SOCIAL GRATIFICATIONS

Especially when considering their ties to orientational gratifications, it is surprising that para-social gratifications have received so little explicit study. Seemingly ignored with regard to gratifications derived from newspaper reading, the para-social relationship described by Horton and Wohl (1956) is an essential ingredient in the identification process that takes place between the audience member and the television newscaster (Levy, 1979). Here the newscaster encourages the relationship by looking directly into the camera while conversing with the viewer in a way that is often perceived as an ongoing reciprocal dialogue. Interaction among members of the now common "news team" also tends to bring about the illusion of regular participation in an extended peer group within which the viewer serves as an "ex-officio" member with the ultimate power to change the composition of the team merely by changing the channel. However, many such relationships are decidedly imbalanced, with the audience member deriving such benefits from the "wisdom" and "advice" of the newscaster, that an ongoing empathy develops (Horton and Wohl, 1956). Of course, such emphatic identification is not limited to the viewer with a favorite newscaster. Para-social relationships are established with many of the people featured regularly in the "content" of news stories, such as political figures, entertainment personalities, and sports heroes. Newspaper political columnists, advice columnists, and humorists are also likely sources of para-social gratifications.

Para-social gratifications have been linked to frequent viewing of early evening television news programs, and this is particularly true for the older segment of the population (Levy, 1979). Dependency on both nightly news programs and weekly news magazine shows is also facilitated by para-social involvement (Wenner, 1982). Further evidence shows that a relative lack of political cynicism is characteristic of people engaging in para-social relationships (Wenner, 1983b). These people also tend to see television as the dominant source of their political information (Wenner, 1984). Most interesting is that para-social gratifications have been shown to be predictive of general political and specific campaign interest, and correspondingly high levels of political discussion (Wenner, 1983b, 1984). These latter findings, which are more typically associated with surveillance and vote guidance gratifications, point out the need to understand the relationship between orientational and para-social gratifications.

Although para-social gratifications are employed in many studies, little is known about the differences among such gratifications. One schema for characterizing para-social gratifications can be applied here is the *supplement, complement, substitute* progression suggested by Rosengren and Windahl (1972). Here the media-person relationship is characterized in terms of the relative dependence people place on mediated versus face-to-face relationships. From this framework, *supplementation* would start at the top near the orientational gratification border where the Leeds *personality identity* category subsets of *reality exploration* and *personal reference* employ para-social elements (Blumler, 1979; McQuail et al., 1972) that are bridged by Levy's (1978b) notion of *reassurance*. *Reality exploration* tips the border, being more orientational than para-social, but with decided identity components that refer to mediated actors and their situations. *Reassurance* is very similar, but has a clearer "person" reference to orientation (Levy, 1978b). *Personal reference* describes even more active real person-media person comparisons (McQuail et al., 1972). When such comparisons are made routinely, the interaction that results defines a *complementary* rather than merely supplementary relationship. Here, *companionship* (Wenner, 1976) and *para-social interaction* (Levy, 1979; Palmgreen et al., 1980, 1981) characterize relationships that become increasingly important with increasing paucity of real-life relationships. Conceptually, *substitution* gratifications should go beyond being merely complementary, but most often (McQuail et al., 1972; Rubin, 1981b) they have been characterized similarly to companionship and para-social interaction. However, *para-social guidance* (Wenner, 1983b, 1984) does describe a relationship approaching substitution for people who are rather exclusively dependent on television news for vote guidance.

PARA-ORIENTATIONAL GRATIFICATIONS

Much as the mapping of para-social gratifications can be characterized by a threefold progression, para-orientational gratifications can be seen as a progression away from gratifications having to do with intrinsic, substantive qualities of news to those that are more extrinsically valued. *Reinforcement* gratifications, which take up the top section near and even crossing the orientational border, give way to ritualized *expressive play* gratifications in the middle, and to diversion strategies aimed at *tension reduction* gratifications near the social gratifications border. All are clearly *para*-orientational in the sense that they are *reactions* to social expectations to use news content for orientational purposes. Reinforcement "reorients" through selective perception strategies that are often important to ego defense. Ritualized expressive play is an interventionist strategy aimed at "subverting" content through playful manipulation. Tension reduction gratifications "divert" orientational messages through a drive to avoid orientational presses by focusing on the decidedly entertaining qualities of news.

Included in this section of the map are three *avoidance* strategies—for reasons of partisanship, political alienation, and preference for relaxation—which have been specifically associated with political news (Becker, 1976, 1979; Blumler and McQuail, 1969; McLeod and Becker, 1974). A variety of other forms of avoidance orientations have been examined, and a common surfacing has been the concept of avoidance or *dissatisfaction* because of perceived media bias or other negative evaluation of the news source (Becker, 1979; Levy 1978b; Wenner, 1983b). Rather than view such avoidances apart from gratifications, or as negative gratifications as has been considered (Becker, 1979; Levy, 1978b), a place for them has been made within the overall gratification mix for news. As voiced in the literature, avoidance dispositions have been cast as "orientations," but from the framework here they are merely *"para*-orientations" that surface as reactions to and alternatives for orientational gratifications. In addition, as Palmgreen et al. (1980) have suggested, segregating avoidances from gratifications becomes unnecessary from a gratifications sought and obtained perspective. By looking at the absolute levels of gratifications sought and obtained, as well as their links to low levels of exposure, gratification explanations for avoiding exposure become readily apparent without measurement of reflective "avoidances."

The avoidances and other para-orientational gratifications have had consistent connections with other variables in a political context. Excitement and entertainment gratifications tend to have a stimulative effect on exposure to, affinity for, and dependency on a variety of types of media news, as well as being indicative of strong partisanship, high levels of political cynicism, relatively poor recall of news items, and frequent political discussions (Gantz, 1978; McLeod et al., 1982; McLeod and Becker, 1974; Rubin, 1981b; Wenner, 1982, 1983b). Selectively derived reinforcement gratifications have been associated with substantial political activity, strong partisanship, and intention to vote, but have also revealed little knowledge gain (Becker, 1976; McLeod and Becker, 1974; Wenner, 1983b). Partisan avoidance is characterized by strong political interest and accurate knowledge of the issues, while alienation avoidance is associated with little attention to or interest in politics, and relaxation avoidance combines this lack of interest with little likelihood of engaging in political discussions or voting (Becker, 1976; McLeod and Becker, 1974, Wenner, 1983b).

These findings help characterize progressive distinctions in para-orientational gratifications. Consistency-linked *reinforcement* gives way to *partisan avoidance* as internally originated needs for consistency come into contact with the external referents of political party affiliation. *Dissatisfactions* (Levy, 1978b) as well, have an external referent—the qualities of the news presentation—which may intertwine with more internal goal orientations, such as those aimed at ego defense. Ego-defensive strategies can also be seen if one returns to and examines the operationalizations of *alienation avoidance* (Blumler and McQuail, 1969; McLeod and Becker, 1974) and *comedy entertainment* (Wenner, 1983b) derived from campaign coverage. *Time consumption, habit,* and *ritual* are decidedly more passive than their expressive counterparts, *excitement* (Blumler and McQuail, 1969; McLeod and Becker, 1974) and *dramatic entertainment* (Wenner, 1983b). *Diversion* (Blumler, 1979; Levy, 1978b; McQuail et al., 1972) and *relaxation avoidance* (Becker, 1976, 1979; Blumler and McQuail, 1969; McLeod and Becker, 1974) take that ritualized and playful expressive strategy and aim it more directly at explicit tension reduction.

As was the case with para-social gratifications, the effort toward an analysis of progressions within para-orientational gratifications is based on considerable extrapolation of an area where much is known, but where many links are not yet clear, and agreed upon definitions are difficult to come by. What does seem clear is that some conceptual ordering within process gratifications categories will be helpful in clarifying links between them and provide fodder for the intensive analysis of critical and cultural studies. In effects studies, such clarification may be even more important if we are to arrive at a clear understanding of how informational orientations are processed en route toward a link with the social gratifications that propel those orientations concerning media content into the individual's interpersonal network.

SOCIAL GRATIFICATIONS

When compared with other gratification categories in which characterization is based on a melding and ordering of considerable conceptual variety, social gratifications can be characterized by a central core in which a cognitive-affective merger takes place in evaluating perceived usefulness of news in interpersonal discussions after exposure. From this central core emerge two types of social gratifications. These are most vividly contrasted in Wenner's (1983b) distinction between *play* and *persuasive* conservation gratifications. *Persuasive social gratifications,* such as those garnering supportive "ammunition" to be used in discussions, are commonly operationalized as *anticipated communication* in studies focusing on political news and information (Becker, 1976; Blumler and McQuail, 1969; Levy, 1978d; McLeod and Becker, 1974). More integrative in character, *play social gratifications* take the form of *interpersonal or social utility* that stress "interesting" things to pass along to friends, and are seen in studies of "everyday" news consumption (Becker, 1979; Levy, 1978b; Levy and Windahl, 1984; McQuail et al., 1972; Palmgreen et al., 1980, 1981; Wenner, 1982, 1983a, 1984).

Social gratifications have their clearest link with exposure to, attention to, and dependency on varying forms of news (Atkin, 1973; Becker, 1976; Wenner, 1982, 1983a). In more politically focused contexts, evidence has shown social gratifications to be indicative of general political and specific campaign interest, guided most likely by related high levels of political activity and partisanship (McLeod and Becker, 1974; Wenner, 1983b, 1984). The relation of social gratifications to the accurate acquisition of knowledge, however, is not clear. While Becker (1976) found evidence that social gratifications were indicative of knowledge of Watergate, McLeod and Becker (1974) found that those using political news on television as a source of "ammunition" for arguments with others did not tend to learn appreciably about the issues. They posit that such lack of learning is related to the tendency to be selective in information held for later discussion.

Finally, there are a number of findings suggesting that social gratifications tend to occur in association with other gratifications. Levy and Windahl (1984) have shown that social gratifications are positively related to both orientational "surveillance" gratifications and to a combination of process gratifications (entertainment/para-social interaction). Palmgreen et al. (1980) find that when sought, social gratifications tend to combine with orientational gratifications, but when obtained, the two tend to split into separate factors. This contrasts markedly with process gratifications, which tend to form separate factors (entertainment and para-social interaction) when sought, but combine into one dimension when obtained (Palmgreen et al., 1980). When taken together, these findings that link social gratifications to all others are most provocative. Palmgreen et al. (1980) suggest that such process gratification links are in good part based on the *structural characteristics* of news and these contribute to the breaking apart of content gratifications into those useful for orientation and those useful for social purposes. Further investigations, by using the theoretical frameworks outlined in the following sections, might well aim at understanding how gratification structures change according to whether they related to the seeking or obtaining phase of the gratifications process.

THEORETICAL IMPLICATIONS
OF THE MEDIA NEWS
GRATIFICATIONS MAP

Perhaps more than any other conceptualization, McGuire's (1974) matrix of human motivation theories provides evidence for Blumler's (1979: 11) observation that "there are many theories about uses and gratifications phenomena, which may well differ with each other over many issues." While McGuire sees each of the sixteen concepts of human motivation as reflective of a "model of man," they are used here as coexisting and overlapping views that have more relevance to certain kinds of news gratifications than others. McGuire's breakdown is structured as a 2×2 table, with each of the categories subdivided further into bipolar opposites. One face of the table distinguishes between *cognitive* and *affective* modes, each of which may stress either *growth* or *preservation* of current equilibrium. The opposing face of the table distinguishes between *active* and *passive* initiation, each of which may take place with either *internal* or *external* goal orientations. Although space limitations prevent going into detail about each theoretical area, each of these theories will be positioned as they relate to the areas in the media news gratifications map (see Figure 9.3). It should be recognized that the concern here is not so much with getting a "perfect" fit, but rather with illuminating a conceptual framework that might serve as the basis for theoretical development in media news gratifications research.

ORIENTATIONAL GRATIFICATIONS

The orientational gratification area represents the most fertile area with reference to McGuire's matrix. Indeed, orientational gratifications can be characterized, in some fashion, by all eight of McGuire's cogni-

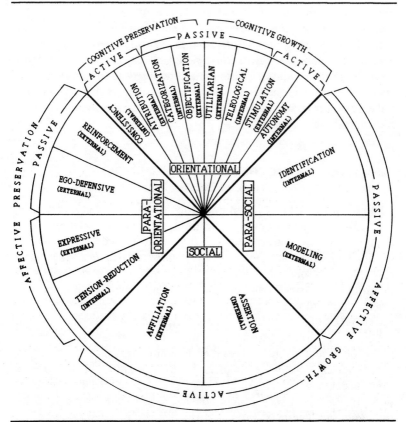

Figure 9.3 Gratifications Map Integrating McGuire (1974) Matrix of Human Motivation Theories

tive theories of motivation. The area is defined by a bifurcation of cognitive growth and preservation theories. Moreover, the area can be characterized by a relatively passive center. At its core are the less well-specified *surveillance* and *information* gratifications that tend to have general external referents in keeping with *utilitarian* theories on the growth side, and *objectification* theories on the preservation side. When more specific orientational gratifications that pertain to decision making come into play (such as *decisional utility, issue guidance,* and *vote guidance*), the range of passive cognition theories expands somewhat to include those with the internal referents that make such decisions possible in a way consistent with *categorization* theories on the preservation side, and *teleological* theories on the growth side. Moving toward the border of para-orientational gratifications, orientational gratifications become more actively preserving in character, and more selective interpretations of the informational content acquired take over in ways consonant with *attribution* and *consistency* theories. On the other side, it can be seen that gratifications such as *curiosity, reality exploration, reassurance, personal identity,* and *personal reference* become progressively more active, and thus have explicit reference to *stimulation* theories with external orientations, and *autonomy* theories with more internal focus as orientational gratifications move closer to and overlap with para-social gratifications.

PARA-SOCIAL GRATIFICATIONS

While the varied theories of both cognitive growth and preservation can be tied to orientational gratifications, the theories that most clearly apply to para-social gratifications have a more limited focus on passive affective growth. The *supplement* to *complement* to *substitute* progression that has been used to describe differences among para-social gratifications is consistent with a gradual shift from *internal* to *external* goal orientations. At one end of the progression, *supplementation* can be seen in terms of *identification* theories. Here, the identity component of the gratification is merely supplemental to the internal goal orientations of the individual. At the other end of the continuum, *substitution* can be seen in terms of *modeling* theories. In this case, internal goal orientations become secondary to the external ones defined by the media personnae upon whom the individual has become more dependent. The individual whose social interactions (of a certain quality and about certain topics) are largely limited to media personnae is likely to receive guidance in those instances where the para-social relationship is longstanding and highly valued. Such guidance may be the basis for a "model" that may be used when opportunities for social interaction with others finally present themselves. In the middle of the continuum, *complementary* para-social relationships involves an *interaction* of the internal goals of identification processes with the external goals that define modeling behavior.

PARA-ORIENTATIONAL GRATIFICATIONS

In contrast with the affective growth involved in para-social gratifications, para-orientational gratifications can be seen as a passive to active progression in affective preservation motives. The theoretical break-down offered by McGuire (1974) mirrors what has been cast earlier as a movement away from the orientational border aligned with gradual transformation from more to less reference on the intrinsic, substantive content characteristics of news. Selectively-based *reinforcement* with external reference aids *ego-defense* with internal focus in the passive "reorientation" of news content. More active, but ritualized, *expressive* motivations "subvert" externally imposed content through playful manipulation. Internally driven "diversion" of content characteristics focuses more on the "structural" entertainment qualities of news in the active search for *tension reduction.*

SOCIAL GRATIFICATIONS

While orientational gratifications reside in remarkably fertile theoretical terrain that impacts upon social gratifications, social motivations have received comparatively little attention as a distinct entity. As social contact implies active growth, social gratifications are pegged into this variety of affectively focused theory, although it would be naive to assume "pure" social motivations without some fuel from the cognitive reference provided by orientational gratifications. As noted earlier, a split in social gratifications can be synopsized by Wenner's (1983b) distinction between *play* and *persuasive* conversation. *Affiliation* theories, with their *external* reference, provide a link to gratifications that stress integrative qualities of using news as the basis for social contact. Using news as "ammunition" in persuasive conversation, however, can hardly be described as integrative. Here, *assertion* theories that focus on *internal* goals related to the needs for power and achievement tend to be more relevant.

NOTES TOWARD A THEORETICAL REDUCTION

As McGuire (1974) has observed, sixteen theoretical positions may err on the overly complex side, even when applied to something as broad as human motivation. When applied to a more limited endeavor, such as the understanding of media news gratifications, the sixteen theories become even more unwieldy. More applicable to research practice may be a theoretical reduction (see Figure 9.4) that encapsulates the main trends seen in both the earlier overlay (see Figure 9.3) and the gratifications map (see Figure 9.2). The abbreviated comments here are limited to four areas (1) within-category reductions, (2) convergent selectivity, (3) ports of entry, and (4) patterns of movement.

WITHIN-CATEGORY REDUCTIONS

Although important from many different theoretical perspectives, *orientational gratifications* can be reduced to two varieties. These have to do with *cognitive growth* as they come near para-social gratifications, and with *cognitive preservation* as they come near para-orientational gratifications. In the affective domain, a related distinction between growth and preservation characterizes the main differences between the two types of *para*-gratifications. *Para-social gratifications* involve *affective growth,* while *para-orientational gratifications* involve *affective preservation.* When sharing many characteristics with orientational gratifications, para-social gratifications tend to be dominated by *internal* goal orientations, but as the identification process gives way to modeling, *external* referents become more important. On the other hand, para-orientational gratifications begin as more *passive* near orientational gratifications, and more *active* as they come closer to social gratifications. Although falling technically under the domain of affective growth theories, *social gratifications* can be seen to be aimed at two types of connections, both of which necessarily involve some degree of information gain, as well as the affective processing of it. Depending on the locus of their drives, these social connections (Katz, Gurevitch, and Haas, 1973) may be either *affiliative* or *assertive* in nature.

CONVERGENT SELECTIVITY

In charting the terrain of the news gratifications maps, four categories of gratifications have been characterized. The major theoretical foci for each of the categories have been suggested. However, it is more likely that news consumption comes about because of a variety of countervailing motivations that simultaneously pull on the individual with different degrees of strength. If the net effect of these countervailing motives pulling against each other on individuals were "averaged" and plotted

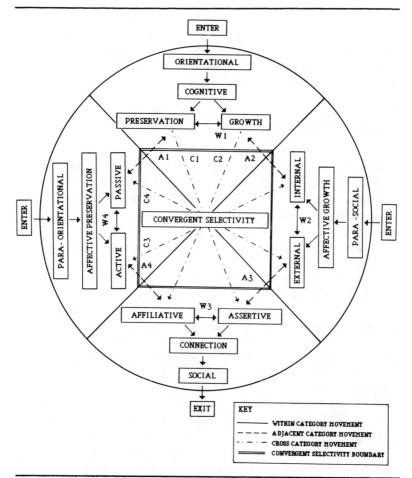

Figure 9.4   Theoretical Reduction of Patterns of Movement Among News Gratifications

on the gratifications map, that plotting would likely show a concentration near the center of the map. Such an idea of mixed motives for news consumption has been called *convergent selectivity* by Stephenson (1967), who was attempting to describe the interaction of the individual's playful intervention with information. The term is used in a broader sense here, representing a convergence of forces propelling the individual, and manifested through content and process gratifications. More simply stated, convergent selectivity is located at the intersection of content and process gratifications (see Figure 9.1) and is an area where the bulk of the population experiences news gratifications. Outlying gratification experiences taking place apart from any points within the intersection, while theoretically possible, in practical terms tend to be infrequent deviations that arise from psychological imbalance or severe social isolation.

PORTS OF ENTRY

As a heuristic concept, the news gratification map can be seen as a piece in the puzzle of explaining media-person relations. Because the map suggests a wide variety of theoretical emphases, it may serve as a piece within either a scientific or cultural model of that puzzle. Regardless of model preference, the research to this point suggests that the map might best be approached from certain points rather than others. As the gratifications that are sought are formed prior to and in pursuit of gratifications that are obtained, they indicate the typical ways in which the "world of gratifications" (as suggested by the map) may be "entered." These *ports of entry* are located outside *orientational, para-orientational,* and *para-social* quadrants, in keeping with the Palmgreen et al. (1980) finding of such a structure for gratifications sought. As social gratifications are not sought as a distinct entity, tending instead to combine with orientational gratifications when sought, no port of entry is located there. Rather, as the Palmgreen et al. (1980) findings suggest, one tends to "exit' the news gratifications experience with uniquely obtained social gratifications that connect the individual to the "outside world." In a very basic sense, the "world of gratifications" could not be exited any other way. The other types of gratifications involve processes or orientations that revolve about the individual's "inner world,' although, as suggested earlier, that world may have external as well as internal referents.

PATTERNS OF MOVEMENT

Through the plotting of survey samples of individual gratifications sought versus those obtained on the news gratifications map, a sought-obtained "shift" or "movement" could be illustrated. Theoretically, this could reveal much about how what people want differs from what they get from media news. For example, the Palmgreen et al. (1980) data, if it had been collected with such plotting in mind, might well indicate a "gravitational flow" pattern between gratifications sought and obtained. The sought-obtained movement here may be thought of as subject to "gravitational flow" in the sense that gratifications in the state of being sought tend to move "down" through the convergent selectivity area and toward social utility as they are obtained. Such "changes" in gratification structure conceptualized as "movement" may well hold the keys to much theoretical development. For instance, such a "gravitational flow" pulling down from an entry point at orientational gratifications to an exit at social gratifications describes the audience experience with information flow that is the concern of researchers with a *scientific* view (see McQuail, this volume). Entering or exiting the gratifications experience may not be of major importance to researchers with a *cultural* view, but understanding patterns of movement, especially within process gratifications, would seem to be at the foundation of any intensive analysis aimed at an accurate reading of the news "text" that the audience is experiencing. Also, these patterns of movement among process gratifications are important from the scientific view if one is to understand how informational orientations come into social use. Theoretical development from either view should benefit from an understanding of "population densities" plotted on the gratifications map, how they come about, where they are located, and how they redistribute over time as cultural changes alter both the definition of news and the ways in which news is useful in society. Three terms are offered that may help structure such theoretical development.

Within-category movement is the most limited in the sense of not involving an intersection of content and process gratifications, and thus, convergent selectivity. Such movement, however, may be substantial. For example, a within para-orientational gratification move from passive to active (W4 in Figure 9.4) involves quite a change from reinforcement and ego defense to playful expression and tension reduction. *Adjacent-category movement* spans no greater distance, but is theoretically more complex because it involves a content and process gratification interaction in a route that passes through the outlying bounds of convergent selectivity. As much evidence suggests that gratifications activity tends to take place at border areas such as the one between orientational and para-social gratifications (A2 in Figure 9.4), understanding the propellants of movement between these areas is central to theoretical development. *Cross-category movement* within content and process gratifications have been the foci, respectively, from the scientific and cultural views. For instance, the content path (C1 in Figure 9.4) linking orientational gratifications, which aid cognitive preservation with consequent assertive social connections, is basic to the study of opinion leadership (Levy, 1978d). On the other hand, understanding relations among process gratifications, such as those which run between active para-orientational gratifications stressing expressive play and passive para-social gratifications stressing identification (C3 in Figure 9.4) are equally important to theoretical development from the cultural view (Glasser, 1980, 1982). The approach here takes into account the concerns of both the scientific and cultural views, but posits that since cross-category movement necessarily involves venturing into the convergent selectivity area, research from either view would be enriched considerably if more explicit attention were paid to the gratification patterns that run perpendicular to those of major concern.

CONCLUDING COMMENTS

In this chapter, a theoretical structure has been developed that may be applied to the study of media news gratifications. It is likely that the framework presented here with regard to media news can be expanded and applied to the broader context of general media gratifications, or narrowed to some smaller subset of media or genre-specific gratifications. An effort has been made to unify the scientific and cultural views of communication by integrating research about news gratifications with the wide variety of human motivation theories that have been structured by McGuire (1974). The appropriateness of this theory about the nature of news gratifications may be tested in a variety of spheres, some of which will be touched upon briefly below.

First, media news gratifications research has been colored by a bias toward focusing on television news gratifications. Attempting to avoid such a bias, the conceptual maps developed here focus on the broad concept of media news, rather than news of any one particular form. Nonetheless, the conceptualization is weakened by the relative paucity of research about news gratifications derived from media other than television. More questions need to be asked about the similarities and differences among gratifications derived from different media, and how these tie into relationships that may give us a more complete picture of the news gratification process within a given society. The media news gratifications maps should be helpful in structuring answers to these kinds of questions by allowing a plotting of such differential patterns of gratifications in reference to a common ground.

Second, although much is known about the range of gratifications that may be derived from news, we know very little about "population densities" for certain kinds of news gratification experiences within a society. How common or uncommon are certain kinds of gratification experiences? How do these "population densities" vary among different segments of the audience? Answers here, as well, may be plotted on the news gratification maps to illuminate what elements of news experience may be shared culturally versus those that may be unique to certain subparts of society.

Third, more questions need to be asked about cross-cultural differences in news gratifications. Here again, the news gratification maps may be used to plot and understand the significance of such cross-cultural differences, as well as the similarities common to different societies.

Fourth, plotting strategies for the media news gratifications maps should be used to illuminate differences between gratifications sought and the gratifications obtained from news. Questions about such relative satisfaction are important in understanding what people are not getting from news. Do expectations change such that gratifications sought over time become aligned with gratifications obtained? When discrepancies between what is sought and what is obtained from news persist over time, how do people compensate for this and what significance does this have culturally?

Finally, much must be learned about how "population densities" for certain kinds of gratifications shift over time. Such longitudinal analysis must relate how structural changes in the presentation of news interacts with changing patterns of exposure to, expectations of, and satisfaction from news.

The preliminary attempt here at outlining a strategy for describing the major types of movement that may occur on the news gratifications map will need to give way to theoretical tests of the reasons behind shifts in gratifications patterns. That the news gratifications maps can help accelerate theoretical development concerning the changes in news gratifications experience is strong reason to consider their employment. While it seems clear that sixteen theories may well be too many to work with in a cohesive fashion in our theoretical efforts, the mapping strategy offers ways to reduce the theoretical divisions to a more limited metatheoretical combination that may provide the kinds of explanations from which researchers with both scientific and cultural views can benefit.

Chapter 10

MEDIA GRATIFICATIONS
THROUGH THE LIFE CYCLE

Alan M. Rubin

CHRONOLOGICAL AGE IS A USEFUL CONCEPT for describing mass media use. This chapter considers some supporting literature for this premise by focusing on the television gratification-seeking behaviors of different chronological age groups. The analysis identifies the salience of younger children's motives for media use, particularly for fantasy, the emergence of informational use in adolescence, the need to consider individual differences, social category and relationship factors in explaining media use, the relative continuity of gratifications sought through the early and middle adult years, and the heightened attention given to the electronic media by the older media audience. However, the essay suggests the limitations of a descriptive chronological age view and argues for alternative life-position explanations of communication behavior through the life cycle. In addition, one salient regularity in media gratification-seeking behavior across the life cycle is suggested.

CHRONOLOGICAL AGE DISTINCTIONS

CHILDREN AND ADOLESCENTS

Beginning in the late 1950s, communication research began to explore the role of television in the lives of children. Early studies reported differences in viewing patterns across child and adolescent age groups. Himmelweit et al. (1958) and Schramm et al. (1961), for example, observed that British, American, and Canadian children and adolescents spend more time watching television than on other leisure activities. Schramm and his colleagues found that television viewing steadily increases until approximately the eighth grade when it begins to decline in a slowly falling slope until the twelfth grade, as print and radio use increases. Lyle and Hoffman (1972) and Greenberg (1974) also noted a peak viewing level reached approximately by age 12. Both the Greenberg study and one by Rubin (1977) found significant negative correlations between age and amount of television viewing for their British and American samples of children and adolescents; the viewing amounts of 9-year-olds average almost twice as much as that of 17-year-olds. Factors in addition to age, such as increased participation in social activities by adolescents, affect mass media use.

Viewing behaviors are complex and cannot be explained simply by examining the number of hours children spend watching television. Lyle (1972: 7) reported that "children become purposeful viewers—having regular viewing times and favorite programs" and that "amounts and times of viewing change almost year to year as the child grows older." Children and adolescents select television and media content "in terms of their own needs and their personal capacity for understanding; in adolescence this involves greater responsiveness to information about personal relationships, and about adult life" (Himmelweit et al., 1958: 32). The early studies by Schramm et al. (1961) and Himmelweit et al. (1958) found that younger children prefer action that does not require understanding complex motives, such as cartoon and animal entertainment shows and westerns; adolescents are less interested in stereotyped plots and straightforward action and prefer more varied action and more complex motivations, such as situation comedies, crime shows, and popular music programs. Any interest in public affairs television is acquired late in adolescence. "Television news is regularly watched by only a rather small minority of the [child] population; educational programs by a still smaller group" (Lyle, 1972: 17). According to Schramm and his colleagues, "any media use centering on something other than entertainment is learned late" (Schramm et al., 1961: 39).

A few more recent studies, though, have noted that television functions as a primary agency of political socialization for children and adolescents (for example, Dominick, 1972; Rubin, 1976, 1978). Rubin reported that although indiscriminate viewing of television may be dysfunctional for a child's political learning, some children and adolescents in his American samples selected certain news and public affairs programs. In these instances, the viewing of selected television content may be functional for a child's political learning. Also, Adoni (1979) found that a sample of Israeli high school students, ages 15 to 17, used the mass media in the formation of national and civic values. Newspapers, television and radio were perceived as useful for the development of civic attitudes about the political system.

It is not age per se that determines media content selection and use, but individual, family, and social factors along with the desire to fulfill gratification-seeking motives. Himmelweit et al. (1958) noted that intelligence and activity are two factors that produce more selective and moderate modes of television use. They also argue that television viewing becomes less important at adolescence because it no longer meets the altered social needs of adolescents. Lyle (1972: 23) observed that variables such as mental ability and social class are related to "attitudes toward the medium and manners of use."

Age, however, is a viable descriptor of attitudes and behavior, partly because an age cohort can tell us something about the role of individual and social factors in the life cycle. Television use is important in the lives of children. Lyle and Hoffman (1972) reported that first graders are more likely to use television content as a model for social play, to dream about what they see on television, and to be frightened by television content. Younger children have a great affinity with television and perceive its content as being realistic (Greenberg, 1974; Rubin, 1977, 1979). The younger children have fewer internal frames of comparison, and similar to immobile adults, fewer external functional alternatives against which to weigh the television experience.

People, including children and adolescents, use the media and their content to satisfy certain personal needs. Schramm et al. (1961) found that children tend to organize their time around television and have a high level of affection for the medium. They discovered a complex relationship whereby television "enters into the whole life of the child" (p. 169). Children use television for entertainment, escape, information, and as a social tool. They found that children's television use is fantasy oriented, providing immediate gratifications, and argued that television more readily meets children's needs for fantasy experiences than for reality experiences. They noted that children do learn from television viewing, and that most learning from fantasy programs is incidental. Himmelweit et al. (1958) found that television is appealing since it is readily available and a good time filler; viewing offers security, reassurance, excitement, suspense, escape, and identification with heroes and television personalities.

Age is also a correlate of motives for television use (gratifications sought from viewing). Greenberg (1974: 84) reported that the "younger child shows more identification with each of the gratifications than does the older child." The findings parallel those for television affinity and perceived realism of television content. Both Greenberg (1974) and Rubin (1977, 1979) have found chronological age to be a consistent and negative correlate of viewing motives—arousal, companionship, relaxation, learning, habit, pass time, and escape. Greenberg (1974: 84) concluded that age is "the only consistent demographic correlate" of the television viewing motives of children and adolescents.

The studies just mentioned observed reduced levels of salience of the viewing motives with increasing age, and consonance in the relative rank positions of the motives across the three age groups. Also similar are the persistent salience of habitual and time-passing uses of the medium for children and adolescents, the decrease in salience of using the medium for excitement from age 9 to age 17, and the low standing of learning and forget (escape) as motives. The salience of motives also correlates with certain program preferences and the attitudes toward the medium, for example, perceived realism of television correlates with watching television to learn, and affinity with the medium correlates with watching television out of habit or to pass the time.

YOUNGER AND MIDDLE-AGE ADULTS

Several studies begin to shift consideration of media motives beyond the child age groups. Across a variety of communication channels, for example, Lometti et al. (1977) observed several relationships between motives for media use and chronological age from middle school to college age groups: Channel use for entertainment/surveillance (to seek information, for companionship, for excitement, and to overcome loneliness) decreased; channel use for affective guidance (guidance and issue decision making) decreased slightly; and channel use for behavioral guidance (for guidance, companionship, and information) increased. Among his samples of college students, Bantz (1982) concluded that there are no clear differences between medium-specific and program type-specific motives for using television; his factor solutions indicate that those in his sample watched television in general or favorite programs for companionship, surveillance, entertainment, voyeurism, and social resource reasons.

In a broader age sample (ages 4 to 89), Rubin (1981a) found that younger persons were more likely than older persons to watch television for reasons of escape, to pass time or out of habit, arousal, and social interaction. Pass time/habit, companionship, and entertainment motives were most strongly and positively correlated with amounts of television viewing. Arousal, pass time/habit and escape motives were most strongly and positively correlated with television affinity. And, information and arousal motives were most strongly and positively correlated with perceived realism of television. In their study of adult television news watching, Palmgreen et al. (1980) determined three structures of motives or gratifications *sought*: interpersonal utility/surveillance, entertainment seeking, and para-social interaction. They noted a contrast between these motives for use and the gratifications *obtained* from the respondents' most watched programs: interpersonal utility, entertainment/para-social interaction, and surveillance.

In general, many of the investigations that have examined adult media use have been guided to varying degrees by typologies offered by Blumler (1979) and McQuail et al. (1972). Blumler summarized three general orientations toward the media: cognitive (surveillance and reality exploration); diversion (boredom relief, escape, entertainment, and arousal); and personal identity (reminders of the past, support for ideas, and behavioral guidance). The earlier typology of McQuail et al. depicts four hypothesized dimensions of media-person interactions. These four suggested uses of the mass media are: diversion (escape from the routine, escape from problems, and emotional release); personal relationships (companionship and social utility); personal identity (personal reference, reality exploration, and value reinforcement); and surveillance. However, the authors add a cautionary note about the universal validity of such a typology of media-person interactions, "since the phenomena in question are to some extent variable according to changes in audience experience and perception and also to the changes in communication content and differences in social context" (p. 162).

Media use has sometimes been related in empirical investigations to some of these differences in audience experience and social context, such as consumer and lifestyle characteristics. Pearlin (1959) found that those with stressful experiences who have a need to forget about their personal problems seek escapist fare from television. For her adult sample, Eastman (1979) reported finding relationships among television use motives and lifestyle traits. For example, those who used television to get away from problems and people, to obtain enjoyment and stimulation, or to provide a substitute for interaction, tended to be people who try different products, have debts, and look for bargains. Although a broader discussion of the value of life-position factors for explaining communication behavior will follow later in this essay, it is important to realize that the relationships between media gratifications and individual behaviors and attitudes are more complex than they have been depicted to be by descriptions based on chronological age.

OLDER ADULTS

During the past two decades, several studies have focused on the upper part of the chronological age spectrum. Similar to the children and adolescent findings, television viewing has been identified as the primary leisure activity of older persons (DeGrazia, 1961; Schramm, 1969). The elderly have been labeled "embracers" of television (Glick and Levy, 1962). A Louis Harris (1975) survey observed that more persons aged 65 and over spend time watching television than with any other mass medium, and that viewing levels are higher for those over age 50 than for younger persons.

What is watched on television by the older age group is somewhat different from what is viewed by younger persons. Meyersohn (1961) found that older persons prefer "concrete, nonfictional entertainment." Preferences typically favor news and information programming, including talk shows and magazine programs, as well as family dramas and light music programs (Davis, 1971; Meyersohn, 1961; A. Rubin and R. Rubin, 1981, 1982b; Wenner, 1976).

Investigations of gratifications sought and of mass media functions have provided explanations for why television is such an important medium of information and entertainment for older persons. Salient television viewing motives of older persons include information seeking, entertainment, inexpensiveness, convenience, companionship, relaxation, and time consumption (A. Rubin and R. Rubin, 1982b). Davis and Edwards (1975) proposed four functions of television for the elderly: television provides a link to the surrounding environment; programming provides a means to bracket or structure the day; viewing enables a sense of keeping occupied; and the medium and its personalities offer a feeling of companionship.

Other studies have looked at the relationships between media use and social connectedness of older persons and have suggested that: media use combats loneliness and alienation by compensating for lost interpersonal communication channels (Schramm, 1969); television entertainment reduces feelings of isolation by offering an illusion of living in a populated world (Hess, 1974); mass media use substitutes for interpersonal contact and participation (Graney and Graney, 1974); and television provides a common basis for social interaction (Meyersohn, 1961). Levy (1979) found that although para-social interaction with television news personae is common for viewers, the degree of para-social interaction increases for older viewers.

LIFE POSITION AND MEDIA USE

THE LIMITATIONS OF CHRONOLOGICAL AGE

Investigations of older persons' uses of television have enhanced alternative explanations of media use through the life cycle. They have pointed to the need to reconceptualize the meaning of *life position*. In particular, chronological age alone is solely an indicant of media behavior. It is not an isolated variable, or even a valid and reliable explanatory variable in the life cycle. This view is supported by Johnsson-Smaragdi (1983: 24):

> [Chronological age is] a temporal dimension along which change is mapped. . . . The important events marking the individual life-span occur at very different chronological ages. Finishing education, entering the labour market, marriage, having children and so forth, are examples of events that occur at a totally different age for each individual. It then becomes of little use to think about age as a demarcation variable of the life-stages of adults.

Chronological age is a marker variable. Although it provides a fairly consistent description of mass media use patterns, its value is restricted for *explaining* and *predicting* life-cycle patterns of media use. It indicates patterns or regularities for why people use the media, what they consume, for how long, and the like, but lacks sufficient explanatory ability. It describes rather than explains. A reliance on chronological age descriptions may hinder explanation and prediction of relationships between consequent mass media uses and effects, and antecedent communication, biophysical and psychosocial factors. Constructs other than chronological age cohorts are required to explain and predict media gratifications through the life cycle. Danowski (1975), for example, has argued that *informational aging* is a more viable construct for life-cycle explanations than is chronological age. Informational aging "assumes that individuals age at different rates along different psychological and social dimensions."

Communication behavior, such as media use, is affected by a host of communication, social, personality, and other factors. Attention to *life-position* factors provides improved indicators of media use and communication behavior across the life cycle and a better means for explaining media use gratifications. Dimmick et al. (1979) have argued that *life-span position* is a more valid concept than chronological age to explain human development processes and media use. They proposed a biophysical and psychosocial spiral of progression model that explains media gratifications in the life cycle as functions of life-span position, shared life events (cohort), and social milieu of the times (history or period). *Life-span position* reflects societal-behavioral expectations as a person progresses along the spiral. *Shared life events* reflects similarities in perceptions of those born within the same birth cohort, but differences of those born in different cohorts. The *social milieu* of the times affects the choices available to a person at different periods. For example, two persons of similar age cohorts, but of different historical periods, might be dissimilar if their socialization experiences are tempered separately by peace and war, economic stability and crisis, moral tolerance and prohibition, or liberal and conservative social environments.

Dimmick et al. (1979: 10) proposed "the salience or importance of needs to change over the life span in response to changes in sociopsychological states and that the changes in need structure would eventuate in a reorganization of need-satisfying activities including the mass media." So, for example, the literature of communication and aging supports the idea that the media, particularly television, may provide a functional means for achieving a sense of social interaction when the traditional social actors become absent from one's life. Studies focusing on television news (Levy, 1979) and talk radio (Turow, 1974) provide support for this proposition.

Research has demonstrated that salient life-position factors include audience members' mobility, interaction, self concept, and life satisfaction. Wenner (1976) identified types of elderly users of television primarily from social mobility and isolation factors. One type of television user substitutes television for interpersonal interaction. Swank (1979) found that less mobile, older individuals tend to rely more on television than on other media channels or social activities. Korzenny and Neuendorf (1980) determined that an older person's self concept varies according to preferred television content and the functions that television serves;

whether a person watches for information or escape, however, a sense of alienation increases.

Societal structure would also be expected to constrain the uses and effects of available communication choices (Rubin and Windahl, 1982). So, factors such as social class, education, and income provide a segment of society with a broader range of potential choices in communication media, but leave others in the same society and in the same chronological age cohort with fewer options. This would result in an uneven spread of information within and across age cohorts, and in societal knowledge gaps. In addition, media use is affected by the interface of personal and mediated channels of communication (Rubin and Rubin, 1985). Individual needs that are met by specific communication choices, and the use and availability of communication functional alternatives vary within and across chronological age cohorts. It is important, then, to consider a variety of factors such as life-span position, shared life events, social milieu, individual needs, individual differences, interpersonal and social relationships, and functional alternatives for valid explanations of gratification-seeking behavior.

CONTEXTUAL AGE

The findings of an investigation of hospitalized patients led to the positing of a *contextual age* construct (Rubin and Rubin, 1981). In that investigation environmental context was a more influential factor than chronological age in determining television viewing motives, program preferences, and viewing behaviors. The results revealed that there were greater differences in the television use patterns of younger than older respondents from home to hospital settings so that, in confinement, younger persons were more likely to use television to compensate for a lack of interaction and social activity. Rubin and Rubin (1981: 13) suggest that "two contextual variates—social conditions (e.g., physical confinement) and communication behaviors (e.g., interpersonal interaction reduction)—would appear . . . to render age differences in television use less meaningful once individuals share similar contextual environments."

In subsequent studies, *contextual age* was developed as a life-position construct to explain communication behavior. The construct includes six dimensions relevant for defining aspects of life position: physical health, interpersonal interaction, mobility, life satisfaction, social activity, and economic security. Two research studies (A. Rubin and R.

Rubin, 1982a; R. Rubin and A. Rubin, 1982) have examined the construct as it relates to television use by an older-age sample (ages 55 to 92) and by a broader-age sample (ages 17 to 83). Factor analyses of the items that make up each dimension produced four interrelated components of contextual age: self-reliance (physical health and mobility), interaction (interpersonal interaction and social activity), life satisfaction, and economic security.

The results of the older-age sample study indicated that the less economically secure, life satisfied, and self-reliant (who also interacted more often with other persons) sought companionship and escape from television, but used the medium less for reasons of relaxation; persons with lower life satisfaction and interaction levels (who also were more economically secure) used television less as an inexpensive means of relaxation and more as a vehicle of escape, time consumption, and social interaction (A. Rubin and R. Rubin, 1982a). The results of the broader-age sample study indicated that the less self-reliant used television as a means to pass the time; persons who were life-satisfied and socially active (but also less self-reliant) sought advertising, relaxation, and behavioral guidance from television, but not escape or social interaction (R. Rubin and A. Rubin, 1982). Factors such as mobility, economic security, social interaction, and life satisfaction, then, provide us with improved explanations of media gratification-seeking behavior compared with the descriptive chronological age variable.

In addition, a combined analysis of the data from both samples of the two previous studies indicated that the associations between these biophysical and psychosocial variables are not always in line with presumed stereotypes. Although older persons were not as mobile or healthy as younger persons, they were more economically secure, satisfied with their lives, and interacted more often with others (Rubin and Rubin, in press). The latter analysis supports the idea that life-position dimensions are more valid for a proper view of adult communication behavior across the life cycle than is chronological age.

RITUALIZED AND INSTRUMENTAL MEDIA USE

Across various chronological age groupings, one consistent finding has been apparent in a series of recent studies. In particular, several separate analyses have indicated that television may be used ritualistically or instrumentally (Rubin, 1981b, 1983, 1984; A. Rubin and R. Rubin, 1982b). *Ritualized* television use entails rather habitual seeking of a variety of interrelated gratifications, such as time consumption, companionship, and entertainment. Typically associated with ritualized use is extended viewing and heightened affinity with the medium; diversionary program correlates are sometimes apparent. *Instrumental* television use entails the seeking of informational gratification. Typically associated with instrumental use is the selection of news, talk, and other information programs, but not heightened affinity or extended viewing.

This distinction is also similar to Cutler and Danowski's (1980) dichotomous differentiation between process gratification—"derived from the extrinsic values that do not bear a direct link to particular substantive characteristics of messages" (p. 270)—and content gratification—"derived from the use of mediated messages for their direct, substantive, intrinsic value for the receiver" (p. 269). Ritualistic media use focuses on the process or experience of using the media to be amused, to relieve boredom, for companionship, and other similar reasons. Instrumental media use focuses on the seeking of certain media content, often informational in nature. However, it is possible to link process and content gratification-seeking behavior so that, for example, an individual would seek entertaining and exciting informational-type messages. This was a finding in one study of a popular American television program, *60 Minutes*, for a sample of people that ranged in age from 14 to 83 (Rubin, 1981b). Chronological age in that study, and in others, had little bearing on the identification of both interrelated media use gratifications and ritualistic or instrumental media use patterns.

Although chronological age may not explain ritualistic or instrumental media use, life-position factors may. For example, social isolation and lack of mobility may lead to extended use of a medium such as television, to heightened affinity with a depended upon medium, and to the seeking of ritualistic-type gratifications such as using the medium for companionship or to pass the time (Rubin and Rubin, 1981; R. Rubin and A. Rubin, 1982; Swank, 1979; Wenner, 1976). One's degree of life satisfaction would also seem to reflect media use for escapist purposes, as life satisfaction and the seeking of escapist gratifications from television are negatively related (A. Rubin and R. Rubin, 1982a; R. Rubin and A. Rubin, 1982).

MEDIA USES AND EFFECTS

This distinction in how media are used across the life cycle has implications for a variety of concepts including audience activity, media effects, functional alternatives, and media dependency. It has been argued elsewhere that audience activity is a variable, not an absolute (Blumler, 1979). Levy and Windahl (1984), for example, were able to distinguish between different periods and correlates of audience activity in relationship to television viewing. They maintained that viewers in their sample actively sought television news to gain information, but did not actively seek diversion. Ritualized and instrumental television use points to differences in aspects of audience activity such as selectivity and goal directedness. Instrumental use might indicate greater selectivity and goal directedness by consumers regardless of their position in the life cycle. Ritualized use might indicate a lower degree of activity and selectivity and present the potential for greater media dependency and influence (Rubin, 1984).

In addition, ritualistic or instrumental media use has implications for media effects. Windahl (1981) argued that different outcomes should result from using a medium ritualistically or instrumentally. He labeled the outcomes of media use as *consequences*, the outcomes of using media content as *effects*, and the outcomes of media and content use as *conseffects*. For example, media dependency might be a consequence of media use, information acquisition or attitude reinforcement might be an effect of using media content, and para-social interaction might be a conseffect of media and content use.

Obviously, the role functional alternatives play in the uses and effects process must be kept in mind. A reduction in the use of alternatives to a medium, if related to either instrumental or ritualized use, should lead to greater dependency on a medium and potentially more influence on an individual's cognitions, attitudes, and behavior (Rubin and Windahl, 1982). The role of functional alternatives also emphasizes the need to consider the interface of personal and mediated channels of communication for explaining media uses and effects, including dependency on communication channels (Rubin and Rubin, 1985). Attention to functional alternatives would also emphasize a dynamic view of the uses and effects process as media users would need constantly to adjust media use expectations and motives to the gratifications received from communication sources, channels, and content.

Toward these ends, two areas of needed research can be identified. First, although interpersonal *interaction* is frequently posited as an important variable in the uses and gratifications process, it seldom shows a strong relationship with media use variables. An apparent, but overlooked reason for this might be that the interaction variable has been operationalized incorrectly. Since uses and gratifications paradigms typically proceed from individual needs and motives for communication to actual communication behavior, both salience of motives and present levels of interaction need to be considered to operationalize interaction more astutely. What needs to be assessed is a *discrepancy* measure between an individual's current level of interaction and his or her desire or drive (motivation) to interact. It is this discrepancy between interaction level and motivation that might lead to improved explanations and predictions of gratification-seeking behavior. A concept such as loneliness, for example, may reflect a discrepancy between a desire for interaction and the lack of interpersonal contact.

Second, uses and gratifications researchers have been remiss in the study of media use as an active *process* (Swanson, 1977). Although uses and gratifications paradigms depict process, empirical investigations have generally not studied process. A dominant reason for this is that process is difficult to observe and measure. Empirical investigations have measured motives for using media and have assumed that individuals use a medium to gratify those motives that reflect individual needs. However, it is safe to assume that motives shift as the communication process unfolds. For example, a medium might be used instrumentally to seek information for decision making. However, what if using the medium's content doesn't fulfill the motive? Traditionally, uses and gratifications models have posited that individuals would then seek different content, a different medium, or a functional alternative. What also needs to be considered, though, is the process of realigned motives to meet the situational constraints. Do motives remain stable but the seeking of media and messages change? Or, might unfulfilled motives themselves be altered? Surely this would affect future communication gratification-seeking behavior.

CONCLUSION

Descriptions of media use behaviors and attitudes within chronological age segments have been provided with a consistent degree of regularity by many empirical investigations. These studies have described the media use patterns of children, adolescents, and adults. A chronological age view, although contributing to a description of life-cycle patterns of media use, fails to explain adequately the multifaceted process of media use or to predict mass media effects. Attention to life-position factors makes possible the heuristic explanation of mass media uses and effects. Life-position factors are related to integral components of uses and gratifications paradigms including individual needs, communication motives, audience activity, interpersonal communication, and functional alternatives. Explanation and prediction of gratification-seeking behavior are enhanced through attention to life-position elements.

Chapter 11

THE NATURALISTIC STUDY
OF MEDIA USE AND
YOUTH CULTURE

James Lull

MANY ADOLESCENTS ARE ENGAGED IN a heroic struggle against what is to them a profoundly irrelevant sociocultural environment, replete with relentless and unreasonable expectations of conformity to dullness. The teenage years provide a first opportunity to explore exciting cultural ground that differs sharply from terrain controlled by the ubiquitous forces of conventionality that surround them. Youth take risks to fulfill the vague, inwardly sensed, largely unreinforced promise of creative expression, personal growth, relevant cultural awareness, meaningful relationships, spontaneity, and fun that lie in consciousness and activity not prescribed by the authoritarian agents that have directed nearly every aspect of their preadolescent lives. For youth in the United States and most of Europe at least, there is a radical discrepancy between behavior expected of them at home and school and what becomes available through peer-group associations and activities during leisure time. The generationally based tension that exists between the worlds of "what's good for you" and "what I want" exacerbates the creation and consumption of striking artifacts of youth culture that energize its members and give meaning to the routine forms of communication in which they engage.

The interpersonal relations and media usages of adolescents reflect the dynamics of their struggle—a search for self-identity and meaning in an increasingly impersonal world and an irrepressible energy that demands change from a resistant environment. This chapter focuses on the role of mass media in these processes and emphasizes one particular content area—music—in a brief analysis of the communicational aspects of adolescents' lives. A second major topic addressed in this chapter is the use of ethnographic data-gathering techniques for the systematic study of communication of youth—their interpersonal relationships, media-use practices, and cultural experiences. The confusion and excitement of adolescence is regarded here as a fascinating domain of social life that is little understood by researchers but holds provocative implications for communication theory.

THE ADOLESCENT, THE FAMILY, AND TELEVISION

Adolescence generally begins with the onset of puberty and lasts until the person assumes a substantial degree of emotional independence. The startling eruption of sexuality is accompanied by an array of changing lifestyle behaviors in the lives of young people. With respect to communication, this period signals a marked alteration in the frequency and types of interactions that many children have with their families. During adolescence, most young people decrease the frequency of contact they have with their parents and increase interactions with peers. Adolescents soon use adult forms of transportation, thereby increasing out-of-home social contact and the routine passing of leisure time. They develop friendships at school and in other environments that begin to occupy much time formerly spent with the family. Consequently, parents' roles in adolescent socialization decrease compared to earlier stages of childhood (McLeod and Brown, 1976).

This redirection in the lives of adolescents has an impact on their media experiences as well. Television viewing acquires new connotations for adolescents. Watching television in most homes is a family activity, signifying a social event that many adolescents no longer find exciting or satisfying. Consequently, the amount of time spent watching television decreases during adolescence (Comstock et al., 1978; McLeod and Brown, 1976). This change in exposure patterns occurs not only in the United States, but also in England (Greenberg, 1974), Israel (Adoni, 1983), and Sweden (Johnson-Smaragdi, 1983; Roe, 1983b), where research has shown that involvement with television decreases sharply between the early and middle stages of adolescence. The time spent viewing television by adolescents also shifts away from co-viewing with parents to more sibling co-viewing and viewing alone (Chaffee et al., 1971).

Interpersonal communication in the family that involves television changes during this period too. Several studies have shown that parental influence on adolescent children is indirect (Chaffee et al., 1971; Chaffee and Tims, 1976; McLeod et al., 1972; McLeod and Brown, 1976). The collective spirit of these studies suggests that in the communication environment of the home (considered in terms of what these authors call "family communication patterns"), direct modeling, in which parental example stimulates patterns of exposure to television, may not accurately characterize the nature of viewing in many homes even before children reach adolescence. By the time children become teenagers, they have established many personal routines, including media-related activities, and may no longer be directly influenced very much by their parents. More likely to affect media behavior is the atmosphere of interpersonal interaction that exists in the home. Varying family communication styles presumably suggest and reinforce values that lead families to differential patterns of media exposure and consumption, even the ways they employ the medium for a wide range of personal and interpersonal purpose (Lull, 1980a).

The American family and television seem to be inseparable. A recent government summary indicates that families in the United States spend about half their free time at home watching television (NIMH, 1982). In many homes, the television set has become a symbol of the family—a medium they experience communally. With two notable exceptions, video games and music—television, the visual medium, offers adolescents very little pertinent content. So for many young people, television represents both the boring social environment of family life and a predictable array of uncompelling images. These circumstances fail to meet the new requirements of youth. For adolescents who desire to establish independence from their families, changes in routine behavior are likely to include retraction from the family-oriented, generally uninspiring experience of television viewing. The family and television are at least temporarily discarded for the far more exciting domain of peers and other media—radio, music, and film.

THE PEER GROUP AND FORMAL EDUCATION

Adolescents who are highly integrated into peer networks use media for a variety of satisfactions and gratifications. They occupy a "role moratorium," a period of life when adult expectations of them are somewhat suspended (Adoni, 1983) and when new socializing agents begin to influence their attitudes and activities. The proliferation of modern media, particularly music-based forms, impinge directly upon their experience—sometimes stimulating behavior, at other times supplementing or complementing their interpersonal activities.

In the study of adolescents, relationships that exist among family life, peer group realities, and formal education must be considered since most young people orient themselves away from their families, toward their friends, and are required to spend much time at school. The very earliest media gratifications studies reflected a communion between the peer group and electronic media use, suggesting that particular patterns of exposure were stimulated by their potential for "peer group utility" (Riley and Riley, 1951). Johnstone found that the highest levels of television viewing among adolescents in his sample were among those boys and girls who were not well integrated into their peer groups (Johnstone, 1974). Peer group networks were reinforced through exposure to music and movies, not television. A recent study of pre-adolescent childrens' time spent outside school indicated that television's primary role for these 11- and 12-year-olds living in California was that it simply filled time (Medrich et al., 1982). For children who do not develop satisfactory peer group ties, television may continue to fill this temporal and psychological void during the teenage years. Peers are most likely to displace parents in conditions where extrafamilial relationships develop satisfactorily. Although adolescents may turn to music privately at home, many of the roles music plays for them obtain in their emerging vibrant social networks.

Alienation directed toward institutions in general, and toward school in particular, is a common stance for adolescents living in nations throughout much of the world. This generalized rebellious attitude involves music. Relationships that exist among peer orientation, interest in music, and educational attainment are not yet clear. However, some Swedish researchers have attempted recently to position these phenomena temporally (Roe, 1983b; Rosengren, Roe, and Sonesson, 1983). Among girls, at least, the survey research in Sweden generally shows that low grades may cause girls to be more peer oriented, a condition that researchers believe leads them to listen to large amounts of pop music. This development presumably "announces to themselves and their surroundings that (the girls) are orienting themselves away from the world of school and parents towards that of peers, pop and pleasure" (Rosengren et al., 1983: 12-13). Throughout the Swedish studies a negative statistical association was found between success at school and amount of music consumed. This negative relationship between music (including its correlates dance, fashion, and language style) and achievement in school also has been demonstrated in England (Sugarman, 1967). Popular music may provide an alternative focus for adolescent school children and prestige for those who are immersed in it (Brown and O'Leary, 1971). Pop music may also provide alternative "solutions" to the dilemmas of American youth who have failed in school (Tanner, 1978).

MUSIC AS A SOCIOCULTURAL RESOURCE

Popular music functioned socially for youth long before the evolution of rock 'n' roll, of course, but when the working-class, hybrid genre that draws from country and blues music emerged in the United States it attracted young people immediately. Considered by some more than thirty years ago to be a "current fad," rock music was recognized for its widespread appeal to young teenagers, easily surpassing more traditional forms of music in popularity. Not only was the beat of rock music appreciated by youth, but the lyrics of popular music generally spoke to their concerns. Horton (1957) recognized popular music as a symbol system that invokes a language useful to adolescents for examining their personal and social existences. Carey (1969) analyzed the lyrics of popular music as critical commentary on personal autonomy and social relationships. The lyrics of popular songs during the activist 1960s in the United States reflected concerns ranging from personal conditions of love and sex to social protest issues and themes of global harmony (Cole, 1971). Lyrical content has shifted since 1955, reflecting the contemporary personal and political circumstances that face youth (Harmon, 1972). It is clear that rock music generally reflects the conditions of youth and provides a cultural rallying point around which personal and group decisions are made about a diverse range of subjects of interest to young people (e.g. Denisoff and Peterson, 1972; Hibbard and Kaleialoha, 1983; Pichaske, 1979).

MUSIC AND SUBCULTURE

Some social groups incorporate music fundamentally into their living conditions, lending additional character to their unique lifestyles, and thereby providing cultural models for youth to imitate. Music has played such a role for the American black population beginning with their efforts to maintain some semblance of cultural identity while bound in the despicable chains of slavery and continuing in the twentieth century with the creation of jazz, rhythm and blues, soul, funk, disco, and rap music. A black subculture living on the island of Jamaica has created the distinctive and important reggae music, a synthesis of influences that includes features of rhythm and blues music of the 1960s received by the islanders from radio stations transmitting in southern Florida (White, 1983). Reggae has become a universally appreciated genre that celebrates Jamaica, particularly its Rastafarian subculture, where the slow, dreamlike rhythms of the music resonate with states of mind induced by the smoking of ganja, the high-quality cannabic herb that grows there in abundance (Davis and Simon, 1982; Faristzaddi, 1982; White, 1983; Winders, 1983). Rastafarianism combines a unique metaphysics with a distinctive lifestyle that encompasses special dietary habits, gender relations, child-rearing practices, and personal appearance (the dreadlock hairstyle, red, green, and yellow clothing). Still, the most common cultural stamp of Rastafarian subculture is "roots reggae" music that its adherents believe unite "Jah's people." Reggae music announces a vivid separateness to the rest of the world culminating in the proposed exodus of the Rastafari from Babylon, the white man's land.

Beyond its subcultural and political functions in Jamaica, reggae signifies a universal sound of protest and is an element of unity and resistance in some white youth cultures in England, Europe, and on the West and East coasts of the United States. A counterpart of reggae, "ska" music has become an important force in the life of the "quasi-delinquent adolescent fringe" of working-class English youth who have embraced its fast-paced cadence (Hebdige, 1979). Some English youth have included these and other genres in the basic practices of their daily lives, using the music to escape, to express public dissatisfaction with their economic circumstances, and to develop desirable social relationships (Frith, 1981).

Though some observers of youth and music hesitate to draw a parallel between the living conditions of English and American adolescents, the American punk rock movement (originating in the English music-based subculture) has attracted many young people to it, forming an alternative subculture with many adolescent members that is identifiable not only by its music, but by other lifestyle features including clothing, hairstyle, and language. Punk rock refers to a type of rock music, but "punk rockers" is understood by most people to represent more than a preference for a particular type of music. Punk is an enduring worldwide phenomenon representing a loosely knit oppositional lifestyle that embodies strong anti-institutional values and employs what appear to be harsh forms of expression. The punk subculture is capable of producing the "requisite outraged responses from parents, teachers, and employers" (Hebdige, 1979).

Reggae and ska have influenced punk music, suggesting a practical class relationship between poor black and white youth, particularly in certain neighborhoods of London (Hebdige, 1979). Punk is more a way of living than a formalized set of sentiments designed to achieve some collectively understood or endorsed objective or objectives. Nonetheless, the socioeconomic conditions of the capitalist world's underclass are expressed in the creation of this music, exacerbated by the biological and mental turmoil of adolescence.

MUSIC AND TASTE CULTURES

Implicit in this discussion is the assertion that culture is, in significant ways, a product of social class generally and of particular social circumstances specifically. The unifying and expressive qualities of American black music, reggae, 1960s protest music, punk rock, and other forms are intimately associated with the common social realities of music makers and listeners. On the other hand, many forms of contemporary popular music appear to transcend boundaries of social class, race, gender, educational level, and nearly every other demographic marker (Lewis, 1982). An important theoretical issue concerning music is whether separate "taste cultures" exist independent from social class in the form of subaudiences who are attracted to particular sounds, songs, and genres. Some communication theorists have argued that these cultural groups exist unaligned with social class (Carey and Kreiling, 1974; Kreiling, 1978). The taste culture perspective places concepts of style and aesthetic preference at the forefront of analysis, replacing the focus on contextually-embedded needs, uses, and gratifications that typify much audience research, including the bulk of that reported in this volume. Taste is regarded by the culture theorists as a self-contained stimulus and response, a motivator and an outcome. This theoretical postulating refuses to position culture subordinate to social structure (Kreiling, 1978).

It is difficult to separate matters of taste from social conditions. Nonetheless, the "socially-shared meanings" and common "states of awareness or consciousness" (Chesebro et al., 1984) that music stimulates in people surely traverse many traditional classifications of socioeconomic status. Indeed, the industry term "crossover music" refers explicitly to diverse audiences that are attracted to particular kinds of music, artists, and individual songs. Michael Jackson, the ultimate crossover artist in the mid-1980s, at least in the Western World, has appealed to millions of fans who are black and white, female and male, very old and very young, rich and poor, straight and gay, old fashioned and modern. The compelling range of influence that the mass media provide through FM and AM radio, records and tapes, and music television increases the potential for audiences "crossing over" in the realm of sound. Thus people from all demographic strata in the more developed countries of the world have access to materials of the popular culture. Regardless of the varying conditions that surround audience members' daily lives, music may "express the images, visions and sentiments of people who find significance in it" (Lewis, 1982: 184).

USES OF MUSIC BY ADOLESCENTS

Whatever the origins of their exposure, it is clear that adolescents listen to a great deal of music, are loyal listeners to specific types of music, and use the sounds for many purposes. Relationships among exposure to cultural materials, the social networks that surround exposure and consumption, and patterns of use have been addressed empirically for many years. Prior to the emergence of rock music, popular music of the Tin Pan Alley era in the United States was used by adolescents. Responding to and using music are adolescent skills. In a classic essay, David Riesman observed that "the same or virtually the same popular culture materials are used by audiences in radically different ways and for radically different purposes" (Riesman, 1950: 360). He commented specifically about the popular music of the 1930s and 1940s and its relationship to American youth, pointing out the utility of music for purposes including identification with singers, as a conversational resource, for demonstrating interpersonal competence by competitively judging which songs will become hits, and for separating oneself from peers by knowing and praising esoteric music and artists. Clearly, Riesman conceptualized adolescent music listeners as an "active audience," a viewpoint that uses and gratifications researchers have repeatedly verified empirically and endorse thoroughly as a theoretical tenet.

In one of the first social-scientific analyses of music, teenage girls from the Chicago area were studied in the early days of rock 'n' roll (Johnstone and Katz, 1957). The researchers demonstrated the significance of the connection between peer group realities and individuals' music preferences, finding that differences in preference existed *within* neighborhoods where choices were affected by peer-group relations, and *between* neighborhoods that were said to represent "culture areas." However, girls who preferred "happy" songs over "blues" songs and who indicated preferences for upbeat lyrics generally were from the South shore, a more wealthy neighborhood than the Hyde Park area, where girls were less optimistic. The culture areas described by these researchers were rooted in varying socioeconomic circumstances.

The intervention of rock 'n' roll upon previous insipid styles of popular music in the 1950s increased the potential for the use of music by adolescents. The agitated beat of rock music resonates with the emotional character of adolescence, providing teenagers with a form of popular culture that they believe speaks to them at gut level. The evolution of rock music and its derivatives, country-rock, punk rock, new wave, and jazz fusion, among others, have made more diverse the kinds of music available for use.

For many adolescents, music is the primary cultural arena in which friendships are consumated (Frith, 1981) and impressions formed (Clarke, 1973). Listening to music (compared to viewing television) makes adolescents feel more open, free, excited, less bored, and is maximally enjoyed when adolescents feel "out of control" (Larson and Kubey, 1983). Affective shifts occur when adolescents listen to popular music, suggesting that the consequences of listening may be particularly gratifying (Gantz et al., 1978). These researchers also found that adolescents believe music makes them feel relaxed, happy, good, and excited. Indeed, when the punk rock and new wave movements were in their early stages in the United States, a study of California college students indicated that a fundamental objection to the new fast-paced music was that it was perceived to be unable to meet the traditional, expected social functions of music (Lull, 1982a).

Music is experienced sensually, appealing to the emotional impulses and cognitive operations of its listeners, affording them countless personal and interpersonal applications. In recent ethnographic research, California adolescents were observed to use music for the following purposes: dancing, exercising, background noise, driving, lessening inhibitions, distraction in uncomfortable social situations, asserting one's personality or image publicly, getting attention and approval, alienating parents, as part of the "cruising" ritual, security in foreign environments, escape from reality, diversion, establishing a mood, changing the mood, enhancing or intensifying a variety of activities including sexual activity and private moments of introspection, to cover up other sounds in the environment, reality exploration, lessening the drudgery of work, stimulating fantasies, passing time, companionship, relaxing, general entertainment, peer-group acceptance and reinforcement, conversational topics, the physiological "buzz" of loud sound, and reminiscing. For adolescents, music—its content, modes of consumption, and use—is extremely hip; television is unspeakably unhip. Particular uses of music are stimulated by a host of considerations. Salient features of a personal or social situation may suggest a use of music to the listener. Pertinent aspects of the message (the lyrics or the feeling of the music) likewise may provide opportunities for application of music as a personal or social resource. Environmental circumstances may provide a context for use, or attributes of the message as it is received may stimulate a particular use.

Music's usefulness is heightened by several factors. The active life of the adolescent nicely matches the flexibility of music. Music is portable, nonfocused, exciting, and associated with hedonistic treasures that exist outside the home. It can be put to use by listeners virtually everywhere on earth and at nearly all times. Unlike television where the sequencing of program materials is controlled almost completely by media sources, songs can be listened to at the times and in the order the listener desires. There is a constantly emerging set of new songs and artists appealing to various audiences for their sound and utility.

During adolescence and in all stages of life, music and other media are employed to satisfy the wants and gratify the needs of the people who use them. Some of the motivations for using media are trivial and fleeting (wants), while other (needs) are steeped in the psychological and social circumstances of life. The systematic employment of media reflects adolescents' immersion in the varying rule-governed environments they occupy, including the family, peer group, and the generalized larger society (Lull, 1982b).

ETHNOGRAPHIES OF YOUTH AND MEDIA

The primary research method employed in uses and gratifications research, the field survey, does not work very well in sweaty environments. The popular British band Au Pairs had just finished an exhilirating set of music closing out a six-hour concert at the Lyceum Theatre near the river in central London. Thousands of English youth had thrashed about the tight quarters for several hours while this band and others relentlessly hammered away at anarchistic themes. As I filed slowly out of the venue shoulder to shoulder that night with some of

England's most intriguing young people, I came to grips fully with the inadequacies of social science methodology as it is taught in the major American graduate schools and practiced by the vast majority of publishing scholars in our field. There simply was no way to represent numerically the essence of what thousands of young people had experienced during the concert or what the cultural meaning of music is to them generally.

Imagine asking punk rockers outside the concert hall how they feel about "slam dancing," for instance, by requiring them to respond to items on a semantic differential. How would they react to a set of Likert-type scale indices? "Would you say that slam dancing makes you feel: (a) very agitated, (b) somewhat agitated, (c) not very agitated, (d) not at all agitated?" At this point in the administration of the question-naire the researcher might suddenly become an involuntary partner in his or her first slam dance. This hypothetical turn of events is presented here to illustrate the enormous gap that exists between some of the most interesting things that take place in various cultures and the ability of quantitative methods of analysis to reflect their nature adequately. The closer one examines culture, the more true this seems to be.

Qualitative methodologies, I believe, are very well suited to the conduct of many kinds of empirical social and cultural research. All measurement begins with observation, the fundamental empirical act. Lately, some scholars in communication have come to believe that dwelling on the observed case *in situ*, however, renders information about social and cultural phenomena that is more theoretically useful than is additional data resulting from further attempts to standardize and quantify the irregular world into cells for statistical treatment. The analysis that many quantified phenomena are given, both the math-ematical and subsequent interpretational aspects, often makes serious a crime of unfaithfulness to the substance of communications processes and events under study. As Cameron (1973: 13) has pointed out, "Not everything that can be counted counts, and not everything that counts can be counted."

True understanding of the "text" of human interaction in which mass mediated symbols and interpersonal relations merge requires a multi-plistic theoretical literacy made up of all forms of evidentiary com-ponents observed to constitute the substance of social practice as best it can be signified through research. Communicational particulars reside in social events and processes ranging from informal conversations to ritualistic interactions such as dance, song, and poetry (Carey, 1979). Research procedures must facilitate the reading of communications episodes as texts, and must attend to social members as authors of those texts. A convergence of quantitative and qualitative research offers the greatest potential for accurate description and explanation of the significance of communications in all contexts.

COMMUNICATION RULES

Many interactions that take place in social environments can be grouped loosely into categories for descriptive purposes. Communication rules, considered within both their microscopic and macroscopic contexts, are patterned indicators of symbolic activity involving media audience members (Lull, 1982b). In the environments of peer groups and families, common microscopic contexts, repeated and strategic communications activity is designed and carried out in order to promote individual and group desires. In macroscopic contexts, patterns of interaction existing between audience members and media, and among audience members stimulated by media content, can be identified, described empirically, and addressed theoretically.

Communication rules are explicit and implicit understandings held by members of social groups that stimulate particular regularities in human action, sometimes termed "patterns," that have meaning in various contexts (Shimanoff, 1980). In the study of music, communication rules govern behavior that ranges from individual decisions about genre and song preferences, and patterns of exposure and consumption, to the often-complex ways in which sound is incorporated interpersonally into the daily routines of listeners. For young people especially, the lifestyle features, behavior of members of friendship groups, and even certain characteristics of national subcultures are rule governed. Patterns of relevance to youth develop in contexts that are influenced by the creation and consumption of music, dance, the aura of entertainment generally, and in situations where possibilities for personal involvement in alternative ways of living are realized.

Communication rules are practical, chosen, modifiable, organizing principles of human interaction that reflect the mental orientations of persons and institutions of power at all social levels. Interaction patterns that emerge in relation to music reveal hierarchies of opinion leadership in the mass-mediated, public context but also in neighborhood or community settings. Particular ways of dressing, dancing, talking, and, more pervasively, selected beliefs and attitudes of audience members are cultivated by the distribution of nonrandom themes and styles that receive exposure via media and merchandising outlets. These combined social operations suggest more than the enactment of cultural trends.

They represent conditions of basic social communication where power is displayed, influence is rendered, consciousness is formed, and routine interactions that inevitably help define the assumptive world of everyday life are perpetually and purposefully invented.

Rules of communication are less contextually variant than are individual acts of communication because a single rule can promote the accomplishment of a wide variety of outcomes. Ethnographic inquiry and other forms of qualitative research can be employed to ascertain these deeply ingrained processes of human interaction. The rules that govern adolescents' interaction with media, music, and each other are considered here to be more central and stable elements of communication than are isolated behaviors existing within the processes of media consumption or explicit gratifications that are said to be associated with consumption. In many cases it is not possible or particularly useful to quantify the presence of rules.

The objectives of ethnographic inquiry are at least twofold. First, researchers can observe complex interrelations that exist between symbol systems and social actors in their natural environments, and can grasp more fully the essence of human communication by probing its depth. Second, subtle operations can be examined carefully to determine what sociocultural patterns exist in the many microscopic and macroscopic contexts of communication. Consideration of these patterns as rules permits theorists to describe and explain many routine characteristics of communications phenomena. The ethnomethodological theoretical perspective (*not* the ethnographic research strategy) is one current approach to the depiction of social activity related to rules that is designed to go beyond "immaculate description of the case" in order to provide evidence of "generic social processes" (Lester and Hadden, 1980).

Human communication is highly irregular not only in form and content, but also in meaning for its participants. One of the goals of ethnographic research, therefore, is to render accurate and insightful distinctions between mundane interactions that carry little meaning and apparently routine interactions that are robust with significance. In this way, the textual saliency of message systems and the receptive potential of social environments in which communications processes unfold can be addressed theoretically in order to describe peculiar events and illustrate meaningful patterns of rule-governed communication. Certain varieties of communication, such as adolescents' experiences with music and their peer group activities in general, are well suited to the methodological and theoretical suggestions put forward here.

Observation in context and depth interviewing of communicators allow the uses and gratifications researcher to avoid some of the problems raised by Elliott (1974) in his exemplary piece of criticism concerning uses and gratifications research. Elliott was correct in his vituperation of empirical research conducted within the then newly emerging theoretical perspective, calling it "mentalistic, individualistic, and static-abstract" (mass communication considered in isolation from other social processes). Ethnographic inquiry responds to some of the shortcomings of quantitative empiricism by directing attention away from mental states toward observed behavior, away from individuals toward social groups, and away from static-abstraction toward process and change interpreted in context.

One methodological challenge for qualitative researchers now is to further develop, employ, and make public the ethnography of communication in media studies wherein evidence and interpretation are integrated in a way that renders accurate and insightful accounts of the intermingling of the symbolic agenda of visual and audio media, interpersonal relationships, and the natural situations of media consumption and use. My own "Social Uses of Television" essay (Lull, 1980b) was an attempt to do this. More recently there have been ethnographic studies of the communicative properties and processes of children's uses of media symbolism in their play activities (Sarett, 1981; James and McCain, 1982); of the ways that television is incorporated into vocational routines (Pacanowsky and Anderson, 1982); of sibling interaction during moments of co-viewing (Alexander et al., 1984); of the orations, dance, sports, music, ritual, and other forms of communication documented by means of culturally reflexive television production (Michaels, 1984); and of the social uses of romance novels by women where the interpretation and employment of fictive content represent varying reader "literacies" (Radway, 1984). Other ethnographic studies have been conducted, but the total so far represents only a very small percentage of the books, book chapters, and journal articles published and convention papers presented regarding media audience activity.

CONCLUDING REMARKS

Logical positivism and its accompanying array of quantitative empirical methods have dominated social research in the United States for the past forty or fifty years, roughly approximating the existence of the electronic mass media. This epistemological and methodological agenda has understandably produced research findings and a system of training in the major graduate schools of this nation regarding mass communication that promote variable identification, hypothesis formulation, testing, and interpretation within the capabilities of quantitative data-gathering approaches and statistical tests of "significance." Most of the studies cited in this chapter and in this book were conducted within such a framework. It is time to expand the scope of research methods into qualitative areas in order to extend the range of research conducted within the uses and gratifications framework generally, and within studies of youth and media specifically.

New areas of analysis in the study of youth culture are now emerging. Television, a medium that has been shown in the research literature to be largely irrelevant to adolescents, has assumed a significant new dimension with the development of music television (MTV), its derivatives, and imitators. Music television presents pop and rock music set to visual imagery and is delivered in a format that approximates the presentational style of contemporary commercial radio stations. There is a playlist, rotation policy, "veejays" (to replace "deejays"), concert news, commercials targeted to young demographics, and other reproductions of the audio medium. Recent research indicates that music television offers a social activity for peers—it is most often watched by adolescents with friends and least often with the family (Miller and Baran, 1984). Numerous studies are under way in the United States to document the impact of this new form of television programming and the patterns that characterize its use by adolescents and others.

Cultural materials designed for consumption by youth are distributed widely via modern communications technologies and access to them is generally available in the more developed countries of the world. Documentation of the comparative social penetration of such materials can be measured quite easily. *How* these cultural fragments are incorporated into the personal and interpersonal lives of adolescents and others, however, is more theoretically and methodologically problematic. Like all mass media, records, tapes, radio, and music television have ideologically loaded content, some of it supportive of prevailing values; some of it standing in opposition to various strains of the dominant culture. It is in audience members' actual uses of cultural forms, particularly those utilizations that involve interpersonal conversations, that the implications of media technologies and their value-laden content often can be observed. These hegemonic processes have been largely overlooked in quantitative empirical research, since it is typically constrained by the ideological biases of institutions that support social research and by the methodological limitations of the field survey.

How the ideological agenda of media content is assimilated by audience members is a subject area that should provoke the interest of uses and gratifications researchers in the future, thereby encouraging a focus on political issues that are now commonly neglected. Youth cultures are lively domains in which many critical issues can be addressed empirically by means of imaginative research strategies, a willingness on the part of researchers to entertain sociocultural phenomena on their own terms, and an orientation toward communication processes that gives proper attention to their political origins and implications. In this way, vivid expressions of mediated culture can be studied vis-à-vis interpersonal relations within a political-economic framework. A research agenda that reflects these priorities could add significant new dimensions to the uses and gratifications perspective, thereby increasing our general understanding of modern communication as a dynamic matrix of intentional symbolism located in the midst of aggressive and imaginative human utility.

Chapter 12

THE EXPERIMENTAL EXPLORATION
OF GRATIFICATIONS FROM
MEDIA ENTERTAINMENT

Dolf Zillmann

THIS VOLUME, ALONG WITH OTHERS (such as Blumler and Katz, 1974), amply documents the great progress made in establishing behavioral patterns of media use. What is consumed, when, by whom, and under what particular circumstances has been ascertained with increasing accuracy. Likewise, the reasons consumers give for their consumption choices have been ascertained and structured with increasing rigor. Numerous projections about the apparent motives for consuming informative and/or entertaining messages have resulted, and intriguing proposals concerning the function and utility of consumption, as well as proposals concerning gratification needs, have emerged (for example, Atkin, in press; Katz, Gurevitch, and Haas, 1973; Palmgreen and Rayburn, 1982; Rubin, in press).

In terms of method, research into media uses and gratifications has relied, for the most part, on survey technique—the instrument of measurement being the questionnaire or some form thereof. The assessment of consumption motives, in particular, has relied totally on soliciting introspection. What has come to be known as uses and gratification research is thus virtually synonymous with questionnaire surveys; or in other words, with asking the consumers of media fare to explain their choices.

The technique has much value. For one thing, it can be used quickly and, comparatively speaking, with minimal expenditure in effort and at low cost. The technique has obvious limitations, however. These limitations are pointed out in occasional self-critical efforts. But criticism, on the whole, tends to be given little credence and is cast aside quickly. The limitations in question concern mainly the validity of inferences from introspective reports of consumption reasons about actual consumption reasons. If uses and gratifications research were to restrict itself to the analysis of media uses and *what people say* motivates them to use the media as they do, the problem would not exist. Prudent as it might be, such restriction of inferences about consumption motives is usually not accepted, and introspection about motives is taken to be veridical information about motives.

At times, introspection concerning motives of message consumption may well reflect the actual motives. It cannot possibly be assumed, however, that they always do or that they do so by necessity. Introspection of motives must, in fact, be considered highly tenuous—for a number of principal reasons. First, message consumers may very simply be unaware of the actual determinants of their choices. Second, they may have learned to think and speak about motives in accord with the ways in which their cultural community thinks and speaks about them; and although "consensual validation" may have occurred to some extent, the perceptions may be erroneous. Third, and perhaps most significantly, in efforts to project a favorable image of themselves to themselves and/or to investigators, respondents may distort any veridical information they might have about their motives for consuming particular messages.

The technique that bypasses these problems with introspective accounts of motives is the experiment. Whether informative or entertaining, messages can be manipulated in critical ways; and respondents who are naive about the manipulations can be observed as they make message choices or react to the messages they have chosen. Any differences in their behavior can then be attributed to the manipulations under control—as there are, or there should be, no other sources for differential behavior. The technique, despite limitations of its own, thus allows inferences about determinants of behavior (such as motives) on the basis of *what people do*. There is no reliance on introspection. Nobody has to take anybody's word for why and for what reasons people do what they do.

The novice to the field might be inclined to believe that those who study media uses and gratifications have embraced whatever methodology holds promise in exploring the issues at hand. Oddly enough, such a novice would and should be bewildered to learn that research tends to progress in traditions that are defined by the use of particular methodologies; and that, once these traditions are formed, alternative approaches are met with indifference. In the study of media uses and gratifications, those who subscribe to survey technique have paid little attention to experimental research on the subject. In fact, many might be surprised to learn that experimental work exists in this area. But those who subscribe to experimentation have been similarly negligent. They paid little attention to the wealth of information that has been aggregated within traditional media uses and gratifications research.

The purpose of this assessment is not to accuse. Rather, it is to point out the need for integrating approaches that in near-complete isolation have been applied to an area of interest. In studying the "hows" and "whys" of message consumption, many research techniques hold promise; and much can be gained from the use of different techniques. Because unique limitations accrue to any specific technique, the use of different methodologies is potentially superior to the use of just one— whichever it may be. Research into media uses and gratifications thus has everything to gain from embracing both survey technique and experimentation. The integration of findings generated by both approaches is likely to give us a far better understanding of why people consume what they consume and why they enjoy what they enjoy than would the findings deriving from either approach alone.

This chapter seeks to serve the needed integration of findings by providing a brief overview of experimentation on uses and gratifications phenomena. It introduces the reader to the experimental work on selective exposure (determinants of consumption choices) and enjoyment (determinants of consumption appreciation). This introduction is necessarily incomplete and selective. Focus is on the consumption of entertaining messages. Nonimmediate effects, such as influences on aggressive or sexual behavior, or on perceptions of reality, are not considered.

MEDIA USES

Consumers of entertainment can be very deliberate in their choices. A particular television program, for instance, may have been considered, a decision to watch it may have been made, and exposure to the program may result as soon as the program becomes available. Not all choices are of this kind, however. It seems that, more often then not, entertainment choices are made impulsively. In sampling television programs by flicking the dial or by pushing buttons, the program that holds the greatest appeal by "instant appraisal" or "gut reaction" is likely to be picked, and the factors that determine this appeal need not be at all clear to the respondent. It should be the exception that viewers, in making entertainment choices, engage in explicit and systematic evaluative comparisons of the options before them. It is more likely that they make these choices rather mindlessly—that is, without using formal and stable criteria in their appeal assessment. If the choice criteria are often vague and unclear, the ends or purposes served by the choices in question can be no clearer. That is, respondents tend to construe their choices as the result of a global desire to be well entertained, but may not comprehend any ulterior functions that might be served by the consumption of specific forms of entertainment or entertainment as such. Particular effects of consumption, then, might be sought without the consumer having awareness of it. But how can such "tacit" understanding of functions, should it exist, develop?

REGULATION OF EXCITATION

Entertaining material can produce considerable excitement in respondents (see Zillmann, 1982). Such excitement manifests itself in obtrusive sympathetic dominance in the autonomic nervous system, among other things, and it produces intense affective reactions. Hedonically speaking, these reactions can be positive or negative, depending upon the respondents' idiosyncratic appraisals of what transpired.

The capacity of entertaining material to produce excitement is obviously greater for persons experiencing low levels of excitation than for persons who experience high levels already. To the extent that this capacity influences entertainment choices, it should do so more strongly for people who suffered through a hapless day characterized by monotonous and boring chores than for people who were confronted with uncertainty, competition, and other pressures—in short, people who suffer from overstimulation and stress.

Under the assumption that levels of excitation that vary within a normal range (nonextreme levels) constitute a necessary though not sufficient condition for an individual's feelings of well-being, it has been proposed (Zillmann and Bryant, in press-a) that entertainment from television or another source might be employed to regulate excitation. Understimulated, bored persons should seek exposure to exciting television programs. Even if the material is not intrinsically pleasant, such exposure should be experienced pleasantly because it brings these persons back to levels of excitation that are more closely linked to "feeling good." If the material is intrinsically enjoyable, all the better. For understimulated, bored persons, exposure to exciting television programs thus can be seen as having the benefit of returning them conveniently (at minimal cost in effort and in complete safety) to a hedonically superior, desirable state.

But entertainment not only has the capacity to excite; it can soothe and calm as well (see Zillmann, 1982). This capacity potentially benefits those who are uptight, upset, annoyed, angry, mad, or otherwise disturbed. All these experiences are associated with sympathetic hyperactivity, and persons who experience such hyperactivity would obviously profit from exposure to nonexciting, relaxing entertainment because this exposure would lower their levels of excitation and return it to more desirable levels. Stressed persons, then, would do well to avoid exciting material and to seek out material capable of calming them instead.

The excitation- and mood-altering effects of entertaining material are not in doubt. But can it be assumed that, in selecting television programs for consumption, people make choices that serve excitatory homeostasis? Do people select what is good for them—spontaneously and without comprehension of purpose? Can it be assumed that bored individuals prefer exciting material over relaxing material and that stressed individuals display the opposite preference? It can indeed, based on the premise that bored persons experience relief when watching exciting programs and stressed individuals experience relief when watching relaxing programs, and that the experience of relief constitutes negative reinforcement that shapes initially random choice patterns into mood-specific entertainment preferences (Zillmann, 1982; Zillmann and Bryant, in press-a).

The proposal that people form mood-specific preferences—that is, behave as if they had a tacit understanding of what is good for them under specific affective circumstances—has been supported by experimental research (Bryant and Zillmann, 1984). Subjects were first placed into a state of boredom or stress. Ostensibly in a waiting period, they were then allowed to watch television as they pleased. Their choice was among three exciting and three relaxing programs. Unbeknownst to the subjects, the programs were prerecorded and fed from videotape recorders to the monitor the subjects were watching. From this monitor, the time of program consumption was unobtrusively recorded. The data revealed that exciting programs attracted bored subjects significantly more than stressed subjects and that relaxing programs attracted stressed subjects significantly more than bored subjects. Effects of self-determined exposure on excitation were assessed as well. It was found that almost all subjects had chosen materials that helped them effectively to escape from undesirable excitatory states. In fact, almost all overcorrected (bored subjects ended up at above-base levels and stressed subjects below-base levels of excitation). Only a few bored subjects failed to behave in line with expectations. They elected to expose themselves to relaxing fare and remained in a state of subnormal excitation as a result.

RELIEF FROM NOXIOUS EXPERIENCE

The tacit understanding of benefits accruing to the consumption of entertainment is not limited to exciting and calming programs, however. It extends to other message characteristics. Among other things, experimental research has provided evidence that persons select programs that are involving to different degrees as a function of persons' affective states. It has been found that persons who would affectively benefit from distraction tend to select highly absorbing material that is capable of providing relief. Those in less need of distraction show less appetite for this kind of material (see Zillmann and Bryant, in press-a). It has also been observed that individuals confronted with acute problems from which distraction through entertainment cannot offer any escape or prompt relief (such as anger from provocation that demands corrective action) tend to stay away from entertainment altogether—at least temporarily (Christ and Medoff, 1984).

For persons seeking mood improvement (such as termination of bad moods, achievement of good moods, or facilitation and extension of good moods), exposure to humor and comedy appears to offer a potent solution. To those in acute need of some cheering up, merriment and laughter on the screen should hold considerable appeal. Generally speaking, entertainment that seems capable of stimulating positive affect immediately and frequently should be the pick of those suffering from bad moods. These people should be strongly inclined to choose comedy and its kin over alternative, competing offerings.

An investigation that establishes that this is indeed the case has been conducted with women at different stages in the menstrual cycle (Meadowcroft and Zillmann, 1984; see also Zillmann and Bryant, in press-a). On the premise that the premenstrual syndrome is created mainly by the rapid withdrawal of progesterone and estrogen that afforded anesthetizing protection earlier, it was argued that premenstrual and menstrual women should suffer from bad moods, if not from feelings of depression. As a result, these women should experience the greatest need for relief through merriment and laughter. Midway through the cycle, when estrogen levels are elevated and progesterone levels rise, this need should be less pronounced, if at all existent. As there is little that premenstrual and menstrual women can do about their misery, comedy of any kind offers a most convenient way out and, consequently, should become highly attractive.

To test this proposition, women were asked to select programs they would enjoy watching. They chose from among known situation comedies, action dramas, and game shows. The position in the cycle was ascertained thereafter. On the basis of the latter information, the women were placed into four-day phase groups throughout the cycle, thus allowing the tracing of programs chosen for consumption as a function of hormonal conditions. In confirmation of the hypothesis it was found that premenstrual and menstrual women selected exposure to comedy programs significantly more often than did women in other phases of the cycle. At midcycle, the women exhibited comparatively little interest in comedy and showed an appetite for serious drama instead. On gloomy premenstrual and menstrual days, then, comedy becomes especially attractive. People who are down on their luck in other ways may similarly be expected to seek (and accomplish) mood lifts from comedy.

But comedy is not by necessity a mood improver. Television comedy, in particular, is laden with testing and demeaning happenings, even with considerable hostility (Zillmann, 1977). Material of this sort is unlikely to amuse persons who have recently been targets of similarly debasing actions because exposure to the material will tend to reinstate the unpleasantness and annoyance from the treatments in question. Acutely angry persons, for example, cannot expect favorable mood changes from comedy that dwells on hostile actions. Angry persons thus would be well advised to refrain from exposure to such comedy, but not to other forms of comedy. Experimental research again shows that people behave as if they had tacit knowledge of these effects. Provoked, angry persons were found to refrain from watching hostile comedy and to turn to alternative offerings (Zillmann et al., 1980).

Interestingly, children as young as four and five years of age are already capable of using television fare to improve their mood states. In an experiment by Masters et al. (1983), boys and girls of this age were placed into a nurturant, neutral, or hostile social environment and then provided with an oportunity to watch children's television programs. Once the different mood states (good, neutral, bad) had been induced, the children were allowed to watch television as long as they pleased. They were free to shut off the monitor on which only one program could be received. This program was either nurturant or neutral. The nurturant one was composed of extremely supportive, nonthreatening, and reassuring segments from "Mister Rogers' Neighborhood." The neutral program consisted of a news show for children that presented world events devoid of emotional content. The length of time the children elected to watch the one or the other program served as a measure of exposure.

The effects were clear-cut and and as expected for boys. Boys treated in a hostile manner, compared to the other boys, stayed with the nurturant program more than twice as long. Boys in a good mood exhibited the least need for exposure to nurturant television material. There were no corresponding differences in exposure to the neutral, nonnurturant program. For girls, in contrast, the mood treatment failed (when subjected to the hostile environment, girls coped effectively with it by distracting themselves), and reliable exposure effects could not be observed as a consequence.

AVOIDING AVERSION

In the investigation by Masters et al., the boys placed into the hostile social environment suffered acute distress, and they then sought to relieve it by exposure to nurturant material. The girls curtailed the distressing experience by busying themselves with puzzles. They might have accomplished the same objective by exposing themselves to an absorbing, distracting television program. But this option was not provided, and other findings that would shed light on this possibility are not available. Research has addressed a related issue, however.

It has been proposed that exposure to entertainment can not only foster relief from acute aversion, but can diminish concerns about possible future aversions (see Zillmann and Wakshlag, in press). The viewers' anticipations of information capable of putting their aversion apprehensions to rest should make entertaining messages containing such information very attractive. The same anticipations should lead viewers to expect being disturbed by exposure to material that gives rise to and boosts their concerns, and this should motivate these viewers to avoid exposure to material that features information they deem distressing. Viewers can thus be expected to make entertainment choices that are likely to minimize discomfort through avoidance of disturbing material and/or to maximize comfort through provision of pacifying information.

An experiment conducted by Wakshlag et al. (1983) shows these selection tendencies very clearly. Male and female adults were or were not placed in a state of apprehension about becoming victims of crime, especially violent crime, and later given an opportunity to select entertaining drama for consumption. The subjects chose from a list of film synopses. These synopses had been pretested and received scores for the degree to which a film was perceived as featuring violent victimization and/or the punitive restoration of justice. Measures of the appeal of violence and justice were obtained by adding the scores of the films that were selected.

The findings revealed strong gender differences in the appeal of both violent victimization and justice restoration. Females responded less favorably to violence than did males, and they were attracted more strongly than males to justice restoration as a salient theme of drama. Regardless of these overall gender differences, both crime-apprehensive males and crime-apprehensive females proved equally sensitive to the drama dimensions under consideration. Apprehensive persons selected drama that was lower in levels of violent victimization and higher in justice restoration than did their nonapprehensive counterparts. Apprehensive individuals, then, did exhibit the proposed tendency to minimize exposure to disturbing events and to maximize exposure to information capable of diminishing their apprehensions. The main message of television's crime drama—namely, that the criminals are being caught and put away, which should make the streets safer—apparently is music to the ears of those who worry about crime (see Zillmann, 1980).

The reader who is interested in a more complete accounting of the research on selective exposure is referred to a recent collection of exposés on that topic (Zillmann and Bryant, in press-c).

MEDIA GRATIFICATIONS

Entertainment offered by the media does not, of course, merely serve the regulation of arousal and associated affect or accomplish a contagion of merriment for persons eager to rid themselves of bad moods. Entertaining messages are capable of gratifying respondents because of unique intrinsic properties. But what are these properties? What is it that makes for good entertainment? And what is it that makes entertainment fail?

The enjoyment of drama, comedy, musicals, games, and sports is undoubtedly influenced by a host of variables. Many of these variables have received attention and have been considered significant (for example, Jauss, 1982; Goldstein, 1979). But none has received more attention and is deemed more significant in its effect on enjoyment than affective dispositions toward interacting parties, especially parties confronted with problems, conflict, and aversive conditions. Human conflict in the raw has often been singled out as the stuff of which all good drama is made. Conflict constitutes only a starting point, however. The portrayal of intense conflict, in and of itself, does not, with any degree of regularity, certainly not by necessity, lead to enjoyment. Enjoyment depends not so much on conflict per se as on its resolution and on what the resolution means to the parties involved. It depends on how much those who come to glory are liked and loved and on how much those who end up humbled, humiliated, and punished are disliked and hated. Good drama relies on positive and negative sentiments toward the parties in conflict and on the extent to which a resolution can be accepted by the audience with its own, idiosyncratic perceptions and judgments. Indifference toward protagonists and antagonists is the antidote to good drama. Strong positive and negative affective dispositions toward the agents in any kind of drama are vital and must be created if the featured events are to evoke strong emotions, great enjoyment included.

DYNAMICS OF AFFECT IN SPECTATORS

"Character development" is the process that controls initial affective responses. The portrayal of goodness in protagonists makes them likable and lovable. Analogously, the portrayal of evil in antagonists makes them unlikable and hateable. To the extent that any intended character development works, it produces positive and negative dispositions toward the agents of a play—or more generally, toward any agent in an exchange that benefits some and harms others, overt competition (as in sports) included.

Character development can be effective because respondents bring empathy and, more importantly, moral considerations to bear on the events. What the agents in a play are doing matters most. Their conduct is the basis for the audience's approval or disapproval. Such approval or disapproval is a moral verdict, of course. The fact that this is not generally recognized by respondents (and those who study their behavior) does not alter that circumstance. Essentially, then, approval of conduct fosters liking; disapproval, in constrast, fosters disliking (see Zillmann, 1980, 1983b).

Once an audience has placed its sentiments, pro and con, with particular characters, enjoyment of conflict and its resolution in drama depends on intermediate outcomes, but mostly on the ultimate outcome, for the loved and hated parties. Positive affective dispositions inspire hopes for positive outcomes and fears of negative ones. Protagonists are deemed deserving of good fortunes and utterly undeserving of bad ones. Negative affective dispositions, on the other hand, activate the opposite inclinations: fear of positive outcomes and hopes for negative ones. Antagonists are deemed utterly undeserving of good fortunes and deserving of bad ones. The hopes and fears, in turn, lead respondents to empathize with the emotions displayed by protagonists. The joys as well as the suffering of liked characters tend to evoke concordant, "shared" affect in the audience. In contrast, these hopes and fears prompt counter-empathic reactions to the emotions experienced by antagonists. The villains' joy is the audience's distress; and the villains' suffering, being brought to justice, and getting their comeuppance is the audience's delight (see Zillmann, 1983b).

These dynamics of affect in spectators—or listeners, for that matter—should be thought of as a dichotomous system (negative, positive) underneath which continuous variables exist. Liking and disliking of characters is obviously a matter of degree, and the projection of consequences for the enjoyment of events and outcomes must take this into account. The following formal predictions are the result (see Zillmann, 1980):

(1) Enjoyment deriving from witnessing the debasement, failure, or defeat of a party, agent, or object increases with the intensity of negative sentiment and decreases with the intensity of positive sentiment toward these entities.

(2) Enjoyment deriving from witnessing the enhancement, success, or victory of a party, agent, or object decreases with the intensity of negative sentiment and increases with the intensity of positive sentiment toward these entities.

(3) Annoyance deriving from witnessing the debasement, failure, or defeat of a party, agent, or object decreases with the intensity of negative sentiment and increases with the intensity of positive sentiment toward these entities.

(4) Annoyance deriving from witnessing the enhancement, success, or victory of a party, agent, or object increases with the intensity of negative sentiment and decreases with the intensity of positive sentiment toward these entities.

(5) Propositions 1 through 4 apply jointly. Consequently, all contributions to enjoyment and/or annoyance combine in total enjoyment or annoyance. In this integration of contributions, annoyance is conceived of as negative enjoyment, and contributions to enjoyment and annoyance are assumed to combine in an additive fashion.

GRATIFYING MAINSTAY

Predictions from this disposition model of enjoyment have been confirmed by numerous experimental investigations. Research support has been obtained not only for the enjoyment of drama (see Zillmann,

1980), but for humor appreciation (Zillmann, 1983a; Zillmann and Cantor, 1976) and the enjoyment of sports events (Bryant and Zillmann, 1983; Zillmann et al., 1979) as well. Comedy can, of course, be construed as a form of drama that differs from drama proper only by the presence of cues indicating that things are not to be taken too seriously. Most tendentious humor (jokes or other formats featuring hostile and/or sexual occurrences in which somebody is victimized) can be similarly construed as dramatic episodes—brief, miniaturized ones—in which there is conflict that is resolved in favor of a deserving party and to the detriment of a victim who had it coming. Setting someone up for the punch line is nothing other than making him or her deserving of the humorous knockdown.

The operation of these dispositional mechanics of enjoyment is most obtrusive in sports spectatorship. Sports fans have favorite players and teams. They also have players and teams that they detest, sometimes intensely. Seeing a beloved competing party humble, humiliate, and destroy a resented one obviously constitutes the ultimate in sports enjoyment. Equally obvious, the reverse outcome provides no joy; it is upsetting, if not depressing. It is clear, in addition, that indifference toward persons or teams in a contest is the kind of condition under which excitement and intense enjoyment cannot materialize. All this is not to say that the enjoyment of athletic events is not influenced by many other factors (see Zillmann et al., 1979). It is to say, however, that the dispositional mechanics of affect seem to be of overriding significance in the enjoyment of sports events—and of dramatic confrontations of any kind.

PARADOXICAL GRATIFICATION

The popularity of suspenseful drama has bewildered many who sought to understand and explain it. The fact that people enjoy such drama seems contradictory, even paradoxical. This is because suspenseful drama features, for most of its duration, the protagonist or protagonists in situations describable as impending disaster. The parties for whom the audience has developed fondness are in peril; they appear to be doomed (Zillmann, 1980). Over considerable periods of time, the heroes are tormented and about to be overpowered and destoyed by malicious beings and/or extraordinary dangers. Dreaded, disastrous happenings are repeatedly imminent. If the latest action-packed raids on the audience are any indication, the audience of future suspenseful drama will confront such happenings almost continually. How can anybody, under these circumstances, enjoy drama? The dominant affective experience should be one of empathic distress—and stress from sheer stimulus bombardment. No doubt, this noxious experience is relieved at times when the feared and seemingly imminent events fail to materialize and, especially in the resolution, the protagonists overcome the dangers that threatened them, destroying any evil forces in the grandest of fashions, and usually against all odds. At times, of course, the resolution is less full-fledged, and the protagonists merely get away with dear life. Contemporary horror movies tend to take that format also, as tormented ladies barely escape the chainsaws, and the villains are spared for the sequel. Yet even in resolutions that do not feature the annihilation of evil forces there is usually cause for jubilation, and the resolution can be deemed satisfying. In summary, then, suspenseful drama dwells on showing a hero or heroes in peril, but it also offers a resolution that is satisfying, if only minimally so. The indicated paradox consists of the fact that drama of this kind tends to evoke empathic distress more often and for longer periods of time than euphoria. Hence, it should be suffered more than it should be enjoyed. How can such a formula work for nonmasochistic audiences?

One explanation is that the persons attracted to suspenseful drama (and to disaster and horror movies, by the same token) are sufficiently understimulated, if not bored, to appreciate any shakeup of their excitatory state (Tannenbaum, 1980; Zuckerman, 1979). If arousal levels are subnormal, excitatory reactions—even when deriving from distress—can help return arousal to more pleasantly experienced levels. The safety and convenience of the exposure situation makes it unlikely that levels rise to uncomfortable heights. Still, the immediate affective experience associated with any arousal kicks is likely to be a noxious one, and this circumstance favors a more elaborate explanation.

According to the alternative account (Zillmann, 1980), residues of excitation from empathic distress and/or from the response to the threatening stimuli persist through resolutions and intensify the euphoric experience that is evoked by these resolutions. As the magnitude of residual excitation is greater than the more intense the distressful experience, it follows that the enjoyment of satisfying resolutions will be the more intensified the greater (and more immediate) the preceding distress reaction. The simple consequence of this is that suspenseful drama will be the more enjoyable, the more the audience is initially made to suffer—through empathy with the endangered protagonists and/or any duress induced by those dangers with which the protagonists struggled. Great enjoyment, then, is expected to derive in part from great distress.

Evidence for the proposed mechanics of the enjoyment of suspenseful drama comes from several experimental investigations (see Zillmann,

1980). Essentially, drama was manipulated to accomplish variations in the appeal of protagonists (for instance, liking, indifference, disliking), in the severity of the dangers confronting them (low, high), in the degree to which the protagonists were vulnerable to the dangers (low, high), and in the efficiency with which they coped with and ultimately neutralized these dangers (low, high). The findings establish a number of things. First of all, they show that empathic distress with a party in peril is clearly a function of affective disposition toward that party. Distress increases with the degree of fondness felt toward a party, and it is virtually absent—both cognitively and in its sympathetic manifestations (for example, as excitation)—when the party is disliked or resented. Second, and most important here, the findings show that, exactly as predicted, the enjoyment of suspenseful drama that features a satisfying resolution increases with the degree of residual excitation from empathic distress. As empathic distress grows with the severity of the dangers that confront liked protagonists and/or with the protagonists' vulnerability of succumbing to these dangers, this amounts to saying that enjoyment of a satisfying resolution to suspenseful drama is greater the more intense the preceding noxious thrill of suspense. Third, the findings indicate that suspenseful drama that fails to feature a satisfying ending, and thus fails to instigate a euphoric reaction in the end, does benefit less, if at all, from residual excitation deriving from empathic distress. For enjoyment to be intensified, enjoyment must be created; and it is usually created—by the presentation of a final outcome that benefits the liked, deserving protagonists and that, as a result, satisfies the audience. Fourth, the findings leave no doubt about the fact that audiences applaud bravery and heroism. Characters who confronted great dangers and/or coped effectively with them are liked the more for it.

REMAINING QUESTIONS

The experimental exploration of gratifications has succeeded in many other areas (see Zillmann and Bryant, in press-b). For instance, the influence of the social conditions under which entertainment is consumed on the enjoyment of the entertaining stimuli has been investigated, and some patterns of effects have been secured. On the other hand, however, many issues have remained unresolved, and some phenomena seem more puzzling than ever. The appeal of tragedy and the popularity of bad news are two of the most bewildering that come to mind.

Although tragedy is rarely full blown (without euphoric moments or cause for relief), the appeal of this genre of entertainment challenges all hedonic considerations. The proper response to tragedy should be profound sadness. If this response is characteristically made (and there is no reason to suppose that it is not), why do people elect to put themselves through such a highly noxious experience? Probably owing to bewilderment, we are inclined to believe there must be some hidden benefits. But what are they?

The appeal of bad news poses similar problems. Surely, some bad news has informational utility and exposure to it is indicated for that reason. But news programs are often laden with reports about others' misfortunes and about those others' anguished reactions to the misfortunes; and these reports are devoid of immediate utility. One is again tempted to look for benefits, especially for hedonic benefits. Could it be there is delayed gratification for the consumption of material that is unpleasant initially? Is sharing the information concerning dreadful events with acquaintances and friends enjoyable to a point that warrants the consumption of distressing materials? Could it be that seeing others suffer fosters the pleasant realization of how good the viewer or listener has it and how much he or she has to be thankful for? Is learning about tragic happenings that victimize others, whether from news reports or from fiction, ultimately gratifying in this sense?

We do not know at present. However, nothing stands in the way of resolving these issues; and a combination of research approaches in which experimentation plays a part would seem to hold great promise in accomplishing this expediently.

Chapter 13

GRATIFICATIONS ASSOCIATED WITH
NEW COMMUNICATION TECHNOLOGIES

Frederick Williams
Amy Friedman Phillips
Patricia Lum

GOING BEYOND MASS COMMUNICATION

Uses and gratifications theory has historically been applied to mass media, but it has always held promise for the study of other media as well, including the so-called "new" technologies. We refer to such visible media as video cassette or disk, cable television, new telephone services, home computers, videotext or teletext services, and to the less visible technologies of digital switching, satellite transmission, and broadband telecommunications networks. Certainly, the proliferation of new communication technologies may affect the structure of communication in society and make available a greater range of choice for satisfying communication needs. New media uses may complement uses already studied. Previously identified uses may shift to new media from old ones, providing fresh insights into the relationship between media use and gratifications. Further, uses and gratifications theory incorporates concepts that provide a base for developing a framework for research into the adoption of new technologies. A challenge, as posed by Palmgreen (1984b), is for researchers to "adapt and mold the current conceptual framework to deal with new communication technologies." In essence, the likely questions raised by this challenge are the topic of this chapter.

One initial observation of this chapter is that there is not so much that is "new" in the aforementioned technologies. To the user, most are merely extensions of existing media, for example, in the sense that video cassettes or disks are related to broadcast television, or the new electronic text services are extensions of traditional print. Most important, and especially relevant to this chapter, is that the new media offer many increased alternatives for both access to and interaction with message stimuli. Some of the technologically based contributions include the following:

- making distance all but irrelevant (communications satellite)
- freeing television from the restrictions of broadcast schedules (videotape)
- providing for nonlinear access to information (computers, video disks)
- offering nearly unlimited availability of two-way voice or text communications (mobile telephone, computer teleconferencing)
- transporting many simultaneous message or program choices (coaxial cable, fiber optics)
- bypassing the printing and transportation requirements for the transmission of textual information (video and teletext)

These new opportunities for access have more generalized psychological and behavioral conseqeunces for the human communicator. There are more choices, and hence, more alternatives for gratifications (as in having thirty rather than five channels of television, or the added alternatives of disks, tapes, cable, and pay-TV channels). Mobility is greatly increased, thereby opening new opportunities to engage in gratifications seeking independent of locational restrictions (as in viewing movies at home rather than at a local theater). There is increased freedom to create personal schedules, as reflected by videotape or in working at home during hours of one's choice. Finally, there is the increased opportunity for interactivity with media (as with random access video disk, or computers) or with people via telecommunications networks (as with teleconferencing).

Such structural considerations are important in determining the path a person will take to gratify a communication need. People make trade-offs between various media according to what is available and accessible to serve a particular perceived need. For example, Blumler (1979) notes that housewives without a telephone show a significantly greater use of television for serving a personal identity function than would otherwise be served by social contact through use of the telephone.

Certainly, then, from the broader environmental view, there is the question of how or whether new technologies will change environmental alternatives for media gratifications. Already, annual Nielsen summaries are showing some trade-off in the United States between audiences' increased use of tape and cable TV alternatives in place of traditional network broadcasting for their entertainment needs. Further, there is the increasing prospect of tape rentals cutting into traditional moviegoing, a condition reminiscent of the effects of television's introduction in this country. Indeed, we are seeing modifications in the choice environment. Some of these may be short-lived, as with video games, and others may change the media environment forever (as television did and as video cassettes now seem likely to do).

Another example of environmental change, although seldom addressed in uses and gratifications research, is the effects of new communications technologies on organizational environments. Management information systems, word processing, electronic mail, and other new technologies of "office automation" are visibly changing the nature of organizational communications, and presumably the associated uses and gratifications as well.

CHOOSING AMONG THE OPTIONS

How do we account for the dynamics of media and content selection from among the greatly expanded array of choices? Van Leuven (1981: 426) presents a two-level expectancy theory "capable of handling media and message selection processes at once." This type of theory, originally suggested by McQuail and Gurevitch (1974), is an action/motivation theory focusing on individual users, their choices of media behavior, and, perhaps in response to Swanson's (1977) criticism regarding lack of attention paid to perception of meaning attached to media and messages, on the meanings and expectations they attach to those choices.

Other authors have proposed expectancy models (Galloway and Meek, 1981; Palmgreen and Rayburn, 1982) but all are similar in that they view either behavior, behavioral intentions, or attitudes as a function of the following: (1) expectancy—the perception of an object's possession of a particular attribute or that a certain behavior will lead to certain consequences—and (2) evaluation—that is, the degree of affect, positive or negative, toward an attribute or behavioral outcome. Palmgreen and Rayburn's (1982) model holds that the products of beliefs and evaluations influence the seeking of gratification, which influence media choice and consumption. This then results in the perception of certain gratifications obtained, which then feed back to reinforce or alter an individual's perceptions of the gratification-related attributes of a particular medium, message (content), or program genre.

To date, we know very little of the beliefs and evaluations associated with new media alternatives. It is possible, however, to conceive of broad dimensions of media attitudes such as those found in Phillips's (1982) pilot research with university students. Multivariate scaling techniques clearly indicated that students differentiated communications alternatives such as video cassettes, cable TV, or even computers along rather basic attitudinal dimensions. This raises questions concerning not only how such attitudes mediate a person's expectations of satisfaction from using a particular medium, but how those attitudes become socialized in the first place.

It has also been shown that content may be perceived not just as information but as other forms of stimulation as well. For example, "social presence" theory (Short et al., 1976) suggests that individuals associate different degrees of personal contact with various media, and that choice of a medium may not be for purposes of informational content but for the affective consequences. This holds particular implications for those new technologies (especially computers) that are felt by some to be markedly "impersonal" media. How can the perceived social presence of a medium be enhanced? Presumably this is as much a question of rhetorical choices and capabilities as it is one of technology. A telephone call, although lacking in visual cues and some paralinguistic ones, can nevertheless be highly personal if the appropriate language is used. The same can be said of cmputer-based teleconferencing.

A GRATIFICATIONS LOOK
AT SELECTED TECHNOLOGIES

Few uses and gratifications researchers have focused on studying new communication technologies. This may be because the most pressing research issues have had less to do with certain types of media than with conceptualizing the behavioral and social processes of selection and gratification. Although uses and gratifications approaches provide descriptive information about media use, media characteristics have changed, and are continuing to change, over time. One reason for studying the new technologies is to examine how, or if, gratifications change with media characteristics. Another reason is to gain further understanding of how new media are perceived and used.

Research into the new technologies falls primarily into the realm of function or utility studies, drawing inferences from uses rather than actually measuring gratifications. These studies are of value, since it is desirable to view uses and gratifications not of one medium alone but within the context of a person's total media environment. Communication needs may be better defined through examining changing human-and-media interactions. In the following few pages, several studies dealing with the uses of new technologies are reviewed.

CABLE TELEVISION

Although cable television has had a long history of simply extending the signals of over-the-air broadcasters, the more modern and ambitious vision is one of wide selection, broadband communications services, including interactive ones. These can range all the way from televised entertainment to interactive banking.

One study that deals directly with expectations associated with cable television emphasizes that researchers must expand their concept of the types of specific gratifications that may be served by new technologies. Shaver (1983) conducted focus group interviews and found certain functions relating to the unique aspects of cable. The two most frequently mentioned motives for viewing cable TV were "variety," provided by the increased number of channels and programming choices and "control over viewing," associated with the flexibility of programming. The various motives identified seem to fall into content (religious programs), structural (variety), service (better reception), and psychological needs (companionship) categories, although Shaver did not group them in this manner. Some of these gratifications have also been associated with traditional broadcast television (such as general surveillance), but others are directly linked to the cable TV medium.

In a study conducted for the NCTA (Opinion Research Corporation, 1983), people who chose whether or not to subscribe to cable TV were loosely classified into five groups. Although better reception was still mentioned as the primary reason for subscribing to cable, certain other distinctions among users were defined. Three user groups reflected the following characteristics:

(1) undifferentiated users of the medium who will watch everything and are early adopters of cable;

(2) the "entertain me" group—those who primarily seek entertainment and diversion and are likely to be pay-TV subscribers; and

(3) the "basic but . . . " group—those who are more differentiating in their use—specifically, they want and choose among sophisticated, intellectually stimulating, children's, family-oriented, or information programming, and are likely to seek out home services and other special services.

These studies show that functions relating both to the form and content of the medium will be associated with a technology. Furthermore, a distinction seems to be evident between people who seek out entertainment or escape and those who seek a variety of specific services, a point we raise later in consideration of the new "text" services.

VIDEO CASSETTES

Video cassettes differ from television as audio cassettes do from radio. Specifically, video cassette recorders, which are rapidly growing in popularity and use, offer the audience the opportunity for "time-shift viewing" (Waterman, 1984). Unlike video disks, which for the present, can only be obtained with prerecorded content, blank video cassettes can be used for recording broadcast or cable TV programs for viewing at a later time.

Studies (for example, university students studied by Phillips, 1982) consistently indicate that time-shifting and prerecorded theatrical films (Waterman, 1984) are the most popular uses of video cassette machines. Further uses include playback of home-produced tapes, self-help programs (such as exercises), educational materials, the newly popular "music videos," and uses coupled with a camera (See also studies by Levy and Fink, 1984, and by Roe, 1983a). These uses of videotapes reflect especially on the factors of choice, time, and mobility mentioned previously. The program content may often be the same as in the older medium (television or films), but advantages spring from the circumstances of use. Nor should we overlook the fact that cost may often be reduced, as with the case of viewing films. In all, the implications here are that a new media technology may offer not only new gratifications but may make traditional gratifications (for example, TV shows, movies) more easily obtainable.

Cassettes also hold implications for the structure of the film and television program industry, thus contributing to media environmental change. One advantage in the production and distribution of video cassettes is that new productions can be economically viable without having to appeal to large audiences. Thus we may see the proliferation of highly specialized cassette programs along with those geared to the mass market.

INTERACTIVE SERVICES

Of course, our most prominent interactive media technology, the telephone, has been with us for over a century. More recent interactive technologies include two-way cable (such as the Warner-Amex "Qube" system) and various forms of text services, both broadcast or cable transmitted (teletext), or available via phone networks (videotext). The interactive capability of such services is used for different ends, ranging from the selection of programs to a full two-way message system. Consequences for audience members include greater selection, more personal control over selection, and the sense that one can be a communications source as well as a receiver.

It is now becoming commonly known that interactive television services such as Qube have not been as popular as originally envisaged. A reason frequently given is that the public has grown to expect mainly entertainment and escape—that television offers respite rather than involvement. Another reason is that for interactive services to hold customers, they must offer advantages in time, convenience, or cost. It is noteworthy that while there has been little growth of interactive television on a mass media scale, there has been steady growth of specialized information services such as those offered by Dow Jones News Retrieval, The Source, or CompuServe.

One study of specialized interactive services bears upon the functional dimensions of their use. Dozier and Ledingham (1982) identified two key dimensions in the use of interactive banking, shopping, and home security in San Diego: surveillance and transaction. The surveillance mode, a "read-only" status, was found to be more attractive to users than the transaction, "read-write" interactive mode. This finding prompted the researchers to predict that, all other factors being equal, the surveillance function of this information utility will be adopted more rapidly than the transaction function. Information retrieval systems, however, are sometimes associated with a "depersonalization" factor, one reflective of social presence studies (Short et al., 1976). Dozier and Ledingham found that while this service provides perceived advantages such as time savings and convenience, such services as electronic banking and shopping are often viewed as not being worth the disadvantage of the loss of social interaction. Thus while the desire for convenience is served, the need for getting out of the house and engaging in daily social interactions is not met for some users.

TELECONFERENCING

New technologies have taken various forms in conferencing applications. These include audio, video, facsimile, data, or text links, as well as combinations of any of them. Most studies of teleconferencing have centered upon factors of effectiveness rather than upon need satisfaction.

Although audio conferencing has long been available through public telephone services, its use has been surprisingly modest, given all the attention devoted to modern teleconferencing. Many studies (such as Dutton et al., 1982) have shown that with proper management, video conferencing can be quite effective in meeting situation-specific communication needs of corporate communication.

Computer teleconferencing has grown in recent years, especially in organizational environments where messages may be stored for forwarding—as in "asynchronous" conferencing. In fact, the computer may be losing its forbidding, impersonal image as more individuals gain experience in computer-mediated communications. Hiltz and Turoff (1978) suggest that there is an affective dimension present in both asynchronous and synchronous computer teleconferencing. People may anthropomorphize and use computers in roles ranging from psychiatrists to "partners in crime."

Computer aided networks such as electronic bulletin boards and services like The Source are becoming more publicly accessible as more people purchase home computers. The choice to use such systems seems to reflect various motives. In addition to accomplishing specific tasks (as discussed with information services), these motives include the desire to establish and maintain contacts outside one's own geographic areas and the need for access to schedules. Hiemstra (1982) and Rice (1980) suggest that such uses do not always depend on interpersonal involvement; hence, the technical restrictions of the medium do not impede effectiveness so much.

Hiltz (1978) and Phillips (1983) found that people are very active in their socio-emotional use of computers for working out problems and in using face-saving tactics or stream-of-consciousness thinking, even when the conference they are involved in is task-oriented. There is also apparently a personal utility type of factor involved. Turkle (1984) points out that familiarity with "computerese" is important because computer-related terms and concepts now permeate our lives. It may be inferred from these and other studies emerging in the literature that there are many different types of needs and gratifications associated with computer-mediated communication that have not yet been assessed.

ELECTRONIC MAIL

Some of the computer based conferencing systems discussed above share many characteristics with "electronic mail." Essentially messages are sent to a central computer where they can be forwarded at the receiver's request. For several years, the U.S. Postal Service offered an "ECOM" service whereby computer originated mail was electronically distributed to the nearest post offices, then printed and mailed first class. Although that service has now been discontinued, various forms of it are offered by Western Union, Federal Express, and MCI. To our knowledge there are no major social scientific studies of electronic mail of this type. Are factors of choice and mobility, or just simple convenience, important here? Or are there other, deeper, satisfactions such as the ease of keeping "in touch" with colleagues or friends? Is electronic mail only perceived as a convenient substitute for traditional forms of postal services, or does it offer new satisfactions?

Computer networks within organizations sometimes offer messaging systems also referred to as electronic mail. In a study of one such system, Steinfield (1983) found that the mail system was used for a wide variety of purposes, some that bore little resemblance to the standard teleconferencing-based uses. A search for major dimensions of use uncovered "task" and "socioemotional" use clusters. The former were self-evident, consisting mostly of the act of transferring or obtaining information. The latter, however, related to the maintaining of personal relationships, feeling a part of the organization, and being "in touch." Social uses were reported almost as frequently as were task-oriented ones. Again, "personalization" is an important gratification associated with some media technologies.

TOWARD A FRAMEWORK FOR STUDYING NEW MEDIA TECHNOLOGIES

What, then, should be considered in the application of uses and gratifications approaches to the study of the new media technologies? Essentially, we see six topics of special concern that are beginning points in the development of a framework for research. These include expanded choice, interactivity, personalness, new types of "personalized" gratifications, audience concepts, and a broadened theoretical focus.

EXPANDED CHOICE

Although we initially took the position that the new media are less "new" than they are extensions of traditional media, there are many new circumstances of use that together contribute to a wide array of new or modified uses and gratifications. In order to understand how these uses fit together and how media are used to satisfy needs, we must look to the individual's total media environment. Changes might have been seen as initially structural, for example, in that there are many more alternatives from which to choose. But they can also be seen in terms of specific modifications of choice, as, for example, in how the introduction of pay cable services have altered the uses of other media. As a result, media use may become more highly differentiated in serving communication needs. To continue the example, some uses of cable may substitute for uses previously assigned to broadcast television, but new uses will also appear that are complementary with and not substitutes for old media uses, as when an individual purchases special informational programs on the stock market.

SPECIAL QUALITIES OF INTERACTIVITY

The literature frequently suggests the importance of the emerging contrast between technologies that are interactive versus those that are noninteractive. Surely, they may serve different communication needs. This contrast is particularly evident in experiences with the new text services. On the one hand, services have been designed to meet a wide variety of media needs (for example, as traditional publishers have attempted to distribute "electronic" magazines), presumably many of which would be definable in terms of traditional uses and gratifications. On the other hand, there are the gratifications associated with specific, utilitarian services (such as banking) that are so specifically task related that more general gratifications concepts seem irrelevant. For example, using videotext to make travel reservations is fundamentally different from deciding to view a movie with your video cassette player.

PERSONALNESS

Interactivity also provides opportunities for interpersonal-like transactions between individuals or among groups of communicators (as in electronic mail). There are also the rhetorical implications of developing "personalized" communication styles for use with new media (as, for example, in teleconferencing).

MORE SPECIFIC AND PERSONALIZED GRATIFICATIONS

There is greater opportunity for unique, personalized gratifications, some of which differ from traditional media rewards. Text services present a potentially infinite range of alternatives for the consumer-user. As contrasted with mass communications in which uses and gratifications research has often associated certain satisfactions with a given medium, text services could offer any gratifications allowed by the nature of the medium (and, of course, viable in the marketplace). This leads media development away from products (especially films and television shows) that must capture a large mass market in order to survive. There is a greater potential in text services for more esoteric materials to be made available. They need not have mass appeal, a characteristic that fits the concept of "demassification" of media.

Interactive media such as computer mail or bulletin board services also allow people the opportunity to be message disseminators. As such, they may help gratify a need to circulate a message to many receivers simultaneously or asynchronously. A characteristic of some of the most used text services is that the satisfied need often reflects accomplishment of a specific task (such as booking theater tickets) rather than a traditional media-related satisfaction (such as being entertained). The task may have emotional dimensions as well, of course. For example, people may use computer bulletin board services to meet new friends (even romantic ones!) or to share ideas concerning a highly specific topic of interest.

THE CONCEPT OF AUDIENCE

The vastly increased choice potential of certain new media (such as video cassettes, text services) changes the concept of the relation of media-and-audience vis-à-vis selection. If this is so, the concept of "audience" itself becomes problematic and future research should look at individuals as participants. Perhaps many assumptions about audiences need to be reexamined. For example, as the degree of media and content selection increases, the "audience" takes on more of the nature of individual "participants" rather than an aggregate group. General models for examining audience gratifications from traditional media become less useful.

AN EXPANSION OF THEORETICAL FOCUS

Given the range of choice and the complementarity of various new media, many intervening variables become important. New models that incorporate utilitarian functions, range of choice, the phenomenon of personalization of a medium, and the temporal dimension of attitude must be posited and tested in the framework of communication gratifications. Such new research must be prepared to map its own way. New dimensions need to be measured that look at the audience as participants. And as the communications choices can be defined in conceptual terms more closely related to basic human needs, perhaps we can map those needs more clearly than in the past, based upon existing social psychological theories of drives and drive reduction behaviors. Only when uses and gratifications theory can be interpreted relative to the larger context of social and psychological theory will it contribute to our greater understanding of the human condition and the complex roles that communications serve therein.

PART IV

LOOKING AHEAD

Chapter 14

REACHING OUT:
A Future for
Gratifications Research

Jay G. Blumler
Michael Gurevitch
Elihu Katz

BIRTHDAYS, BAR MITZVAHS, and anniversaries are notoriously unreliable as *significant* staging posts in the lives of peoples, societies, and scientific paradigms. They descend upon us arbitrarily, involuntarily, uninvited. Although such milestones are supposed to mark change, they do not necessarily coincide with the onset of *meaningful* change. Yet such is their symbolic significance in our culture, that at the very least they induce introspection: Where have we been and where do we aim to go? They prompt reflection on the wisdom we have accumulated and kindle hope that an even better course may be charted in the future.

The tenth anniversary of the publication of *The Uses of Mass Communications* (Blumler and Katz, 1974), which preparation of the present volume celebrates, has all the hallmarks of such a milestone. The terrain that has been traversed and conquered so far is clearly mapped out in the preceding pages. "Gratifying" progress is recorded—in theory, methodology, and findings. The uses and gratifications paradigm evidently stands confidently on its own feet, generating its characteristic questions, refining its guiding concepts, building its house of data cumulatively. Palmgreen, Wenner, and Rosengren's general gratifications model (see Chapter 1) demonstrates how effectively the present crop of uses and gratifications researchers have (literally) got their act together. Yet, writing in late 1984, and asked to contemplate the future of this tradition, we discern both a troubling danger and an exciting opportunity.

Our tack in this chapter is selective. We neither reprise past work on audience gratifications nor respond to long-running criticisms of the approach nor review all prospective items for a new research agenda. Instead we pose the following question: Is it sufficient for uses and gratifications research to continue on its merry way (whether along the path defined originally by Katz et al., (1974), or along that modeled later by Palmgreen and his associates), working within its own bounded and manageable area, elaborating its own terms, problems, and measures? Or should it aim to address some of the core issues and concerns that are currently surfacing in other productive and provocative lines of mass communication analysis?

THE PRESENT RESEARCH SCENE

This question reflects our awareness that the landscape of mass communication research has been transformed in the past ten years. While uses and gratificationists were cultivating their vineyard, the field as a whole has been invigorated by major developments on several other fronts. New models of audience effects have taken account of characteristic mass media work ways and their likely societal implications—as in theories of agenda-setting (Chapter 5), "spirals of silence" (Noelle-Neumann, 1974), media dependency (Ball-Rokeach and DeFleur, 1976), political malaise (Robinson, 1976), and the like. Meanwhile, critical theorists and neo-Marxists have been raising issues about the ideological role of the media, the location of media organizations in the nexus of power relations in society, the nature of the production process and the values of media professionals. It is true that few critical scholars have yet managed to deal at length with media audiences, betraying at times the uncertainty of novices when invited to dive into the pool of audience experience. (For a perceptive discussion by one such scholar of the problem of the "disappearing audience" in the critical paradigm, see Fejes, 1984.) Yet appreciation of a need to examine audience roles in mass media systems is now increasing among many members of the critical school themselves.

On our side, the essays in this volume show that the uses and gratifications approach is alive and thriving, and suggest that it will continue to produce significant insights into audience experience. The danger is that we may lapse into a self-contained insularity and fail to seize the opportunity now at hand to gain a wider hearing and influence. If our approach is indeed significant, it should be able, not only to resonate within its own ranks, but also to reach out to address a larger array of concerns emerging from other paradigms.

With such an outgoing prospect in mind, let us consult four lines of relevant development in the field.

First, there is the growth of work on "reading" texts and the attendant issue of the meanings that are conveyed by and extracted from them. Probably the most important stimulus for such work has been the application of semiotics to the study of mass media messages. Unlike conventional content analysis, which aspired to develop objective and replicable measures of manifest content, semiotics approached texts as polysemic, offering in principle a multiplicity of meanings, albeit not necessarily equal in prominence or weight. To that extent, it highlights the role of the reader in the decoding process, one that should be ringing bells with gratificationists, precisely because, among audience researchers, they are the most experienced in dealing with a multiplicity of responses.

Second, there is increasing interest in the mass media as propagators of ideological messages. In the first instance, this stemmed from Marxist doctrines of hegemony. But in a period when many forces would appear to be undermining political legitimacy—apathy, volatility, skepticism, privatization, and a sense of powerlessness and intensified inter-group hostility—non-Marxists may also appreciate the ideological role of mass communication. But how does the audience member actually receive an ideological message? Semioticians are coming to realize that the answer cannot be drawn solely from analyses of media content— that "characteristics other than textual ones play a part in the way viewers make sense of a text" (Ang, 1984). Uses and gratificationists could therefore help to identify those audience orientations that filter reception of the presumed ideological message.

Third, there has been increasing concern with television as a potential carrier of a global culture. Sensitive to the debate about media imperialism on the one hand, and to issues over media roles in the construction of reality on the other, researchers have begun to ask questions about the messages conveyed to audiences in other societies by globally diffused, largely Anglo-American, television technologies, professional practices, genres, and programs. A focal hub of such research is how media fare, which apparently crosses linguistic frontiers with consummate ease (Katz and Liebes, 1984), impinges on or is bent by the diverse cultures they enter. Here, too, the distinctive concern of gratificationists for modes of audience use, involvement, and response is apposite.

Fourth, there is a more holistic awareness of systemic influences on mass communication patterns. Increasing attention is consequently being paid to: (1) links of media institutions with other institutional orders in the environment (economic, political, cultural), (2) the functions performed by media institutions in upholding or disrupting such orders and (3) national system characteristics that may shape and constrain communication contents and effects. Uses and gratifications researchers are correspondingly invited to study audiences more often in system-aware contexts—as holders of systemically defined roles and as carriers of systemically spawned cultures.

Our opportunities to operate on a broader canvas are enhanced by yet another recent development in the field. Spokesmen of diverse positions are now showing signs of sharing at least certain postulates about the nature of the mass communication process. This strengthens the prospects of a meaningful cross-paradigm dialogue. In this connection, three more or less shared assumptions are significant.

One is that entertainment is, or may be, political. The implication is that we should look more subtly at the latent meanings of messages, not only at messages as classified by *TV Guide* distinctions. Of course proponents of cultural studies have long recognized that soap operas, adventure serials, family comedies, and popular songs purvey messages about class, gender, and power relations, project presumed national values and norms, and portray ideal-typical social roles. But the proposition that entertainment is political also undergirds the approach termed as cultivation analysis, taken by Gerbner et al. (1979), which alleges that television programming as a whole uniformly indoctrinates (false) images of reality—as well as the quite different view of television as a "cultural forum," being propounded by Newcomb and Hirsch (1983), who assert that, "Conflicting viewpoints of social issues are . . . the elements that structure most television programs."

Second, on all sides, media impact is increasingly being regarded as "interactive," that is, as a product of the interplay of content features and audience dispositions. This notion has a long pedigree, reaching back at least to Bauer's (1964) definition of communication itself as a transactional process, through McQuail et al.'s (1972) designation of their schema of audience gratifications as a "typology of media-person interactions," to McLeod's and Becker's (1974) advocacy of a "transactional" model of media effects, to Graber's (1984) analysis of news processing as interactive, "in which the predispositions of various audiences interact with incoming messages," and, most recently, to Wenner's exploration in Chapter 4 of this volume of a transactional merger of uses and effects orientations. But essentially the same notion is implicit in the concerns of those semioticians, who are keen to learn "what happens when the text is 'realized' as a 'live' discourse" (Hartley, 1982), and for whom the ideological work of the media message is not accomplished, until it is decoded by audience members with options to respond in more than just one way (Hall, 1980; Morley, 1980). Actually, the latter speak more often of "negotiation" than of "interaction," but, whatever the terminology, *we* should note how it reinstates our view of audience members as active—as "more than just passive receivers of already fixed 'messages' or mere textual constructions" (Ang, 1984).

Third, critical theorists and pluralists are even converging on a similarly complex sense of the relationship between media discourse and the surrounding social order. Although for Hall (1982), for example, mass communications are largely structured in ideological dominance, space for a certain amount of message diversity is opened by this treatment of the mass media as sites of cultural conflict and a "class struggle in discourse." And although Newcomb and Hirsch (1983) treat television as a "cultural forum," in which a wide range of textual offerings appear, they have also acknowledged that such "variety works for the most part within the limits of American monopoly capitalism and within the range of American pluralism." Thus scholars in both camps are poised to explore how the mass media may be simultaneously involved in processes of social control and social change.

We conclude from this review of the field's current preoccupations and presuppositions that uses and gratifications researchers are challenged in the coming period to situate the active audience member within a media system (tied reciprocally to political, economic, social, and cultural systems), which, though responsive to some of his interests, does not dance to his tune alone. Four priorities of future emphasis would flow from acceptance of such a challenge.

DOWN WITH "VULGAR GRATIFICATIONISM"

Philosophically, lingering traces of "vulgar gratificationism" should be purged from our outlook. This implies the following:

(1) Rejection of audience imperialism. Our stress on audience activity should not be equated with a serene faith in the full or easy realization of audience autonomy. The audience member is not unconstrainedly master of his or her cultural fate, as if surrounded by a wealth of benign communication instrumentalities, all at her or his service. The audience member assuredly has a degree of control—that of patronage, opinion, sheer cussedness—to exercise the on/off switch, select, talk, and judge. But the individual must pursue goals in a communications arena, where

he or she is the target of a host of more organized interests, whose aims are not necessarily those of the audience member, who has to find the way, then, in a world of grinding axes, conflicting claims, confusing voices, and often only partially satisfying messages.

(2) Social roles constrain audience needs, opportunities, and choices. We never meant to talk about abstracted individuals, but about people in social situations that give rise to their needs. The individual is part of a social structure, and his or her choices are less free and less random than a vulgar gratificationism would presume.

(3) Texts are also to some extent constraining. In our zeal to deny a one-to-one relationship between media content and audience motivation, we have sometimes appeared to slip into the less warranted claim that "almost any type of content may serve practically any type of function" (Rosengren and Windahl, 1972). Consequently, we are often dismissed for implying that "almost any television program or newspaper . . . can be used for almost any function and hence, can be interpreted in almost any way" (Becker, 1984). We must therefore build into our outlook an explicit recognition that texts are not infinitely open and may allow a limited number of possible readings. Perhaps the *New York Times* can be read as pornography, but that is unlikely to be its statistically dominant use.

Taken together, these limitations undermine the projective-test perception of media as lending themselves to any use. They also hold open, in its full complexity, the issue of where power lies in media systems: with the audience, we say, insofar as sufficiently diverse material is provided and is actively selected and processed; but also with the producer of texts, insofar as media images and agendas are narrowly and repeatedly structured; and hence (in the latter case), with those whose interests are served by such patterns. In conjunction, then, these propositions inject into the uses and gratifications paradigm an essential (but sometimes neglected) element of *realism*—without reducing, however, our normative commitment to the would-be active audience member and to the provision of media materials designed to enable him or her to realize her or his purposes.

REINSTATE THE "DISAPPEARING MESSAGE"

Typically, contributors to this volume have paid only glancing attention to any body of communication output (notable exceptions include

Attention to content
may be a control or
manipulation device

Wenner's treatise on the nature of television news gratifications in Chapter 9 of this volume and Zillmann's discussion of experimental research on TV drama in Chapter 12). Such neglect of the message may seem surprising, for the pioneers of uses and gratifications research referred richly to reciprocal relations of audience motivation and media content—how *Big Sister* plots enhanced the status of listeners' house-wifely roles (Warner and Henry, 1948) and *Hilltop House* let listeners compare their own problems with those of the serial's long-suffering heroes and heroines (Herzog, 1944). Losing sight of the message is also at odds with more recent exhortations "to unravel how far, and in what ways, perceptions of content meanings contribute to media motiva-tions" (Blumler, 1979); to forge closer ties "between differing patterns of gratifications sought and the meanings and interpretations given spe-cific media messages" (McLeod and Becker, 1981); and to undertake more studies "of the role of motivation in the processing of media messages" (Palmgreen, 1984b).

Despite such precedents and recommendations, however, uses and gratifications scholars have been slow to engage in making likely con-nections between motivations and meanings. Why is that? How might the deficiency be put right?   *Need it be put right*

Perhaps three features of our approach best explain why we have paid so little attention to media content:

(1) We have often written as if uses and gratifications models were principally designed to explain the process of media *consumption*. We have appeared more interested in learning why television was heavily used or why *Dallas* was heavily viewed, than in the meanings associated with such activities. The latter were treated as out of (our) bounds.

(2) "Meanings" could have crept in through our interest in the role of audience gratifications in mediating the process of communication effect. Nevertheless, they were kept out due to our reliance on rather gross measures or effect. Preoccupied with such "mega-effects" as information gain or reinforcement, we have lost sight of questions about how a person's *particular* perceptions of the world might have been confirmed or altered by virtue of his/her exposure to mass communica-tions. As McLeod and Becker (1981) note, more fine-grained research into the mediating effects of audience motives in the interpretation of *specific* messages is required, if "the gap between social scientists in the uses and gratifications tradition and exponents of popular culture" is to be narrowed.

(3) Emphasis has often been put on how socially and psychologically determined needs generate impulses to patronize certain media and contents without adequate explanation of why *those* media materials

attract such needs. In principle, the expectancy-value approach to media gratification (Palmgreen and Rayburn, Chapter 3, this volume) could counter this bias, for it maintains that "beliefs about a source are the primary informational components determining the seeking of gratifications." However, little has so far been done to examine, within an expectancy-value framework, beliefs about what media materials stand for (for example, the images and values associated with preferred newspapers, magazines, television programs, and so on). As Palmgreen and Rayburn point out, this is an area "where a merger of cultural and gratifications studies could yield rich dividends."

But why should uses and gratifications researchers take the trouble to embroil themselves in interpretations, readings, meanings, and decodings, looking at texts as well as consumers in the process? Is it just because others find such pursuits so fascinating? Or in order to fashion hitherto elusive alliances with humanists and cultural studies enthusiasts?

No, the reasons lie deeper. For one thing, if we are really concerned with the active audience, then study of the reader-text relationship should form a part of our brief. "After all, it is the distinctive mission of uses and gratifications research to get to grips with the nature of audience experience itself, which is ever in danger of being ignored or misread" (Blumler, 1979)—or of being postulated from on high by devotees of hegemonic dominance and from below by plumbers of deep structures in textual symbols!

For another, there is undoubtedly a relationship—possibly an intimate one at times—between how people tune in to mass media materials and the meanings they derive from them. If so, we should be studying that relationship in all its examinable aspects. Four angles of attack on it strike us as promising:

(1) Texts may be part and parcel of the very process of media motivation—sources of sought gratifications, not just objects of them. In other words, a "text" will sometimes be chosen by a consumer for the relevance of a possible reading of it to needs springing from that person's social situation or role and/or the world view allied to it. A vivid example appears in Radway's (1984) ethnographic account of the absorption in romance fiction of a group of young housewives and mothers. For them, the rewards of reading romantic novels were inseparable from the notions of love and male-female relations they conveyed. One could say that in the first instance the readers were seeking not certain rewards (such as escape or affirmation of identity), but what in the texts offered the reward. (According to Radway, these women fell into a wider class of "category readers," individuals who tended to

choose books from only a certain category, "because essential features of their social life create needs and demands that are somehow addressed and fulfilled by these books.")

But how widespread might such a close involvement of features of the text in reasons for attending to it be? Clearly, it often manifests itself among the more engrossed fans of some well-defined body of material. Seekers of what Blumler (Chapter 2, this volume) terms "social identity" might therefore be especially likely to relate to texts in such a manner. However, McGuire (1974) hints that many other audience members may do so as well, when proposing that gratifications are chiefly involved not in initiating exposure, but in "maintaining continued exposure *once appropriate mass communication material*" has been found. Further clarification could be sought by eliciting people's perceptions of various mass media genres, and ascertaining how far their definitions of them include reasons for patronizing them.

(2) Motives may guide textual interpretations. Radway's (1984) romance fiction fans richly exemplify this process as well. For one thing, the plot summaries they proffered were motivationally selective and controlled. The typical definition—"a man and a woman meeting, the problems they encountered, whether the relationship will gel or not"— ignored the many foil figures with whom the hero and heroine were often entangled. In Radway's view, their refusal to acknowledge such elements stemmed "from a deep-seated need to see an ideal relationship worked out between a man and a woman." Other signs of motivational effects on interpretations appeared in readers' perceptions of the novels as "primers about the world" (as encyclopedias of historical and geographical knowledge); and in their treatment of the stories as celebrating a triumph of women's values over the male hero's initial insensitivity to feminine principles (rather than as symbolizing a relinquishing of the weak female self in the arms of a more important man).

Two lessons may be drawn from this case study. Methodologically, it shows that an ethnographic approach should be added to those three strategies of gratifications data collection that are often specified in the literature—self-report, inference from related variables, and experimental manipulation (Becker, 1979). Substantively, it suggests that "personal identity" needs are particularly likely to shape people's textual readings.

We wonder, however, whether other commonly detected gratifications might guide people's interpretations of mass media materials as well. One could postulate, for example, that different readings of the value system represented by quiz programs would be associated with the four distinct gratifications for viewing such programs found by McQuail et al. (1972):

Quiz Gratifications	*Associated Values*
self-rating appeal	achievement
basis for social interaction	sociability/affiliation
excitement appeal	competition
educational appeal	education/culture

Or substitute companionship and para-social interaction gratifications might be equated with perceptions of the values and standards that the favored personalities and characters embody. In fact, a quite extended chain of phenomena might be traced in such a process: from a motive (relief of loneliness); to a use (viewing for para-social interaction); to a reading (perception of the values and standards of favorite characters); to an effect (adoption of those values and standards). Even Noelle-Neumann's spiral of silence theory implies a motive for media use with corresponding textual interpretations—surveillance-to-find-out-what-is-in-vogue-these-days! (See McCombs and Weaver in Chapter 5 and Wenner in Chapter 9.)

(3) The interaction between reader and text will differ according to crucial sources of variation on both sides of the equation (though we are far from knowing what those may be). We have already argued that readers will be socially constrained in how they approach texts and that texts will be constrained in the readings they make available. We are now introducing the likelihood of variability in both sets of constraining forces. Of course, uses and gratifications researchers are accustomed to dealing with variation in audience approaches to media fare. Similarly, texts (media, genres, programs, items) may vary in the degree and manner in which they constrain. Eventually, we should therefore be able to ascribe different interpretative outcomes to how these two sets of (varying) constraints come together.

The task is formidable, however, and exploratory approaches are advisable in the first instance, working with gross distinctions across readers and texts. On the reader's side, we might postulate, for example, that audience orientations that are highly specific, or salient, or require a measure of self-awareness (value reinforcement? social identity?), should facilitate user control over the text. Conversely, gratifications requiring little selectivity, or involving a degree of audience dependence (pass time? scanning modes of news surveillance? substitute companionship?), might virtually invite domination by the text.

On the textual side, certain materials are probably designed to restrict the range of possible readings (more closed), while others extend it, in some cases deliberately so (more open). For example, it is often alleged that television news approximates the first type, due to its seeming objectivity and the straightforwardness of its format and presentation (but see Wenner, Chapter 9). Examples of the second type might include certain fictional materials, the richness of which is suggested by the way in which multilayered plots, subtleties of characterization, and ambiguities of narrative lend themselves to a multiplicity of interpretations. Although television fiction rarely rises to Shakespearean heights, Arlen (1980) claims that the fascination of *Dallas* stems from its moral equivocation (unlike daytime soap operas), while *Charlie's Angels* could plausibly be read as sexist, decadent, liberationist, or escapist. At any rate, closed texts are presumably decoded in accepting or rejecting modes, while more open ones serve more like cafeterias, with something for everyone.

Further possibilities of exploring such interaction may be illustrated by three scenarios that could apply to a confrontation of textual and audience roles in the field of election communication. When considering the examples, it should be borne in mind that past research has highlighted four different roles that audience members can adopt when following a campaign (Blumler and McQuail, 1968)—those of a monitor (seeking information about the political environment); a spectator (seeking excitement); a partisan (seeking reinforcement of his/her preferences); and a liberal citizen (seeking guidance in deciding how to vote).

Suppose first, then, a case of campaign coverage dominated by horse race reporting and corresponding invitations to electors to don spectator roles. Seekers of excitement would be readily served, but would-be holders of monitor and liberal citizen roles would have to either give them up, channel them to other sources, or work harder. Reinforcement seekers, however, could derive affective gratifications from rooting for their side in the contest and concluding that it had won the argument.

A second scenario derives from a view of the jounalistic function as providing "sweeteners" to get people involved in politics. By embedding informational nuggets in dramatic reporting forms, apparently catering to a spectator role expected to be initially salient, audience members might be induced to adopt some different stance—perhaps that of a monitor or even a deliberating liberal citizen. In other words, authors may sometimes try to lead the reader by the hand from one mind-set to another: Does such textual seduction work, in what circumstances, and with whom?

Yet another scenario applies to communication forms that seem to favor the normative decision-making role—as in the League of Women Voters' view of the purpose of candidate debates. Presumably these would serve "liberal citizens" in the audience, and might erode partisan roles (an impact that is sometimes alleged for the evenhanded medium of television in politics). Spectators, however, might best be placed to arrive at an oppositional reading—from their more detached vantage point, regarding the choice as illusory, all window-dressing, contrived and manipulative, and not worthy of serious attention.

(4) Perhaps if entertainment is now thought to be "political," this should be checked against audience experience. For whom is it true, for example, and in relation to what materials? Does the determinedly anti-political streak in our culture and the personal/domestic focus of much entertainment limit its applicability? After all, some people may actively resist being sucked into reflection on the deeper meanings of fare that they just want to enjoy. Would "pure" escapists be untouched by the political messages supposedly carried by mass entertainment—or would they be taken in by them? Reinforcement seekers have emerged from gratification studies of both overtly political and apolitical materials. But what about their political opposite numbers—the vote-guidance seekers? Is there an equivalent among patrons of entertainment—someone, that is, whose motivation for following a serial (for example) might include an interest in exploring the pros and cons of the social and value conflicts displayed? All this might best be examined in relation to one of those key cultural products, which occassionally rise above more run-of-the-mill entertainment provisions—something that is long-running, highly popular, much talked about, and preferably readable in either a dominant or a pluralist mode.

Questions could also be explored about the nature of the political message projected and received. Radway's (1984) work warns us not to expect a straight-line path from audience orientation to communication content to a political reading. In the novels consumed so avidly by her respondents, there was no direct celebration of patriarchal marital relations. Instead, the stories appeared to facilitate both resisting responses to conventional marriage (in Radway's terms, a "tacit . . . protest against the patriarchal condition of women") and accepting ones (by suggesting that the sphere they occupied could be "right and fulfilling"). According to this study, then, patriarchal marriage had generated certain female roles, creating needs for a literature that was open to both conservative and subversive interpretations, ones that could simultaneously appeal to the same women, though neither stemmed very directly from a literal reading of the text.

This analysis reminds us of a pervasive distinction threading through the several levels of our field. Whereas some sociologists of mass communication are impressed with its power to uphold the prevailing institutional order, others draw attention to its function of channelling pressures for change. Whereas many analysts of mass media content emphasize its organically interconnected uniformity, others find a greater diversity in the options and viewpoints presented. And turning to the audience level, McGuire (1974) has divided sixteen psychological theories of human motivation, which may underpin gratifications sought, between those that stress self-preservation (stability, equilibrium) and those that feature self-growth (change, exploration, curiosity). Whether, and in what ways, these three polarities are interwoven in actual mass media systems is an open question.

If much that has been explored in this section could be boiled down to the terms of a prescriptive statement to guide our tradition in the future, it might read as follows: Uses and gratifications researchers should be concerned with the dependence of media-use motives on systemically determined social roles; how these encourage patronage of media materials of certain kinds; how such motives guided readings and interpretations of such materials; how media texts shape and limit motives, expectations, roles, uses; and with what consequences for the self and for acceptance or rejection of the social status quo.

CROSS-CULTURAL COMPARISONS

Most uses and gratifications research is culturally blinkered, because it is confined to single societies. It therefore cannot distinguish those features of audience-media relationships that transcend national boundaries from those that are country-specific.

In the next ten years we therefore urge the conduct of more cross-cultural studies of audience orientations. Such work could be designed to test whether certain media functions that have regularly surfaced across diverse bodies of content in a few societies (surveillance, diversion, identity) are in fact universals (Katz, 1979). It could test whether the same media serve different functions in different societal contexts and whether the same functions are directed to different media in different contexts. It could test whether different cultural values and beliefs influence the mesh of audience motivations and decodings (as preliminary work on audience responses to *Dallas* in the United States and Israel is suggesting; see Katz and Liebes, 1984).

There is also an underlying issue to be explored in such work, which only comparative analysis can address. Beyond the constraints on audience roles that stem from social roles and those that inhere in texts, there is yet another level of constraints—those that arise from the manner in which national communication systems are organized. Broadly, two kinds of system factors could have a bearing on audience expectations and dispositions. One is a media factor per se, reflecting differences in how content offerings are structured and supplied by nationally dominant mass media in different societies. These may differentially favor certain audience roles by rewarding them more often and more accessibly (for instance, does American TV privilege the pass time gratification?). The other is a cultural factor, insofar as different national traditions and norms may favor certain ways of using and responding to media materials (for instance, does American culture privilege spectator roles?). Thus comparative analysis would enable the validity of the so-called structural-cultural explanation of audience behavior (advanced by McQuail and Gurevitch, 1974) to be tested.

However, none of the above should be taken as a recommendation for quick and dirty comparative research, whereby measures of audience gratifications, designed for one national setting, are dropped into a survey in another country, just to see what turns up. There is no reason a researcher in Taiwan, say, should seek respondents' reactions to gratification statements reflecting Israelis' pride in their statehood.

Two precepts follow from this caution. One is that, before comparative inquiry is undertaken, uses and gratifications researchers should ask basic questions about the nature of audience experience with the media *in their own societies,* liberating themselves for the time being from the lure of typologies produced in other countries. The other is that comparative research should be based on a certain amount of prior theorizing about how national system differences might shape audience uses and gratifications. Only then can findings contribute, through confirmation and falsification, to a cumulating body of propositions about system influences on audience behavior.

MACRO-LEVEL ANALYSIS

The prime stuff of uses and gratifications research is micro-level data—evidence from and conclusions about individual audience members. Yet media provision often serves collective as well as individual ends. Popular culture may be used to define the boundaries of youth groups (Murdock and Phelps, 1973). Societies at war appear to have special communication needs (Peled and Katz, 1974). Societies seem to use special media events to steer them through crises (Greenberg and Parker, 1965), focus on external values (Shils and Young, 1953) or to mark transitions. Some cultural forms appear to represent salient features of their social systems. Thus, during the transition to capitalism, the minuet—reflecting the ascriptive, hierarchical stable structure of the noble court—made way for the waltz, which granted access to the new bourgeoisie and rewarded achievement within the dance, just as the larger society was beginning to do (Katz, 1973).

It is time we broke through the micro barrier, then, and took greater account of the macro level when relevant to our concerns. To that end, three possible steps occur to us.

One is to trace the macro in the micro. This is not to imply that macro institutions and occasions are merely aggregates of micro responses. For they do form patterns at the macro level, situating the individual within them in prescribed roles. Nevertheless, by tracing the macro in the micro we can aim to see what social meanings collective experiences and events have for individuals. For example, audiences are presumed by their participation in the national culture to vibrate to the ceremonies and rituals organized by their political leaders and media moguls. But how far that presumption is correct can only be established at the micro level. In a sense, further opportunities are thus afforded to study a significant relationship between the text and the reader, where the former is highly prescriptive, while some among the latter may be annoyed that regularly scheduled programs have been cancelled!

Second, we could more often examine how media service for certain collectivities impinges on the abililty of communication to cater to individual audience member needs. Political communication is a classic case in point. What electoral audiences can get out of it is highly dependent on how it has been designed to serve the sometimes conflicting, sometimes converging requirements of political parties and professional journalists (Katz, 1971). Such an approach would act as a realistic antidote to the simplistic notion of media utility for audience needs, highlighting the vulnerability of the latter to power plays, in which other interests are centrally involved.

Finally, uses and gratifications scholars, sensitive to the interplay of micro and macro forces, could occasionally make contributions to policy debates about mass media roles in society. Consider the communication requirements of institutions such as democracy or market systems. A properly functioning democracy may require a certain proportion of electoral audience "monitors," partisans and uncommitted "liberal citizens." It may be of little interest who plays these roles. But do the news media of democracy produce and sustain these types in adequate proportions, nourishing them with the informational materials they require? And how does such service relate to what other organized actors can legitimately expect to find in a democratic publicity system (whether it be adequate access, fairness of treatment, absence of undue stereotyping and trivialization, etc.)? Similarly, for classic market systems to function properly, there must be available media to provide immediate and complete access to price differences; a different kind of market might require more chances to build brand loyalty than give price information. It is time we gave some thought to the media needs and problems of a range of social institutions and to the extent of their coincidence with the needs and uses of individual audience members.

TO SUM UP

This has not been a very open text, we know, and was not meant to be. In fact, we are performing here as senior citizens, invited to try to light the way before handing over the torch. That does not leave much room for oppositional readings.

We hope, nevertheless, that we have also been persuasive in answering the question posed at the outset whether gratifications research should prefer its own imminent development or attempt to work toward convergences with other paradigms. Our advice, resoundingly, is to try the latter course.

We have intentionally drawn heavily, in these pages, on a research tradition that ostensibly would seem altogether incompatible with our own, one that earlier attributed hegemonic effects to the media based on content analysis alone. But the fact is, ironically, that scholars in this tradition have made certain moves in "our direction," which merit a response from us. For some years now, neo-Marxist theorists have argued for the empirical study of decoding. Note how unlike Gerbner's hypnotic cultivation this is, wherein the viewer is presumed to be altogether unaware of the polluted sights and sounds he or she is inhaling. Moreover, this paradigm has now made explicit space for multiple decodings, including oppositional and other alternatives to dominant readings.

Are we still gratificationists? Or course we are. We are merely proposing certain extensions of principles that were there from the start—albeit neglected sometimes—and proposing additions that are compatible with these first principles in an effort, also, to benefit from serious work being done by others.

Thus, (1) we are consistent with ourselves in urging that individuals come to the media constrained by social and psychological attributes: gratifications sought and obtained are neither random nor individualistic but patterned and clustered. We urge (2) that these social constraints be more often translated into the language of roles. We mean both audience roles (spectator, guidance seeker, escapist, and others) and institutional roles (citizen, consumer, white-collar worker, religious observant), the latter to connect the norms and roles of media institutions with those of other institutions.

(3) We are consistent in our interest in the gamut of audience experience as the primary focus of gratifications research. Audience research, like content analysis, should be aware of affective and social functions and effects, not just cognitive ones. Entertainment may have cognitive uses and effects, but it also has ludic and emotional ones that we need to know more about. The psychology of drama—concepts such as identification, empathy, enthrallment, and others—is so close to the

gratifications formula, yet is largely neglected (but see Zillmann's chapter in this volume).

(4) On the cognitive level, we call for a return to a more specific sensitivity to textual messages and analysis of their uses. Just as content analysts had lost sight of the audience, audience research lost sight of the message. This leads to dialogue of the deaf, with ideological theorists positing the effects of particular messages (see, for example, Thomas and Callahan's [1982] interest in the lesson to be drawn from many family serials, that since the rich are unhappy, the poor are better off); and empirical audience researchers, gratificationists among them, generalizing about mega-effects, such as reinforcement, persuasion, agenda-setting, etc. Gratifications researchers, in their paradigmatic personae, have lost sight of what the media are purveying, in part because of an overcommitment to the endless freedom of the audience to reinvent the text, in part because of a too rapid leap to mega-functions, such as surveillance or self-identity.

(5) We direct attention to the study of decoding or "reading," because it is a natural extension of the idea of "uses." It is not identical with use: Renting the earphones so as to not have to talk with one's fellow passenger is not a "reading" of the in-flight music offerings, but listening to music with an ear to whether it fits the current tastes of one's peer group surely is. The use of communication as content—not as media, not as social context—is closely associated with "reading" (Katz et al., 1973).

(6) Study of decoding leads to the study of "texts," the extent to which they attract certain kinds of needs, and (7) the extent to which they constrain their own decoding. We are listening here with interest to the possibility that certain texts, perhaps certain media, call for certain kinds of readers, or privilege certain kinds of readers, and discourage others or actively force them into opposition.

(8) We propose that gratifications research be perceived as a negotiation between real readers, approaching texts in audience and institutional roles, and texts that have certain kinds of readers in mind. (9) We believe that such negotiations may go on in everyday social interaction and sometimes in interpretive communities that grow up in relationship to a text or genre.

(10) The process of communication, then, may involve multiple steps: motives, uses, readings, and effects. For example, following Noelle-Neumann (1974), we might suggest the following: (a) Other-directed or otherwise insecure individuals have a need to assess the relative

popularity of their beliefs; (b) they search the media in order to do so; (c) the text may greet them with the news that surely most of us are Social Democrats; (d) they will so read the text; and (e) they will be persuaded thereby not to speak (if they are Christian Democrats). Obviously, the variations are many.

(11) The next ten years deserve to see more daring attempts to transplant gratification studies to more macro levels, both by aggregating individuals in their roles, and by giving consideration to the possibility that societies, institutions, and groups have requirements, which are served by mass communications independent of (sometimes in line, sometimes at odds with) the needs of their individual members.

The past ten years will seem like a vacation by comparison.

Chapter 15

GROWTH OF A
RESEARCH TRADITION:
Some Concluding Remarks

Karl Erik Rosengren

THE TRADITION CALLED uses and gratifications research has been developing for about forty years—at first slowly and hesitantly, but during the past ten or fifteen years at a very quick pace. Research traditions grow and develop in at least three different ways: through differentiation, integration, and expansion. During its history, uses and gratifications research has demonstrated all three types of development.

At the end of a volume such as this one, it is only natural to ask what general developments may be found in the body of research presented in the volume, presumably representing the present state of uses and gratifications research. What signs of continued differentiation, integration, and expansion may be found? In order to answer the question, these three vague terms must first be qualified.

One instrument of scientific differentiation is clarification by means of conceptual analysis. Overviews and theory building are the main instruments of integration. Expansion comes about by means of exploration into unchartered territories, resulting in amplication of the stock of knowledge. In a productive research tradition, all these types of activities are going on all the time, but in a given period one type of activity tends to be predominant, presumably because at that time it is the most important and rewarding one. To what extent do we find attempts at clarification, integration, exploration, and amplification in the research presented and reviewed in this volume? Which of these activities is predominant today? Which one should preferably be increasingly cultivated?

CLARIFICATION AND INTEGRATION

Let us start with clarification. At the most basic level, clarification means better conceptualization. In our volume, the most striking case of this type of clarification is represented by the Levy and Windahl chapter, "The Concept of Audience Activity." Activity is a central concept indeed in the study of individual use of the mass media—yet it has not been made the object of any detailed scrutiny until now. It is true that heated debates have been carried out about whether the audience of the mass media should be characterized as active or passive, but only passing efforts have been made at clarification of the concept of activity as such.

It may seem paradoxical that one of the central concepts of a research tradition should have remained unexamined for such a long time, yet it is not uncommon in the history of science. Now that Levy and Windahl have opened up the matter, no doubt others will follow suit, providing yet other—and probably even better—theoretical and empirical definitions of the central concept of activity. In the end, such clarifications will lead to an increased understanding of the whole phenomenon of individual media use, much as the clarification of the gratification concept in the early distinction between gratifications sought and obtained produced a host of theoretically underpinned empirical studies in the late 1970s and early 1980s (see section on GS-GO in the introductory chapter).

Often the clarification of a single concept leads to the creation of a typology in which the original concept finds its logical place in a conceptual space populated by related concepts. Levy and Windahl clarify the concept of activity by analyzing it into nine different subtypes ordered into a two-dimensional typology. Thus typological work may be important in more than one way. Unfortunately, the state of the art in uses and gratifications research is not very advanced when it comes to typological work. It is not much better or worse, however, than in the rest of mass communication research, often mistaking more or less haphazard lists of mutually related concepts for *typologies* of logically ordered concepts (on typologies, see, for instance, Bailey, 1973).

It is a promising sign that typologies of various phenomena relevant to uses and gratifications research are being developed in several of the chapters in this volume (for instance, in Wenner's chapter on news gratifications, and in the chapters by McQuail, Palmgreen and Rayburn, and McCombs and Weaver). But it is a sad fact that many so-called typologies of mass communication research—including such basic and famous ones as, say, Lasswell's mass media functions— are really not typologies at all, but just lists.

The pedantic taxonomist is often looked down upon by more adventurous and ambitious researchers, but the fact is that mass communication research, like many other social sciences, is still waiting for its Linnaeus to step forward—or, at least, another Merton. The day when the many more or less classic lists of functions, motives, and gratifications abounding in our field will be transformed into typologies proper will mark an important step in the development of mass communication research in general, and uses and gratifications research in particular. Many of our concepts would be clarified and better understood by being logically related to adjacent ones in a typology. And some typologies would give rise to new concepts hitherto unheeded by research.

Typological efforts serve a double purpose. They both clarify and integrate. Another instrument of integration is the overview, summarizing and ordering a number of earlier studies. In a sense, all chapters in this volume may be said to be such overviews, and it is in the nature of things that they should vary considerably in scope and degree of generality, the broad and general ones having to give up detailed specificity, the more specific ones paying for their specificity by means of less scope and generality.

In terms of this continuum, Rubin's review of media gratifications through the life cycle is perhaps the most specific; McQuail's discussion of subtraditions within gratifications research and their location within a multidimensional property space is perhaps the most general. In spite of the great differences between the two, each serves its purpose equally well. Reviews falling in between these two end-points include, for instance, the introductory chapter of the volume, and Wenner's review of news gratifications studies.

Other ways of integrating the tradition of uses and gratifications include the following variants:

(1) regarding gratifications studies as a specific case of a more general approach

(2) relating gratification studies to another, parallel tradition of research

The second approach is applied in an ingenious way by McCombs and Weaver, who in their chapter use the basic concepts of agenda-setting research, inaugurated a dozen years ago by McCombs, to build a bridge between uses and gratifications research and effects research.

The first type of integration mentioned above entails integration in another direction. Uses and gratification research is regarded as a special case of a more general type of social or behavioral science. Integration of this type is vital to any applied research tradition. To quote Fred Williams and his associates in the chapter on new communications technologies: "Only when uses and gratifications theory can be interpreted relative to the larger context of social and psychological theory will it contribute to our greater understanding of the human condition and the complex roles that communications serve therein."

In this volume, two major attempts at this type of integration are represented. Wenner regards gratifications research in the light of John Dewey's transactionalism as developed and transformed by Ittelson, Cantril, Toch and MacLean, Bauer and others. Palmgreen and Rayburn apply an expectancy-value perspective to media gratifications, building on Fishbein's specific version of that general approach.

Of the two efforts, Wenner's is the grander, but the very *grandeur* of the attempt prevents it from leaving the level of general analogies presented in verbal models. The Palmgreen and Rayburn chapter is less grandiose, perhaps, but on the other hand it presents a graphic model translatable into a mathematical one that has been tested and gradually revised in a series of empirical reports. That is, a central part of the uses and gratifications approach has been definitively tied in with theories of a type generally accepted in social psychology. This is probably the most important integrative achievement accomplished in the uses and gratifications research of the last few years. Its importance is enhanced by the fact that it was independently arrived at by three different groups using somewhat different versions of the expectancy-value model (Galloway and Meek, 1981; Palmgreen and Rayburn, 1982; Van Leuven, 1981). This is a fine illustration of the integrative power of formalized and generalized theory, and it also forcefully demonstrates the basic soundness of the gratifications approach.

Yet another type of integration may be seen as coming from the outside—both outside the collection of essays in this volume and outside the traditional boundaries of media gratifications research. A particularly noteworthy example here is Janice Radway's (1984) study of the functions of romance reading referred to in passing by James Lull and more extensively by Blumler, Gurevitch, and Katz. In her way, Radway has reinvented uses and gratifications research. Her description of female romance readers is strongly reminiscent of Warner and Henry's (1948) analysis of those same serials. Thus Radway's work indirectly offers strong validation of the general soundness of the basic ideas of uses and gratifications research. In return, uses and gratifications research will be able to offer a host of methodological devices and theoretical concepts that should be highly relevant to continued humanistic research on the use made of various types of literature by many types of readers. The outcome of such an integrative process may well be an amplification of the field, ultimately bringing about a higher level of generality in our understanding of individual use made of the mass media.

EXPLORATION AND AMPLIFICATION

Parallel to the clarifying and integrative efforts summarily outlined in the previous section have run a number of quite different efforts in uses and gratifications research, efforts at exploration and ensuing amplification of the field. The line between clarification and integration on the one hand and exploration and amplification on the other is by no means very sharp. But, in general, the two latter types of development may be characterized as centrifugal and the former two as centripetal. In efforts aimed at clarification and integration the researcher turns toward the center of the field, cultivating the existing subfields incessantly, and relating its peripheral parts to its more central ones. In efforts of exploration and amplification, however, the researcher struggles forward and outward, always on the lookout for new areas to be explored and ultimately incorporated so that the field may be enlarged. The title of the chapter by Blumler, Gurevitch, and Katz, "Reaching Out", is a good catchword for such exploratory efforts. They may be theoretical, empirical, or methodological in character.

Empirical amplification occurs when new areas of reality are made subject to the approach in question. The chapter by Williams, Phillips, and Lum on gratifications associated with new communications technologies is a good example of this type of amplification, absolutely necessary if a research tradition is to live on in a society sometimes changing faster than the research that is expected to describe and analyze that society. In his chapter on the social character of media gratifications, Blumler points to another way of amplification, that of studying the communication patterns of various subgroups who, by way of specific mass media use, may be able to build and express their identity, both as groups and as individual members of such groups. Yet other ways of amplification may still be found by the perceptive cultivator of the field.

In such amplificatory efforts, considerable methological finesse and ingenuity are demanded. Often the researchers may have to turn to means of collecting their information other than traditional survey and experimental techniques. Various types of naturalistic, ethnographic, "qualitative" research may have to be used, as James Lull so forcefully argues in his chapter. Interestingly enough, the type of research advocated by Lull is rather similar to the type of research through which the tradition of uses and gratifications research was initiated some forty years ago. Thus we certainly know that such research may offer a rich harvest of empirical and theoretical results.

Experimentation is a less time-honored methodological approach in gratifications studies than are naturalistic studies (although, of course, it has been with psychology for a long time indeed). Recently, however, psychologists of communication have devoted considerable energy and talent to the experimental study of mass media gratifications. The result of this methodological amplification of uses and gratifications studies is presented in Dolf Zillmann's chapter.

As Zillmann rightly points out, the experimental approach bypasses the criticism often directed against uses and gratifications studies that motives and other relevant concepts are studied by means of introspective self-reports. The advantage, of course, is bought at a price: the problem of ecological validity, always salient in laboratory research, and the inferential nature of the conclusions drawn. As Zillmann repeatedly underlines, the solution to this dilemma must lie in closer cooperation between scholars versed in experimental and survey techniques. Experiments may be complemented with measurements of motives by means of combined Likert and Lisrel techniques, and the actual incidence of the psychological mechanisms inferred from behavior in the laboratory may be estimated by means of field research.

In such a cooperation between experimental and survey techniques, it is to be expected that the strong theories of the psychology of communication, once their ecological validity has been ascertained, will contribute to very considerable theoretical advances in uses and gratifications research, just as expectancy-value theory has already done.

This is good news indeed, for theoretical amplifications tend to be very difficult to bring about without support from strong theory already in existence. There are no easily applied rules of thumb for path-breaking theoretical explorations. All the same, some of us cannot give up hoping that if only we keep exploring, some day our eyes will behold, if not the source of the Nile, at least some characteristic but distinctly different pattern of reader-text interaction still awaiting discovery. That is one of the avenues suggested by Blumler, Gurevitch, and Katz in their chapter on a future for gratifications research. Somewhat later in the same chapter, however, the authors point to a much grander task of exploration.

Almost by definition, uses and gratifications research is micro-oriented. Yet most models of individual mass media use and gratifications include a societal framework around the individual processes. (See for instance, the "general model" of the introductory chapter, building on, and developing, a number of similar ones.) Blumler, Gurevitch, and Katz suggest that at long last we take that framework seriously. Let gratifications research look for the macro in the micro. This is a challenging task indeed, and it calls for comparative research (see Rosengren, 1974).

In order to include a macro perspective, individual use in two or more societal structures must be studied. This has seldom been done (see, however, Edelstein, 1982); in this volume only Lennart Weibull's chapter attempts to do so. Characteristically, it concerns the use of newspapers, a medium that has not been represented strongly in uses and gratifications studies but in the study of which a structural, macro perspective has always been prominent. Weibull's chapter convincingly shows that increased attention to the macro perspective in studies of mass media use will be able to enrich the tradition of uses and gratifications research, and also, perhaps, in its turn to cast new light on approaches that traditionally have been more macro-oriented.

As Weibull points out, comparative studies of individual media use may come in two other variants. Media use in the same society at different points of time may be studied, and truly different societies may be compared, not just different communities or regions within the same country. Both these types are very weakly represented in present uses and gratifications research; the latter type, in fact, is not presented at all in this volume. One reason for their present absence is that they are very demanding with respect to temporal, economic, and intellectual resources. Panel studies are becoming increasingly frequent, however, and under certain conditions they may be used to demonstrate the influence of changes in situational, macro characteristics. (For good examples of panel studies, see Johnsson-Smaragdi, 1983; Roe, 1983b.) As to comparisons among truly different societies, it may be recalled that the introductory overview demonstrated several findings to have been replicable in societies as different as Sweden, England, the United States, Israel, and Japan. It is hoped that such comparisons over time and space as panel studies and replications are able to offer will pave the way for truly comparative studies.

LINES OF FUTURE DEVELOPMENT

In the preceding sections of this chapter four different ways in which a research tradition may grow and develop have been discussed: clarification, integration, exploration, and amplification. While the lines separating the four types are by no means very sharp, it is quite clear that clarification and integration go together, as do exploration and amplification. The former two types of development have been called "centripetal"; the latter two, "centrifugal." In the first section of the chapter I noted that while all types of research activities go on at the same time, in most research traditions one or two types are predominant at a given time, because at that time they are felt to be most relevant and most productive.

Before asking the two questions regarding which types of development are predominant in uses and gratifications research today and which ones may be most relevant and productive, I must hasten to add that the relationship between the various types of development is, of course, reciprocal, not to say dialectical. Exploration and amplification always call for clarification and integration. Clarification and integration point at new avenues of exploration, leading to renewed amplification. The end result of this dialectical interaction—to the extent that there is any end result at all—is truly cumulative: increased generality and a higher level of abstraction in our stock of certified knowledge.

When all this is said, the two questions remain. Which type of development is predominant in uses and gratifications research today? Which one should be seen as most relevant, because it will probably be most productive, right now and in the nearest future?

There is hardly any doubt that over the years uses and gratifications investigations have been characterized more by exploration and amplification than by clarification and integration. There is no doubt at all, however, that the 1974 volume edited by Blumler and Katz marked the beginning of a trend toward clarification and integration. In the late 1970s and early 1980s this development has been followed up by continued efforts in the same direction; for instance, the many empirical studies based on the distinction between gratifications sought and obtained, and the integration of uses and gratifications research with expectancy-value theories.

In this volume the tendency toward continuing and increasing clarification and integration has been carried yet a few steps further. It is a rather safe guess that the tendency will continue for some time. Increasingly, more concepts will be clarified and differentiated and related to other concepts in typologies and theoretical models of increasing sophistication. This is also what McQuail suggests in his thoughtful chapter: that the uses and gratifications tradition take care of its own theory building. Such a development will be able to draw upon the decisive breakthrough that has occurred in multivariate statistical analysis of linear structural equations (such as LISREL). Such analysis will make this type of theory development rest on less sandy foundations than is often the case with theories that have been verbally formulated and qualitatively illustrated only (see Rosengren, 1983).

Obviously, there is a risk in such a development. Just as with all other types of development, there is a tendency toward diminishing returns in clarification and integration. The distinctions made tend to be ever more minute, the typologies ever more intricate, the statistical models ever more complicated. As a result of such developments, the questions asked and the answers obtained run the risk of becoming ever more trivial. Two things should be said in reply to this sketch of a possible future development.

In the first place, there is very probably a great deal of distance to be covered before uses and gratifications research will meet with any serious problem of diminishing returns as a result of clarification and integration. In the second place, no single type of development, however relevant and productive, is ever in undisputed possession of the field. Complementary to clarification and integrative efforts, therefore, will always be a number of exploratory and amplificatory ones. We have also seen that the present volume does indeed offer a number of creative suggestions for such activities. If properly followed up, such suggestions will ensure that for quite some time there will be enough results to be clarified and integrated with the existing stock of knowledge.

In the final analysis, then, it would seem that the growing tendency to stress clarification and integration as the predominant ways of developing uses and gratifications research will continue for some time, and that all this is to the best advantage of the field. The present volume promises to help strengthen and enrich such a development. Perhaps it will also be able to inhibit another tendency that has been with the field for a long time.

The phrase "uses and gratifications" has functioned as a banner under which some different but related approaches have rallied (neatly ordered in a multidimensional typology by Denis McQuail in his chapter). To raise a banner in the field often means that one will be shot at. This may be an awkward situation, but it is not an entirely negative experience. For one thing it is a way to prove one's existence and relevance. Not even social scientists or scholars of communication shoot at irrelevant, stillborn, dwindling, or even dying enemies.

In this respect, the adherents of the uses and gratifications banner have been richly blessed. Their opponents have been generous in demonstrating that the tradition is alive and kicking, well worth shooting at. It has been a vitalizing experience, and no doubt the tradition has thrived from it. In any case it can hardly be said that the criticism has not been heeded by those rallying under the banner. If students of uses and gratifications should be criticized for anything in this connection, it may well be that they have been only too willing to accept the criticism humbly and turn it toward themselves and their ideas (witness the Blumler, Gurevitch, and Katz chapter). Like another train of medieval flagellants, they have proceeded singing hymns of wail, only too willingly accepting the scourges so generously offered by those who themselves might have had some use for those scourges.

Perhaps the time has come when this curious situation will gradually disappear. Like other research traditions, uses and gratifications must accept, and is willing to accept, a fair amount of well-grounded criticism. But there is no particular reason that students of the individual use made of, and the gratifications derived from, the mass media should be the continuous target of criticism from other quarters of the mass communications field. Indeed, there are some signs in the sky indicating the possibility that the situation could very well be turned around. In any case, the development within uses and gratifications studies has by now probably reached the point where adjacent fields will be able to draw upon, rather than just find fault with, the results of these studies. Such a development may well result in increased clarification and integration, not only in uses and gratifications studies, but also in adjacent fields.

Let us hope this volume will contribute to such a development. If our hopes in this and other respects should be met, the volume will have served its purpose well. The sister volume, presumably to be edited in another ten years' time by another group of editors, will be worth looking forward to.

long term effects is adjacent field.

REFERENCES

ADONI, H. (1983) "The social context of youth culture." Presented at the meeting of the International Communication Association, Dallas.
———(1979) "The functions of mass media in the political socialization of adolescents." Communication Research 16: 84-106.
AGAR, M. H. (1983) "Ethnographic evidence." Urban Life 12: 32-48.
ALEXANDER, A., M. S. RYAN, and P. MUNOZ (1984) "Creating the learning context: investigations on the interactions of siblings during co-viewing." Critical Studies in Mass Communication 1: 345-364.
ALLPORT, F. F. (1955) Theories of Perception and the Concept of Structure. New York: John Wiley.
ANDERSON, D. (1979) "Active and passive processes in children's TV viewing." Presented at the meeting of the American Psychological Association, New York.
ANDERSON, J. A. and T. P. MEYER (1975) "Functionalism and the mass media." Journal of Broadcasting 19: 11-22.
ANG, I. (1984) "The battle between television and its audience: the politics of watching television." Presented to the International Television Studies Conference, London.
ARLEN, M. (1980) "Smooth pebbles at Southfork," in M. Arlen, The Camera Age: Essays on Television. New York: Farrar, Straus & Giroux.
ASP, K. (1985) "Mäktiga massmedier. Studier i politisk opinions-bildning." Department of Political Science, University of Göteborg. (mimeo)
———and A. MILLER (1980) "Learning about politics from the media in Sweden and the United States." Department of Political Science, University of Göteborg. (mimeo)
ATKIN, C. (in press) "Informational utility and selective exposure to entertainment media," in D. Zillmann and J. Bryant (eds.) Selective Exposure to Communication. Hillsdale, NJ: Erlbaum.
ATKIN, C. K. (1973) "Instrumental utilities and information seeking," in P. Clarke (ed.) New Models for Mass Communication Research. Beverly Hills, CA: Sage.
———L. BOWEN, O. B. NAYMAN, and K. G. SHEINKOPF (1973) "Quality versus quantity in televised political ads." Public Opinion Quarterly 37: 209-224.
ATKIN, C. K. and G. HEALD (1976) "Effects of political advertising." Public Opinion Quarterly 40: 216-228.
ATKINSON, J. W. (1957) "Motivational determinants of risk-taking behavior." Psychological Review 64: 359-379.
ATWOOD, R. and B. DERVIN (1981) "Challenges to sociocultural predictors of information seeking: a test of race versus situation movement state," in Michael Burgoon (ed.) Communication Yearbook 5. New Brunswick, NJ: Transaction.
AVERY, R. (1979) "Adolescents' use of the mass media." American Behavioral Scientist 23: 53-70.

BABROW, A. and D. L. SWANSON (1984) "Disentangling the antecedents of media exposure: an extension of expectancy-value analyses of uses and gratifications." Presented at the meeting of the Speech Communication Association, Chicago.

BAILEY, K. D. (1973) "Monothetic and polythetic typologies and their relation to conceptualization, measurement and scaling." American Sociological Review 38: 18-33.

BALL-ROKEACH, S. and M. L. DeFLEUR (1976) "A dependency model of mass media effects." Communication Research 3: 3-21.

BANTZ, C. R. (1982) "Exploring uses and gratifications: a comparison of reported uses of television and reported uses of favorite program type." Communication Research 9: 352-379.

BARNLUND, D. (1970) "A transactional model of communication," in K. K. Sereno and C. D. Mortensen (eds.) Foundations of Communication Theory. New York: Harper & Row.

BARWISE, T. P., A.S.C. EHRENBERG, and G. J. GOODHARDT (1982) "Glued to the box? Patterns of TV repeat-viewing." Journal of Communication 32: 22-29.

BAUER, R. A. (1973) "The audience," in I. de Sola Pool and W. Schramm (eds.) Handbook of Communication. Chicago: Rand McNally.

———(1964a) "The communicator and his audience," in L. Dexter and D. M. White (eds.) People, Society, and Mass Communication. New York: Free Press.

———(1964b) "The obstinate audience: the influence process from the point of view of social communication." American Psychologist 19: 319-328.

———(1963) "The initiative of the audience." Journal of Advertising Research 3: 2-7.

BECKER, L. B. (1979) "Measurement of gratifications." Communication Research 6: 54-73.

———(1976) "Two tests of media gratifications: Watergate and the 1974 election." Journalism Quarterly 53: 28-33.

———and J. W. FRUIT (1982) "Understanding media selection from a uses and motives perspective." Presented at the meeting of the International Communication Association, Boston.

BECKER, S. (1984) "Marxist approaches to media studies: the British experience." Critical Studies in Mass Communication 1: 66-80.

———R. PEPPER, L. WENNER, and J. K. KIM (1979) "Information flow and the shaping of meanings," in S. Kraus (ed.) The Great Debates: Carter vs. Ford, 1976. Bloomington: Indiana University Press.

BELMAN, L. S. (1977) "John Dewey's concept of communication." Journal of Communication 27: 29-37.

BERELSON, B. (1959) "The state of communication research." Public Opinion Quarterly 23: 1-15.

———(1949) "What 'missing' the newspaper means," in P. F. Lazarsfeld and F. N. Stanton (eds.), Communications Research 1948-1949. New York: Harper.

———P. F. LAZARSFELD, and W. N. McPHEE (1954) Voting. Chicago: University of Chicago Press.

BERG, U. and B. HÖIJER (1972a) Publikmekanismer och programval. Stockholm: Swedish Broadcasting Corporation.

———(1972b) Radio och TV—det dagliga mönstret. Stockholm: Swedish Broadcasting Corporation.

BERLYNE, D. E. (1960) Conflict, Arousal and Curiosity. New York: McGraw-Hill.

BLOOD, R. W. (1981) "Unobtrusive issues in the agenda-setting role of the press." Ph.D. dissertation, Syracuse University.

———and J. J. GALLOWAY (1983) "Expectancy-value measures of audience uses and gratifications for media content." Presented at the meeting of the International Communication Association, Dallas.

BLUMLER, J. G. (1979) "The role of theory in uses and gratifications studies." Communication Research 6: 9-36.

———(1973) "Audience roles in political communication: some reflections on their structure, antecedents and consequences." Presented to the International Political Science Congress, Montreal.

———J. R. BROWN, and D. McQUAIL (1971) "Television as a focus of audience gratifications: a proposal for research." University of Leeds. (mimeo)

BLUMLER, J. G. and E. KATZ [eds.] (1974) The Uses of Mass Communications: Current Perspectives on Gratifications Research. Beverly Hills, CA: Sage.

BLUMLER, J. G. and D. McQUAIL (1968) Television in Politics: Its Uses and Influences. Chicago: University of Chicago Press.

———and T. J. NOSSITER (1976) "Political communication and the young voter in the general election of February 1974." Social Science Research Council Report, Leeds.

BOGART, L. (1981) Press and Public. Hillsdale, NJ: Erlbaum.

———(1965) "The mass media and the blue-collar worker," in A. Bennett and W. Gomberg (eds.) The Blue Collar World. Englewood Cliffs, NJ: Prentice-Hall.

BOULDING, K. E. (1965) "General systems theory—the skeleton of science." Management Science 2: 197-208.

BOULIN-DARTEVELL, R. (1978) "Quelque relexions sur a methode des 'usages et satisfactions': en tant qu'instrument d'investigation des mass media." Revue de l'Intitut de Sociologie 1-2: 121-132.

BROWN, J. R. (1976) Children and Television. London: Collier-Macmillan.

———J. K. CRAMOND, and R. J. WILDE (1974) "Displacement effects of television and the child's functional orientation to media," in J. G. Blumler and E. Katz (eds.) The Uses of Mass Communications: Current Perspectives on Gratifications Research. Beverly Hills, CA: Sage.

BROWN, R. L., and M. O'LEARY (1971) "Pop music in an English secondary school," in F. G. Kline and P. Clarke (eds.) Mass Communications and Youth: Some Current Perspectives. Beverly Hills, CA: Sage.

BRYANT, J. and D. ZILLMANN (1984) "Using television to alleviate boredom and stress: selective exposure as a function of induced excitational states." Journal of Broadcasting 28: 1-20.

———(1983) "Sports violence and the media," in J. H. Goldstein (ed.) Sports Violence. New York: Springer-Verlag.

BURRELL, G. and G. MORGAN (1979) Sociological Paradigms and Organisational Analysis. London: Heinmann.

CAMERON, W. (1973) Informal Sociology. New York: Random House.

CANCIAN, F. M. (1968) "Variables of functional analysis," in D. L. Sills (ed.) International Encyclopedia of the Social Sciences. New York: Macmillan.

CANTRIL, H. (1950) The "Why" of Man's Experience. New York: Macmillan.

———A. AMES, A. H. HASTORF, and W. H. ITTELSON (1961) "Psychology and scientific research," in F. P. Kilpatrick (ed.) Explorations in Transactional Psychology. New York: New York University Press.

CAREY, J. W. (1979) "The ideology of autonomy in popular lyrics: a content analysis." Psychiatry 32: 150-164.

———(1977) "Mass communication research and cultural studies: an American view," in J. Curran et al. (eds.) Mass Communication and Society. Beverly Hills, CA: Sage.

———(1975) "A cultural approach to communication." Communication 2: 1-22.

———(1969) "The communication revolution and the professional communicator," in P. Halmos (ed.) The Sociology of Mass Media Communicators, Sociological Review Monograph 13, Keele.

———and A. L. KREILING (1974) "Popular culture and uses and gratifications: notes toward an accommodation," in J. G. Blumler and E. Katz (eds.) The Uses of Mass Communications: Current Perspectives on Gratifications Research. Beverly Hills, CA: Sage.

CHAFFEE, S. H. and J. M. McLEOD (1973) "Individual vs. social predictors of information seeking." Journalism Quarterly 50: 237-245.

———and C. ATKIN (1971) "Parental influence on adolescent media use." American Behavioral Scientist 14: 232-240.

CHAFFEE, S. and A. TIMS (1976) "Interpersonal factors in adolescent television use." Journal of Social Issues 32: 98-115.

CHANEY, D. (1972) Processes of Mass Communication. London: Macmillan.

CHESEBRO, J. W., J. E. NACHMAN, A. YANNELLI, and D. A. FOUGLER (1984) "Popular music as a mode of communication, 1955-1982." Presented at the Burke Conference, Philadelphia.

CHRIST, W. G. and N. J. MEDOFF (1984) "Affective state and selective exposure to and use of television." Journal of Broadcasting 28: 51-63.

CLARKE, P. (1973) "Teenagers' coorientation and information seeking about pop music." American Behavioral Scientist 16: 551-556.

COBBEY, R. (1980) "Audience attitudes and readership." ANPA News Research Reports 29: 8-9.

COLE, R. (1971) "Top songs in the sixties: a content analysis of popular lyrics." American Behavioral Scientist 14: 389-400.

COLLINS, W. (1979) "Children's comprehension of television content," in E. Wartella (ed.) Children Communicating: Media and Development of Thought Speech, and Understanding. Beverly Hills, CA: Sage.

COMSTOCK, G., S. CHAFFEE, N. KATZMAN, and D. ROBERTS (1978) Television and Human Behavior. New York: Columbia University Press.

CUTLER, N. E. and J. A. DANOWSKI (1980) "Process gratifications in aging cohorts." Journalism Quarterly 57: 269-277.

DANOWSKI, J. A. (1975) "Informational aging: implications for alternative futures of societal information systems." Presented at the meeting of the International Communication Association, Portland, OR.

DAVIS, D. K. and W. G. WOODALL (1982) "Uses of television news: gratification or edification?" Presented at the annual meeting of the International Communication Association, Boston.

DAVIS, R. H. (1971) "Television and the older adult." Journal of Broadcasting 15: 153-159.

DAVIS, R. H. and A. E. EDWARDS (1975) Television: A Therapeutic Tool for the Aged. Los Angeles: University of Southern California.

DAVIS, S. and P. SIMMON (1982) Reggae International. New York: Roger & Bernhard GMBH.

DAVISON, W. P. (1959) "On the effects of communication." Public Opinion Quarterly 23: 343-360.

DE BOCK, H. (1980) "Gratification during a newspaper strike and a TV black-out." Journalism Quarterly 57: 61-66, 78.

DeFLEUR, M. L. (1966) Theories of Mass Communication. New York: McKay.

DeGRAZIA, S. (1961) "The uses of time," in R. W. Kleemeier (ed.) Aging and Leisure. New York: Oxford University Press.

DELIA, J. (1977) "Constructivism and the study of human communication." Quarterly Journal of Speech 63: 66-83.

DENISOFF, R. S. and R. A. PETERSON (1972) Sound of Social Change. Chicago: Rand McNally.

DERVIN, B. (1981) "Mass communicating: changing conceptions of the audience," in R. Rice and W. Paisley (eds.) Public Communication Campaigns. Beverly Hills, CA: Sage.

DEWEY, J. (1946) "Pierce's theory of linguistics signs, thought, and meaning." Journal of Philosophy 43: 85-95.

———(1938) Logic: The Theory of Inquiry. New York: Holt, Rinehart & Winston.

———(1930) "Conduct and experience." Psychologies of 1930. Worchester, MA.

———(1925) Experience and Nature. Chicago: Open Court.

———and A. F. BENTLEY (1949) Knowing and the Known. Boston: Beacon.

DIMMICK; J., T. McCAIN, and T. BOLTON (1979) "Media use and the life span: notes on theory and method." American Behavioral Scientist 23: 7-31.

DIXON, R. D., F. R. INGRAM, R. M. LEVINSON, and C. L. PUTNAM (1979) "The culture diffusion of punk rock in the United States." Popular Music and Society 6: 210-218.

DOMINICK, J. R. (1972) "Television and political socialization." Educational Broadcasting Review 6 (February): 48-56.

DONOHEW, L. and L. TIPTON (1973) "A conceptual model of information seeking, avoiding and processing," in P. Clarke (ed.) New Models for Mass Communication Research. Beverly Hills, CA: Sage.

DOVIFAT, E. (1967) Zeitungslehre I Theoretische und Rechtliche Grundlagen. Nachricht und Meinung. Sprache und Form. Berlin: Samlung Göschen.

DOZIER, D. M. and J. A. LEDINGHAM (1982) "Perceived attributes of interactive cable services among potential adopters." Presented at the meeting of the Human Communication Technology Special Interest Group, International Communication Association Annual Convention, Boston.

DUTTON, W. H., J. FULK, and C. STEINFIELD (1982) "Utilization of video conferencing." Telecommunications Policy 6: 164-178.

EASTMAN, S. T. (1979) "Uses of television viewing and consumer life styles: a multivariate analysis." Journal of Broadcasting 23: 491-500.

EDELSTEIN, A. S. (1982) Comparative Communication Research. Beverly Hills, CA: Sage.

ELLIOT, P. (1974) "Uses and gratifications research: a critique and a sociological alternative," in J. G. Blumler and E. Katz [eds.] The Uses of Mass Communications: Current Perspectives on Gratifications Research. Beverly Hills, CA: Sage.

ERBRING, L., E. GOLDENBERG and A. MILLER (1980) "Front-page news and real world cues: a new look at agenda-setting by the media." American Journal of Political Science 24: 16-49.

ESCARPIT, R. (1977) "The concept of 'mass.' " Journal of Communication 27: 44-47.

EYENGAR, S., M. PETERS, and M. KINDER (1983) "Experimental demonstrations of the 'not-so-minimal' consequences of television news programs," in E. Wartella and D. C. Whitney (eds.) Mass Communication Review Yearbook, Vol. 4. Beverly Hills, CA: Sage.

FARISTZADDI, M. (1982) Itations of Jamaica and Rastafari. New York: Grove.

von FEILITZEN, C. and O. LINNE (1972) "Masskommunikationsteorier," in Radio-TV
möter publiken. Stockholm: Swedish Broadcasting Corporation.

FEJES, F. (1984) Critical Mass Communication Research and Media Effects: Its Uses
and Influence. London: Faber & Faber.

FESTINGER, L. (1957) A Theory of Cognitive Dissonance. Evanston, IL: Row Peterson.

FISHBEIN, M. (1963) "An investigation of the relationships between beliefs about an
object and the attitude toward that object." Human Relations, 16: 233-240.

———and I. AJZEN (1975) Belief, Attitude, Intention and Behavior. Reading, MA:
Addison-Wesley.

FISHER, B. A. (1978) Perspectives on Human Communication. New York: Macmillan.

FRANK, R. and M. GREENBERG (1980) The Public's Use of Television: Who Watches
and Why. Beverly Hills, CA: Sage.

FREIDSON, E. (1954) "Communication research and the concept of mass." American
Sociological Review 28: 313-317.

———(1953) "The relation of the social situation of contact to the media of mass
communication." Public Opinion Quarterly 17: 230-238.

FREUD, S. (1934) "Formations regarding the two principles in mental functioning."
Collected Papers 4.

FRITH, S. (1981) Sound Effects: Youth, Leisure, and the Politics of Rock and Roll. New
York: Pantheon.

GALLOWAY, J. J., and F. L. MEEK (1981) "Audience uses and gratifications: an
expectancy model." Communication Research 8: 435-450.

GANS, H. (1980) "The audience for television—and in television research," in S. Withey
and R. Abeles (eds.) Television and Social Behavior: Beyond Violence and Children.
Hillsdale, NJ: Erlbaum.

———(1974) Popular Culture and High Culture. New York; Basic Books.

GANTZ, W. (1981) "An exploration of viewing motives and behaviors associated with
television sports." Journal of Broadcasting 25: 263-275.

———(1978) "How uses and gratifications affect recall of television news." Journalism
Quarterly 55: 664-672, 681.

GARFINKEL, H. (1967) Studies in Ethnomethodology. Englewood Cliffs, NJ:
Prentice-Hall.

GARRAMONE, G. M. (1983) "Issues versus image orientation and effects of political
advertising." Communication Research 10: 59-76.

GERBNER, G. (1969) "Toward 'cultural indicators': the analysis of mass mediated
message systems." Audio-Visual Communication Review 17: 137-148.

———L. GROSS, N. SIGNORELLI, M. MORGAN, and M. JACKSON-BEECK
(1979) "The demonstration of power: violence profile No. 10." Journal of Communication 29: 177-196.

GLASSER, T. L. (1982) "Play, pleasure and the value of newsreading." Communication
Quarterly 30: 101-107.

———(1980) "The aesthetics of news." ETC.: A Review of General Semantics 37: 238-247.

GLICK, I. O. and S. J. LEVY (1962) Living with Television. Chicago: Aldine.

GOLDSTEIN, J. H. [ed.] (1979) Sports, Games, and Play: Social and Psychological
Viewpoints. Hillsdale, NJ: Erlbaum.

GOODHART, G. J., M. A. COLLINS, and A.S.C. EHERNBERG (1975) The Television
Audience: Patterns of Viewing. Lexington, MA: D. C. Heath.

GOODHART, G. J., and A.S.C. EHERNBERG (1969) "Duplication of television
viewing between and within channels." Journal of Marketing Research 6: 169-178.

GOULDNER, A. (1976) The Dialect of Ideology and Technology. London: Macmillan.

GRABER, D. A. (1984) Processing the News: How People Tame the Information Tide. New York: Longman.

GRANEY, M. J. and E. E. GRANEY (1974) "Communications activity substitutions in aging." Journal of Communication 24: 88-96.

GREENBERG, B. S. (1974) "Gratifications of television viewing and their correlates for British children," in J. G. Blumler and E. Katz (eds.) The Uses of Mass Communications: Current Perspectives on Gratifications Research. Beverly Hills, CA: Sage.

——and E. PARKER (1965) The Kennedy Assassination and the American Public. Stanford: Stanford University Press.

GUNTER, B., A. FURNHAM, and J. JARRETT (1984) "Personality, time of day and delayed memory for television news." Personality and Individual Differences 5: 35-39.

GUNTER, B., J. JARRETT, and A. FRUNHAM (1983) "Time of day effects on immediate memory for television news." Human Learning 2: 261-267.

GUREVITCH, M., T. BENNETT, J. CURRAN, and J. WOOLACOTT [eds.] (1982) Culture, Society, and the Media. London: Methuen.

GUREVITCH, M. and J. G. BLUMLER (1977) "Linkages between the mass media and politics: a model for the analyis of political communication systems," in J. Curran et al. (eds.) Mass Communication and Society. London: Edward Arnold.

HACKMAN, J. R. and L. W. PORTER (1968) "Expectancy theory predictors of work effectiveness." Organizational Behavior and Human Performance 3: 417-426.

HADENIUS, S. (1983) "The rise and possible fall of the Swedish Party Press." Communication Research 10: 21-52.

HALL, S. (1980) "Encoding and decoding in the television discourse," in S. Hall et al. (eds.) Culture, Media, Language. London: Hutchinson.

——(1977) "Culture, the media and the 'ideological effect,' " in J. Curran et al. (eds.) Mass Communication and Society. Beverly Hills, CA: Sage.

——and T. JEFFERSON [eds.] (1975) Resistance Through Ritual. London: Hutchinson.

HARMON, J. (1972) "The new music and counter-culture values." Youth and Society 4: 61-83.

Louis Harris and Associates (1975) The Myth and Reality of Aging in America. Washington, DC: National Council on Aging.

HARTLEY, J. (1982) Understanding News. New York: Methuen.

HASTORF, A. H. and H. CANTRIL (1954) "They saw a game: a case study." Journal of Abnormal and Social Psychology 2: 129-134.

HAWKINS, C. K. and J. T. LANZETTA (1965) "Uncertainty, importance and arousal as determinants for pre-decisional information search." Psychological Reports 17: 791-800.

HAYAKAWA S. I. (1955) "Foreward to special issue on transactional psychology." ETC.: A Review of General Semantics 12: 243-244.

HEBDIGE, D. (1979) Subculture: The Meaning of Style. London: Methuen.

HEDINSSON, E. (1981) TV, Family and Society: The Social Origins and Effects of Adolescents' TV Use. Stockholm: Almqvist & Wiksell International.

HEETER, C., D. D'ALLESSIO, B. S. GREENBERG, and D. S. McVOY (1983) "Cable-viewing." Presented at the meeting of the International Communication Association, Dallas.

HEIDER, F. (1946) "Attitudes and cognitive organization." Journal of Psychology 21: 107-112.

HENRY, H. (1982) Readership Research: Theory and Practice, Proceedings of the First Symposium. London: Sigmatext.

HERZOG, H. (1944) "What do we really know about daytime serial listeners," in P. F. Lazarsfeld and F. N. Stanton (eds.) Radio Research, 1942-1943. New York: Duell, Sloan & Pearce.

———(1942) "Professor quiz: a gratification study," in P. F. Lazarsfeld and F. N. Stanton (eds.) Radio Research, 1941. New York: Duell, Sloan & Pearce.

HESS, B. B. (1974) "Stereotypes of the aged." Journal of Communication 24: 76-85.

HIBBARD, D. and C. KALEIALOHA (1983) The Role of Rock. Englewood Cliffs, NJ: Prentice-Hall.

HIEMSTRA, G. (1982) "Teleconferencing concern for face and organizational culture," in Michael Burgoon (ed.) Communication Yearbook 6. Beverly Hills, CA: Sage.

HILTZ, S. R. (1978) "Controlled experiments with computerized conferencing: results of a pilot study." Bulletin of the American Society for Information Science 4: 11-12.

———and M. TUROFF (1978) The Network Nation: Human Communication via Computer. Reading, MA: Addison-Wesley.

HIMMELWEIT, H. T., A. N. OPPENHEIM, and P. VINCE (1958) Television and the Child. London: Oxford University Press.

HOLZER, H. (1973) "Politik and Unterhaltung in den Massenmedien: Reaktionen des Publikums," in D. Prokop [ed.] Massenkommunikationsforschung 2: Konsumtion. Frankfurt am Main: Fischer.

HORTON, D. (1957) "The dialogue of courtship in popular songs." American Journal of Sociology 62: 569-578.

———and R. R. WOHL (1956) "Mass communication and para-social interaction." Psychiatry 19: 215-229.

HUR, K. K. and J. P. ROBINSON (1981) "A uses and gratifications analysis of viewing of 'Roots' in Britain." Journalism Quarterly 58: 582-588.

HVITFELT, H. (1977) Verklighetsförträngning. Lund: CWK Gleerup.

INNIS, H. (1951) The Bias of Communication. Toronto: University of Toronto Press.

ITTELSON, W. H. (1961) "The constancies in visual perception," in F. P. Kilpatrick (ed.) Explorations in Transactional Psychology. New York: New York University Press.

———and H. CANTRIL (1954) Perception: A Transactional Approach. Garden City, NY: Doubleday.

IYENGAR, S., M. PETERS, and M. KINDER (1983) "Experimental demonstrations of the 'not-so-minimal' consequences of television news programs," in E. Wartella and D. C. Whitney (eds.) Mass Communication Review Yearbook, Vol. 4. Beverly Hills, CA: Sage.

JAMES, N. C. and T. A. McCAIN (1982) "Television games preschool children play: patterns, themes and uses." Journal of Broadcasting 26: 783-800.

JANOWITZ, M. (1981) "Mass media: Institutional trends and their consequences," in M. Janowitz and P. M. Hirsch (eds.) Reader in Public Opinion and Communication. New York: Free Press.

JAUSS, H. R. (1982) Aesthetic Experience and Literacy Hermeneutics, Vol. 3: Theory of History of Literature (M. Shaw, trans.). Minneapolis: University of Minnesota Press.

JAY, M. (1973) The Dialectical Imagination. London: Heinemann.

JOHNSSON-SMARAGDI, U. (1983) TV Use and Social Interaction in Adolescence. Stockholm: Almqvist & Wiksell International.

JOHNSTONE, J. W. C. (1974) "Social integration and mass media use among adolescents: a case study," in J. G. Blumler and E. Katz (eds.) The Uses of Mass Communications: Current Perspectives on Gratifications Research. Beverly Hills, CA: Sage.

———(1961) "Social structure and patterns of mass media consumption." Ph.D. dissertation, University of Chicago.

JOHNSTONE, J. and E. KATZ (1957) "Youth and popular music: a study in the sociology of taste." American Journal of Sociology 62: 563-568.

JONES, E. E. and H. B. GERARD (1967) Foundations of Social Psychology. New York: John Wiley.

KATZ, E. (1979) "The uses of Becker, Blumler and Swanson." Communication Research 6: 74-83.

———(1971) "Platforms and windows: reflections on the role of broadcasting in election campaigns." Journalism Quarterly 48: 304-314.

———H. ADONI, and P. PARNESS (1977) "Remembering the news: what the picture adds to recall." Journalism Quarterly 54: 231-239.

KATZ, E., J. G. BLUMLER, and M. GUREVITCH (1974) "Utilization of mass communication by the individual," in J. G. Blumler and E. Katz (eds.) The Uses of Mass Communications: Current Perspectives on Gratifications Research. Beverly Hills, CA: Sage.

———(1973) "Utilization of mass communication by the individual." Presented at the Arden House Conference on Directions in Mass Communication Research, Harriman, New York.

KATZ, E., M. GUREVITCH, and H. HAAS (1973) "On the use of mass media for important things." American Sociological Review 38: 164-181.

KATZ, E. and P. LAZARSFELD (1955) Personal Influence. New York: Free Press.

KATZ, E. and T. LIEBES (1984) "Once upon a time, in Dallas." Intermedia 12: 28-32.

KATZ, R. (1973) "The egalitarian waltz." Comparative Studies in Society and History 15: 368-377.

KAY, H. (1954) "Toward an understanding of news-reading behavior." Journalism Quarterly 31: 15-32.

KELLER, S. (1976) "The telephone in new (and old) communities," in I. Pool (ed.) The Social Impact of the Telephone. Cambridge: MIT Press.

KELLEY, H. H. (1973) "The processes of causal attribution." American Psychologist 28: 107-128.

KILPATRICK, F. P. [ed.] (1961) Explorations in Transactional Psychology. New York: New York University Press.

———and H. CANTRIL (1961) "The constancies of social perception," in F. P. Kilpatrick (ed.) Explorations in Transactional Psychology. New York: New York University Press.

KIMBALL, P. (1959) "People without papers." Public Opinion Quarterly 23: 389-403.

KIPPAX, S., and J. P. MURRAY (1980) "Using the mass media: need gratification and perceived utility." Communication Research 7: 335-360.

KLAPPER, J. (1963) "Mass communication research: an old road surveyed." Public Opinion Quarterly 27: 515-527.

———(1960) The Effects of Mass Communication. New York: Free Press.

KLINE, F. G. (1974) "Time in communication research," in P. F. Hirsch et al. (eds.) Strategies for Communications Research. Beverly Hills, CA: Sage.

———(1971) "Media time budgeting as a function of demographies and life styles." Journalism Quarterly 48: 211-221.

———P. V. MILLER and A. J. MORRISON (1974) "Adolescents and family planning information: an exploration of audience needs and media effects," in J. G. Blumler and E. Katz (eds.) The Uses of Mass Communications: Current Perspectives on Gratifications Research. Beverly Hills, CA: Sage.

KOFFKA, K. (1935) Principles of Gestalt Psychology. New York: Harcourt Brace Jovanovich.

KOHLER, W. (1947) Gestalt Psychology. New York: Liveright.

KORZENNY, F. and K. NEUENDORF (1980) "Television viewing and self-concept of the elderly." Journal of Communication 30: 71-80.

KREILING, A. (1978) "Toward a cultural studies approach for the sociology of popular culture." Communication Research 5: 240-263.

KRULL, R., J. WATT, and L. LICHTY (1977) "Structure and complexity: two measures of complexity in television programs." Communication Research 4: 61-86.

KUHN, A. (1974) The Logic of Social Systems. San Francisco: Jossey-Bass.

KUHN, T. S. (1962) The Structure of Scientific Revolutions. Chicago: University of Chicago Press.

LANG, K. and G. E. LANG (1953) "The unique perspective of television and its effects: a pilot study." American Sociological Review 18: 3-12.

LARSON, R. and R. KUBEY (1983) "Television and music as contrasting experiential media in adolescent life." Youth and Society 15: 13-32.

LASSWELL, H. (1948) "The structure and function of communications in society," in L. Bryson (ed.) The Communication of Ideas. New York; Harper & Row.

LAZARSFELD, P. F., B. BERELSON, and H. GAUDET (1944) The People's Choice. New York: Columbia University Press.

LEMISH, D. (1982) "The rules of viewing television in public places." Journal of Broadcasting 26: 575-581.

LESTER, M. and S. C. HADDEN (1980) "Ethnomethodology and grounded theory methodology." Urban Life 9: 3-33.

LEVY, M. R. and J. ROBINSON (in press) "Comprehension of a week's news," in J. Robinson et al. (eds.) The Main Source: Learning from Television News. Beverly Hills, CA: Sage.

———(1983) "Conceptualizing and measuring aspects of audience 'activity.'" Journalism Quarterly 60: 109-114.

———(1979) "Watching TV news as para-social interaction." Journal of Broadcasting 23: 69-80.

———(1978a) "The 'active' audience considered: the case of televison news." Presented at the annual meeting of the American Association for Public Opinion Research, Roanoke, VA.

———(1978b) "The audience experience with television news." Journalism Monographs 55.

———(1978c) "The audience for television news interview programs." Journal of Broadcasting 22: 339-347.

———(1978d) "Opinion leadership and television news uses." Public Opinion Quarterly 42: 402-406.

———(1978e) "Television news uses: a cross-national comparison." Journalism Quarterly 55: 334-337.

———(1977a) "Experiencing television news." Journal of Communication 27: 112-117.

———(1977b) "The uses and gratifications of television news." Ph.D. dissertation, Columbia University.

———and E. FINK (1984) "Home video recorders and the transience of television broadcasts." Journal of Communication 34: 56-71.

———(1983) "The transience of mass media messages: a model of video recorder use." Presented at the meeting of the International Communication Association, Dallas.

LEVY, M. R. and S. WINDAHL (1984) "Audience activity and gratifications: a conceptual clarification and exploration." Communication Research 11: 51-78.

LEWIN, K. (1947) "Channels of group life." Human Relations 1.

LEWIS, G. (1982) "Popular music: symbolic resources and transformer of meaning in society." International Review of the Aesthetics and Sociology of Music 13: 183-189.

LEWIS, G. H. (1981) "Tastes, cultures and the composition: towards a new theoretical perspective," in E. Katz and T. Szecsko (eds.) Mass Media and Social Change. Beverly Hills, CA: Sage.

LICHTENSTEIN, S. L. and L. B. ROSENFELD (1983) "Uses and misuses of gratifications research: an explication of media functions." Communication Research 10: 97-109.

LIN, N. (1977) "Communication effects: review and commentary." in B. Ruben (ed.) Communication Yearbook 1. New Brunswick, NJ: Transaction.

LIPPMAN, W. (1922) Public Opinion. New York: Free Press.

LITTLEJOHN, S. W. (1983) Theories of Human Communication. Belmont, CA: Wadsworth.

LOMETTI, G. E., B. REEVES and C. R. BYBEE (1977) "Investigating the assumptions of uses and gratifications research." Communication Research 4: 321-338.

LULL, J. (1982a) "Popular music: resistance to new wave." Journal of Communication 32: 121-131.

———(1982b) "A rules approach to the study of television and society." Human Communication Research 9: 3-16.

———(1980a) "Family communication patterns and the social uses of television." Communication Research 7: 319-334.

———(1980b) "The social uses of television." Human Communication Research 6: 197-209.

LUM, P. (1984) "Telephone use by senior citizens: community snapshot." Annenberg School of Communications, University of Southern California. (unpublished)

LUNDBERG, D. and O. HULTEN (1968) Indiveden och Massmedie. Stockholm: Norstedt.

LYLE, J. (1972) "Television in daily life: patterns of use overview," pp. 1-32 in E. A. Rubinstein et al. (eds.) Television and Social Behavior, Vol. 4. Rockville, MD: National Institute of Mental Health.

———and H.R. HOFFMAN (1972) "Children's use of television and other media," pp. 129-256 in E. A. Rubinstein et al. (eds.) Television and Social Behavior, Vol. 4. Rockville, MD: National Institute of Mental Health.

MACCOBY, E. E. (1954) "Why do children watch TV?" Public Opinion Quarterly 18: 239-244.

MacKUEN, M. and S. COOMBS (1981) More than News: Media Power in Public Affairs. Beverly Hills, CA: Sage.

McCOMBS, M. E. (1967) "Editorial endorsements: a study of influence." Journalism Quarterly 44: 545-548.

———and D. SHAW (1972) "The agenda-setting function of mass media." Public Opinion Quarterly 36: 176-187.

McCOMBS, M. E. and L. WASHINGTON (1983) "Opinion surveys offer conflicting clues as to how public views press." Presstime (February): 4-9.

McCOMBS, M. E. and D. H. WEAVER (1973) " 'Voters' need for orientation and use of mass communication." Presented at the annual meeting of the International Communication Association, Montreal.

McCORMACK, T. (1961) "Social theory and the mass media." Canadian Journal of Economics and Political Science 4: 479-489.

McGUIRE, W. J. (1974) "Psychological motives and communication gratification," in J. G. Blumler and E. Katz (eds.) The Uses of Mass Communications: Current Perspectives on Gratifications Research. Beverly Hills, CA: Sage.

McILWRAITE, R. and J. SCHALLOW (1983) "Adult fantasy life and patterns of media use." Journal of Communication 33: 78-91.

McLEOD, J. M., C. ATKIN, and S. CHAFFEE (1972) "Adolescents, parents, and television use: self-report and other-report measures from the Wisconsin sample," pp. 173-183 in G. A. Comstock and E. A. Rubinstein (eds.) Television and Social Behavior, Vol. 3: Television and Adolescent Aggressiveness. Washington, DC: Government Printing Office.

McLEOD, J. M. and L. B. BECKER (1981) "The uses and gratifications approach," in D. D. Nimmo and K. R. Sanders (eds.) Handbook of Political Communication. Beverly Hills, CA: Sage.

——— (1974) "Testing the validity of gratification measures through political effects analysis," in J. G. Blumler and E. Katz (eds.) The Uses of Mass Communications: Current Perspectives on Gratifications Research. Beverly Hills, CA: Sage.

——— and J. E. BYRNES (1974) "Another look at the agenda-setting function of the press." Communication Research 1: 131-166.

McLEOD, J. M. and J. D. BROWN (1976) "The family environment and adolescent television use," in R. Brown (ed.) Children and Television. Beverly Hills, CA: Sage.

——— L. B. BECKER, and D.A ZIEMKE (1977) "Decline and fall at the White House: a longitudinal analysis of communication effects." Communication Research 4: 3-22.

McLEOD, J. M., C. R. BYBEE, and J. A. DURALL (1982) "Evaluating media performance by gratifications sought and received." Journalism Quarterly 59: 3-12.

McLEOD, J. M., J. A. DURALL, D. A. ZIEMKE, and C. R. BYBEE (1979) "Expanding the context of debate effects," in S. Kraus (ed.) The Great Debates: Carter vs. Ford, 1976. Bloomington: Indiana University Press.

McLEOD, J. M., W. D. LUETSCHER, and D. G. McDONALD (1980) "Beyond mere exposure: media orientations and their impact on political processes." Presented at the meeting of the Association for Education in Journalism, Boston.

McLUHAN, M.J (1964) Understanding Media. London: Routledge & Kegan Paul.

McQUAIL, D. (1984) "With the benefit of hindsight: the uses and gratifications research tradition." Critical Studies in Mass Communication 1: 177-193.

——— (1983) Mass Communication Theory. Beverly Hills, CA: Sage.

——— (1979) "The uses and gratifications approach: past, troubles, and future." Massa Communicatie 2: 73-89.

——— (1977) "The influence and effects of mass media," in J. Curran et al. (eds.) Mass Communication and Society. London: Arnold.

——— J. G. BLUMLER, and J. BROWN (1972) "The television audience: a revised perspective," in D. McQuail (ed.) Sociology of Mass Communications. Harmondsworth, England: Penguin.

McQUAIL, D. and M. GUREVITCH (1974) "Explaining audience behavior: three approaches considered," in J. G. Blumler and E. Katz (eds.) The Uses of Mass Communications: Current Perspectives on Gratifications Research. Beverly Hills, CA: Sage.

McQUAIL, D. and S. WINDAHL (1982) Communication Models. London: Longman.

MALETZKE, G. (1963) Psychologies der Massenkommunikation. Hamburg: Hans Bredow Institut.

MALONEY, M. (1955) "Experience as transaction." ETC: A Review of General Semantics 12: 318-322.

MASTERS, J. C., M. E. FORD, and R. A. AREND (1983) "Children's strategies for controlling affective responses to aversive social experience." Motivation and Emotion 7: 103-116.

MAXWELL, C. (1877) Matter and Motion.

MEADOWCROFT, J. and D. ZILLMANN (1984) "The influence of hormonal fluctuations on women's selection and enjoyment of television programs." Presented at the meeting of the Association for Education in Journalism and Mass Communication, Gainesville, FL.

MEDRICH, E. A., J. A. ROIZEN, V. RUBIN, and S. BUCKLEY (1982) The Serious Business of Growing Up. Berkeley: University of California Press.

MELISCHEK, G., K. E. ROSENGREN, and J. STAPPERS [eds.] (1974) Cultural Indicators: An International Symposium. Vienna: Akademie der Wissenschaften.

MENDELSOHN, H. (1974) "Some policy implications for the uses and gratifications paradigm," in J. G. Blumler and E. Katz (eds.) The Uses of Mass Communications: Current Perspectives on Gratifications Research. Beverly Hills, CA: Sage.

———and G. J. O'KEEFE (1976) The People Choose a President. New York: Praeger.

MERTON, R. K. (1949) "Patterns of influence," in P. F. Lazarsfeld and F. N. Stanton (eds.) Communications Research 1948-1949. New York: Harper & Row.

MESSARIS, P. (1977) "Biases of self reported functions and gratification of media use." ETC: A Review of General Semantics 34: 316-329.

MEYERSOHN, R. (1961) "A critical examination of commercial entertainment," in R. W. Kleemeir (ed.) Aging and Leisure. New York: Oxford. University Press.

MICHAELS, E. (1984) "Aboriginal television: notes from the field." Presented at the meeting of the Annenberg Scholars Program, Los Angeles.

MILLER, D. and S. BARAN (1984) "Music television: an assessment of aesthetic and functional attributes." Presented at the meeting of the International Communication Association, San Francisco.

MORLEY, D. (1980) "The 'nationwide' audience: structure and decoding." British Film Institute Television Monograph 11, London.

MORRIS, C. (1946) Signs, Language, and Behavior. Englewood Cliffs, NJ: Prentice-Hall.

MORTENSON, C. D. (1974) "A transactional paradigm of verbalized social conflict," in G. Miller and H. Simons (eds.) Perspectives on Communication in Conflict. Englewood Cliffs, NJ: Prentice-Hall.

MUELLER, J. E. (1970) "Choosing among 133 candidates." Public Opinion Quarterly 34: 395-402.

MURDOCK, G. and P. GOLDING (1978) "Theories of communication and theories of society." Communication Research 5: 339-356.

MURDOCK, G. and G. PHELPS (1973) Mass Media and the Secondary School. London: Macmillan.

National Institute of Mental Health (1982) Television and Behavior: Ten Years of Scientific Progress and Implications for the Eighties. Washington, DC: Government Printing Office.

NEWCOMB, H. and P. HIRSCH (1983) "Television as a cultural forum: implications for research." Quarterly Review of Film Studies 8: 45-55.

NEWCOMB, T. T. (1953) "An approach to the study of communication acts." Psychological Review 60: 393-404.

NOBLE, G. (1975) Children in Front of the Small Screen. London: Constable.

NOELLE-NEUMANN, E. (1984) The Spiral of Silence: Public Opinion—Our Social Skin. Chicago: University of Chicago Press.

————(1978) "Public opinion and the classic tradition: a re-evaluation." Public Opinion Quarterly 43, 2: 143-156.

————(1974) "The spiral of silence: a theory of public opinion." Journal of Communication 24: 43-51.

————(1973) "Return to the concept of powerful mass media." Studies of Broadcasting 9: 66-112.

NORDLUND, J. E. (1978) "Media interaction." Communication Research 5: 150-175.

————(1976) Mediaumgänge: En Explorativ Studie. Lund: Student-litteratur.

NOWAK, K. (1979) "Massmedierna effekter: en Snabbskiss," in Att studera massmediernas effekter. Rapport fran ett symposium anordnat av föreningen Svenska Masskommunikationsforskare. Stockholm: Akademilitteratuur.

OLSSON, C. O. and L. WEIBULL (1973) "The reporting of news in Scandinavian countries." Scandinavian Political Studies 8.

Opinion Research Corporation (1983) Segementation Study of the Urban/Suburban Cable Television Market. Prepared for the National Cable Television Association. Princeton, NJ: Author.

OSGOOD, C. E. and P. H. TANNENBAUM (1955) "The principle of congruity in the prediction of attitude change." Psychological Review 62: 42-55.

OWEN, B., J. BEEBE, and W. MANNING (1974) Television Economics. Lexington, MA: D. C. Heath.

OZBEKHAN, H. (1971) "Planning and human action," in P. A. Weiss (ed.) Hierarchically Organized Systems in Theory and Practice. New York: Hafner.

PACANOWSKY, M. and J. A. ANDERSON (1982) "Cop talk and media use." Journal of Broadcasting 26: 757-781.

PALMGREEN, P. (1984a) "Der 'uses and gratifications approach': theoretische perspektiven und praktische relevanz." Rundfunk und Fernsehen 32: 51-62.

————(1984b) "Uses and gratifications: a theoretical perspective," in R. N. Bostrom (ed.) Communication Yearbook 8. Beverly Hills, CA: Sage.

————(1983) "The uses and gratifications approach: theoretical perspectives and practice relevance." Presented at Hans-Bredow-Institut Symposium on Empirical Audience Research, Hamburg.

————and J. D. RAYBURN (1984) "A comparison of gratification models of media satisfaction." Presented at the meeting of the Association for Education in Journalism and Mass Communication, Gainesville, FL.

————(1983) "A response to Stanford." Communication Research 10: 253-257.

————(1982) "Gratifications sought and media exposure: an expectancy value model." Communication Research 9: 561-580.

————(1979) "Uses and gratifications and exposure to public television: a discrepancy approach." Communication Research 6: 155-180.

PALMGREEN, P., L. A. WENNER, and J. D. RAYBURN (1981) "Gratifications discrepancies and news program choice." Communication Research 8: 451-478.

————(1980) "Relations between gratifications sought and obtained: a study of television news." Communication Research 7: 161-192.

PARKIN, F. (1972) Class, Inequality and Political Order. London: Paladin.

PATTEE, H. H. [ed.](1973) Hierarchy Theory: The Challenge of Complex Systems. New York: George Braziller.

PATTERSON, T. E. (1980) The Mass Media Election: How Americans Choose Their President. New York: Praeger.

PEARLIN, L. I. (1959) "Social and personality stress and escape television viewing." Public Opinion Quarterly 23: 255-259.

PELED, T. and E. KATZ (1974) "Media functions in wartime: the Israel homefront in October 1973," in J. G. Blumler and E. Katz (eds.) The Uses of Mass Communications: Current Perspectives on Gratifications Research. Beverly Hills, CA: Sage.

PETERSON, R. A. (1981) "Measuring culture, leisure and time use." Annals of the American Academy of Political and Social Science 453: 169-179.

PHILLIPS, A. F. (1983) "Computer conferences: success or failure?" in R. Bostrom (ed.) Communication Yearbook 7. Beverly Hills, CA: Sage.

———(1982) "Attitude correlates of selected media technologies: a pilot study." Annenberg School of Communications, University of Southern California. (unpublished)

———P. LUM and D. LAWRENCE (1983) "An ethnographic study of telephone use." Presented at the Fifth Annual Conference on Culture and Communication, Philadelphia.

PIATT, D. A. (1955) "The import of the word 'transaction' in Dewey's philosophy." ETC.: A Review of General Semantics 12: 299-308.

PICHASKE, D. (1979) A Generation in Motion: Popular Music and Culture in the Sixties. New York: Macmillan.

PIEPE, A., M. EMERSON, and J. LANNON (1975) Television and the Working Class. Farnborough: Saxon House.

PLAMENATZ, J. (1958) The English Utilitarians. Oxford: Basil Blackwell.

PROKOP, D. (1973a) Massendommunikationsforschung 2: Konsumtion. Frankfurt am Main: Fischer.

———(1973b) "Zum Problem von Konsumtion und Fetischcharakter im Bereich Massenmedien," in D. Prokop (ed.) Massenkommunikationsforschung 2: Konsumtion. Frankfurt am Main: Fischer.

PRYLUCK, C. (1975) "Functions of functional analysis: comments on Anderson-Meyer." Journal of Broadcasting 19: 413-420.

RADWAY, J. (1984) "Interpretive communities and variables literacies: the functions of romance reading." Daedulus 113: 49-71.

RAYBURN, J. D. and P. PALMGREEN (1984) "Merging uses and gratifications and expectancy value theory." Communication Research 11: 537-562.

———(1983) "Uses and gratifications and expectancy value theory: merging two traditions." Presented to the Broadcast Education Association, Las Vegas.

———(1981) "Dimensions of gratifications sought and obtained: a study of *Good Morning* and *Today.*" Presented at the annual meeting of the Association for Education in Journalism, East Lansing, MI.

———and T. ACKER (1984) "Media gratifications and choosing a morning news program." Journalism Quarterly 61: 149-156.

REIMER, B. (1985) "Influencing the reader: content profile as predictor of reading profile." Unit of Mass Communication Research, University of Göteborg. (mimeo)

———(1984) "Tidningsläsning i Södra Halland." Unit for Mass Communication Research, University of Göteborg.

RICE, R. E. (1980) "The impacts of computer-mediated organizational and interpersonal communication." Annual Review of Information Science and Technology 15: 221-249.

RIESMAN, D. (1950) "Listening to popular music." American Quarterly 2: 359-371.

RILEY, M. W., and J. W. RILEY (1951) "A sociological approach to communication research." Public Opinion Quarterly 15: 444-460.

ROBERTS, D. L. and C. M. BACHEN (1981) "Mass communication effects." Annual Review of Psychology 32: 307-356.

✓ROBINSON, J. (1981) "Television and leisure time: a new scenario." Journal of Communication 31: 120-131.

ROBINSON, M. (1976) "American political legitimacy in an era of electronic journalism." in D. Carter and R. Adler (eds.) Television as a Social Force: New Approaches to TV Criticism. New York: Praeger.

ROE, K. (1983a) "The influence of video technology in adolescence." Media Panel Report 27, Vaxjo University College and Lund University.

———(1983b) Mass Media and Adolescent Schooling: Conflict or Co-Existence? Stockholm: Almqvist & Wiksell International.

ROSENGREN, K. E. (1984) "Communication research: one paradigm, or four?" in E. M. Rogers and F. Balle [eds.] Mass Communication Research in the United States and Western Europe. Norwood, NJ: Ablex.

———(1983) "Communication research: one paradigm, or four?" Journal of Communication 33: 185-207.

———(1974) "Uses and gratifications: a paradigm outlined," in J. G. Blumler and E. Katz [eds.] The Uses of Mass Communications: Current Perspectives on Gratifications Research. Beverly Hills, CA: Sage.

———K. ROE, and I. SONESSON (1983) "Finality and causality in adolescents' mass media use." Media Panel Report 24, Växjö University College and Lund University.

ROSENGREN, K. E. and S. WINDAHL (1977) "Mass media use: causes and effects." Communications: International Journal of Communication Research 3: 336-351.

———(1973) "Mass media use: causes and effects," in Uses and Gratification Studies: A Symposium. Stockholm: Swedish Broadcasting Corporation, Audience and Programme Research Department.

———(1972) "Mass media consumption as a functional alternative," in D. McQuail (ed.) Sociology of Mass Communications. Harmondsworth, England: Penguin.

———P. A. HAKANSSON, and U. JOHNSSON-SMARAGDI (1976) "Adolescents' TV relations: three scales." Communication Research 3: 347-366.

ROTTER, J. B. (1954) Social Learning and Clinical Psychology. Englewood Cliffs, NJ: Prentice-Hall.

RUBIN, A. M. (in press) "Uses, gratifications, and media effects research," in J. Bryant and D. Zillman (eds.) Perspectives on Media Effects. Hillsdale, NJ: Erlbaum.

———(1984) "Ritualized and instrumental television viewing." Journal of Communication 34 (3): 67-77.

———(1983) "Television uses and gratifications: the interaction of viewing patterns and motivations." Journal of Broadcasting 27: 37-51.

———(1982) "Directions in television and aging research." Journal of Broadcasting 26: 537-551.

———(1981a) "An examination of television viewing motivations." Communication Research 8: 141-165.

———(1981b) "A multivariate analysis of 60 Minutes viewing motivations." Journalism Quarterly 58: 529-534.

———(1979) "Television use by children and adolescents." Human Communication Research 5: 109-120.

———(1978) "Child and adolescent television use and political socialization." Journalism Quarterly 55: 125-129.

———(1977) "Television usage, attitudes and viewing behaviors of children and adolescents." Journal of Broadcasting 21: 355-369.

————(1976) "Television in children's political socialization." Journal of Broadcasting 20: 51-60.

————and R. B. RUBIN (in press) "Contextual age as a life-position index." International Journal of Aging and Human Development.

————(1985) "The interface of personal and mediated communication." Critical Studies in Mass Communication 2: 36-53.

————(1982a) "Contextual age and television use." Human Communication Research 88: 228-244.

————(1982b) "Older persons' TV viewing patterns and motivations." Communication Research 9: 287-313.

————(1981) "Age, context and TV use." Journal of Broadcasting 25: 1-15.

RUBIN, A. M. and S. WINDAHL (1982) "Mass media uses and dependency." Presented at the meeting of the International Communication Association, Boston.

RUBIN, R. B. and A. M. RUBIN (1982) "Contextual age and television use: re-examining a life-position indicator," in M. Burgoon (ed.) Communication Yearbook 6. Beverly Hills, CA: Sage.

RUNDFUNK und FERNSEHEN (1980) "Holocaust" in Westeuropa: Zentrale Ergebnisse der Begleituntersuchungen in Belgien, der Bundersrepublik, Grossbritannien, den Niederlanden und Österreich.

SARETT, C. (1981) "Socialization patterns and pre-school children's television and film related play behavior." Ph.D. dissertation, University of Pennsylvania.

SCHOENBACH, K. and D. H. WEAVER (1983) "Cognitive bonding and need for orientation during political campaigns." Presented at the meeting of the International Communication Association, Dallas.

SCHRAMM, W. (1969) "Aging and mass communication," in M. W. Riley et al. [eds.] Aging and Society, Vol. 2: Aging and the Professions. New York: Russell Sage Foundation.

————(1949) "The nature of news." Journalism Quarterly 26: 259-269.

————J. LYLE, and E. B. PARKER (1961) Television in the Lives of Our Children. Chicago: University of Chicago Press.

SCHUTZ, A. (1972) The Phenomenology of the Social World. London: Heinemann.

SEARS, D. and J. FREEDMAN (1967) "Selective exposure to information: a critical review." Public Opinion Quarterly 31: 194-213.

————(1965) "Selective exposure," in L. Berkowitz [ed.] Advances in Experimental Social Psychology. New York: Academic.

SHAVER, J. L. (1983) "The uses of cable TV." Master's thesis, University of Kentucky.

SHILS, E. and M. YOUNG (1953) "The meaning of the coronation." Sociological Review 1: 63-81.

SHIMANOFF, S. B. (1980) Communication Rules: Theory and Research. Beverly Hills, CA: Sage.

SHORT, J., E. WILLIAMS, and B. CHRISTIE (1976) The Social Psychology of Telecommunications. New York: John Wiley.

SIEBERT, F. S., T. PETERSON, and W. SCHRAMM (1956) Four Theories of the Press. Urbana: University of Illinois Press.

SINGER, J. (1980) "The power and limitations for TV: A cognitive-affective analysis," in P. Tannenbaum (ed.) The Entertainment Functions of Television. Hillsdale, NJ: Erlbaum.

STEINFIELD, C. S. (1983) "Communicating via electronic mail: patterns and predictions of use in organizations." Ph.D. dissertation, Annenberg School of Communications, University of Southern California.

STEPHENSON, W. (1967) The Play Theory of Mass Communication. Chicago: University of Chicago Press.

———(1964) "The ludenic theory of newsreading." Journalism Quarterly 41: 367-374.

STINCHCOMBE, A. L. (1968) Constructing Social Theories. New York: Harcourt Brace Jovanovich.

STRID, I. and L. WEIBULL (1983) MedieSverige. En systematisk översikt. Stockholm: Tiden.

SUCHMAN, E. (1942) "An invitation to music," in P. F. Lazarsfeld and F. N. Stanton (eds.) Radio Research, 1941. New York: Duell, Sloan & Pearce.

SUGARMAN, B. (1967) "Involvement in youth culture: academic achievement and conformity in school." British Journal of Sociology 18: 151-164.

SWANK, C. (1979) "Media uses and gratifications: need salience and source dependence in a sample of the elderly." American Behavioral Scientist 23: 95-117.

SWANSON, D. L. (1979a) "The continuing evolution of the uses and gratifications approach." Communication Research 6: 3-7.

———(1979b) "Political communication research and the uses and gratifications model: a critique." Communication Research 6: 37-53.

———(1977) "The uses and misuses of uses and gratifications." Human Communication 3: 214-221.

———(1976) "Information utility: an alternative perspective in political communication." Central States Speech Journal 27: 95-101.

SWINGEWOOD, A. (1977) The Myth of Mass Culture. London: Macmillan.

SZASZ, T. S. (1957) Pain and Pleasure. New York: Basic Books.

TAGG, P. (1981) "The analysis of title music as a method of decoding implicit ideological message on TV," in G. Andren and H. Strand [eds] Mass Communication and Culture. Stockholm: University of Stockholm.

TANNENBAUM, P. H. (1980) "An unstructured introduction to an amorphous area," in P. H. Tannenbaum (eds.) The Entertainment Functions of Television. Hillsdale, NJ: Erlbaum.

TANNER, J. (1978) "Pop, punk, and subcultural solutions." Popular Music and Society 6: 68-71.

THUNBERG, A. M., K. NOWAK, K. E. ROSENGREN, and B. SIGURD (1982) Communication and Equality: A Swedish Perspective. Stockholm: Almqvist & Wiksell International.

THOMAS, S. and B. COLLAHAN (1982) "Allocating happiness: TV families and social class." Journal of Communication 32: 184-190.

TICHENOR, P., C. OLIEN, and G. DONOHUE (1980) Community Conflict and the Press. Beverly Hills, CA: Sage.

TILLMAN, R. (1980) "Punk rock and the contruction of 'pseudo-political' movements." Popular Music and Society 7: 165-175.

TOCH, H. and M. S. MacLEAN (1962) "Perception, communication, and educational research." Audio-Visual Communication Review 10: 55-77.

TOLMAN, E. C. (1948) "Cognitive maps in rats and men." Psychological Review 55: 189-208.

———(1932) Purposive Behavior in Animals and Men. New York: Appleton-Century-Crofts.

TOYNBEE, A. J. (1952) Greek Historical Thought. Boston: Beacon.

TRENAMAN, J. and D. McQUAIL (1961) Television and the Political Image. London: Methuen.

TURKLE, S. (1984) The Second Self: Computers and the Human Spirit. New York: Simon & Schuster.

TURNER, M. A. (1958) "News-reading behavior and social adjustment." Journalism Quarterly 35: 199-204.

TUROW, J. (1974) "Talk show radio as interpersonal communication." Journal of Broadcasting 18: 171-179.

VAN LEUVEN, J. (1981) "Expectancy theory in media and message selection." Communication Research 8: 425-434.

VARIS, T. (1974) "Global traffic in television." Journal of Communication 24: 102-109.

VIDMAR, N. and M. ROKEACH (1974) "Archie Bunker's bigotry: a study in selective perception and exposure." Journal of Communication 24: 36-37.

VON BERTALANFFY, L. (1968) General Systems Theory: Foundations, Development, Applications. New York: George Braziller.

VROOM, V. H. (1964) Work and Motivation. New York: John Wiley.

WACHTMEISTER, A. M. (1972) "Televisions publik," in Radio-TV möter publiken. Stockholm: Swedish Broadcasting Corporation, Audience Research Department.

WAKSHLAG, J., V. VIAL, and R. TAMBORNI (1983) "Selecting crime drama and apprehension about crime." Human Communication Research 10: 227-242.

WAPLES, D., B. BERELSON, and F. R. BRADSHAW (1940) What Reading Does to People. Chicago: University of Chicago Press.

WARNER, W. and W. HENRY (1948) "The radio daytime serial: a symbolic analysis." Genetic Psychology Monographs 37: 3-71.

WATERMAN, D. (1984) "The prerecorded home video and the distribution of theatrical feature films." Presented to the Arden House Conference on Rivalry Among Video Media, Harriman, NY.

WEAVER, D. H. (1980) "Audience need for orientation and media effects." Communication Research 7: 361-376.

———(1977a) "Political issues and voter need for orientation," in D. L. Shaw and M. E. McCombs (eds.) The Emergence of American Public Issues. St. Paul, MN: West.

———(1977b) "Voters' need for orientation, media uses and gratifications, and learning of issue importance during the 1976 presidential campaign." Presented at the meeting of the Speech Communication Association, Washington, DC.

———and J. M. BUDDENBAUM (1980) "Newspapers and television: a review of research on uses and effects," in G. C. Wilhoit (ed.) Mass Communication Review Yearbook 1. Beverly Hills, CA: Sage.

WEAVER, D. H. and H. DE BOCK (1980) "Personal needs and media use in the Netherlands and the United States." Gazette 26: 171-194.

WEAVER, D. H., D. A. GRABER, M. E. McCOMBS, and C. H. EYAL (1981) Media Agenda-Setting in a Presidential election: Issues, Images, and Interest. New York: Praeger.

WEAVER, D. H., M. E. McCOMBS, and C. SPELLMAN (1975) "Watergate and the media: a case study of agenda-setting." American Politics Quarterly 3: 458-572.

WEAVER, D. H., J. C. SCHWEITZER, and G. C. STONE (1977) "Content appearance and circulation: an analysis of individual newspaper characteristics." ANPA Research Report 2.

WEBSTER, J. and J. WAKSHLAG (1983) "The impact of group viewing on patterns of television program choice." Journal of Broadcasting 26: 445-455.

WEIBULL, L. (1984) "Dagspress och etermedier i Sverige 1979-1983." Unit for Mass Communication Research, University of Göteborg. (mimeo)

———(1983a) Tidningsläsning i Sverige. Tidningsinnehave Tidningsval Lasvanor. Stockholm: Liber.

———(1983b) "Newspaper readership in Sweden." Newspaper Research Journal 4: 53-64.

———(1983c) "Political factors in newspaper readership." Communication Research 10: 311-331.

———(1980a) "Den dagliga tidningsläsningen. Analys av tidningsläsning och annan mediekonsumtion en genomsnittlig dag i oktober 1979." Department for Political Science, University of Göteborg. (mimeo)

———(1980b) "Dagspressens lasare. En rapport om intressen och lasvanor hosten 1979." Department for Political Science, University of Göteborg. (mimeo)

WENNER, L. A. (1984) "Using gratifications sought and obtained transactional modeling in 'conseffects' analysis: a study of political interest, discussion and media source evaluation." Presented at the annual meeting of the International Communication Association, San Francisco.

———(1983a) "Gratifications sought and obtained: model specification and theoretical development." Presented at the annual meeting of the International Communication Association, Dallas.

———(1983b) "Political news on television: a reconsideration of audience orientations." Western Journal of Speech Communication 47: 380-395.

———(1982) "Gratifications sought and obtained in program dependency: a study of network evening news and *60 Minutes*." Communication Research 9: 539-560.

———(1977) "Political news on television: a uses and gratifications study." Ph.D. dissertation, University of Iowa.

———(1976) "Functional analysis of TV viewing for older adults." Journal of Broadcasting 20: 77-88.

WESTERSTÅHL, J. (1969) "Comparative political communication." Scandinavian Political Studies 3: 9-14.

WESTLEY, B. H. and L. C. BARROW (1959) "An investigation of news-seeking behavior." Journalism Quarterly 36: 431-438.

WESTLEY, B. H. and M. S. MacLEAN (1957) "A conceptual model for communications research." Journalism Quarterly 34: 31-38.

WHITE, D. M. (1964) "The gatekeeper: a case study in selection of news," in L. Dexter and D. M. White (eds.) People, Society, and Mass Communication. New York: Free Press.

WHITE, T. (1983) Catch a Fire. New York: Holt, Rinehart & Winston.

WHITEHEAD, A. N. (1925) The Principles of Natural Knowledge. Cambridge: Cambridge University Press.

WIGGINS, J. S. (1973) Personality and Prediction: Principles of Personality Assessment. Reading, MA: Addison-Wesley.

WILLIAMS, F., A. F. PHILLIPS, and P. LUM (1982) "Some extensions of uses and gratifications research." Annenberg School of Communication, University of Southern California. (unpublished)

WINDAHL, S, (1981) "Uses and gratifications at the crossroads," in G. C. Wilhoit and H. de Bock (eds.) Mass Communication Review Yearbook. Beverly Hills, CA: Sage.

———E. HEDINSSON, I. HÖJERBACK, and E. NORD (1983) "Perceived deprivation and alternate activities during a television strike." Presented at the meeting of the International Communication Association, Dallas.

WINDERS, J. A. (1983) "Raggae, rastafarians, revolution: rock music in the third world." Journal of Popular Culture 17: 61-73.

WINTER, J. P. and C. H. EYAL (1981) "Agenda-setting for the civil rights issue." Public Opinion Quarterly 36: 431-438.

WOLFE, K. M. and M. FISKE (1949) "Why children read comics," in P. F. Lazarsfeld and K. M. Stanton (eds.) Communications Research, 1948-1949. New York: Harper & Row.

WRIGHT, C. R. (1960) "Functional analysis and mass communication." Public Opinion Quarterly 24: 605-620.

WURTZEL, A. H. and C. TURNER (1977) "What missing the telephone means." Journal of Communication 27: 48-56.

ZILLMANN, D. (1983a) "Disparagement humor," in P. E. McGhee and J. H. Goldstein (eds.) Handbook of Humor Research, Vol. 1: Basic Issues. New York: Springer-Verlag.

——(1983b) "Three-factor theory of empathetic delight and distress." Presented at the National Institute of Mental Health Conference on Affect, Santa Barbara, CA.

——(1982) "Television viewing and arousal," in D. Pearl et al. (eds.) Television and Behavior: Ten Years of Scientific Progress and Implications for the Eighties, Vol. 2. Technical Reviews. U.S. Public Health Service Publication ADM 82-1196. Washington, DC: Government Printing Office.

——(1980) "Anatomy of suspense," in P. H. Tannenbaum (ed.) The Entertainment Functions of Television. Hillsdale, NJ: Erlbaum.

——(1977) "Humor and communication," in A. J. Chapman and H. C. Foot (eds.) It's a Funny Thing, Humour. Oxford: Pergamon.

——and J. BRYANT (in press a) "Affect, mood, and emotion as determinants of selective exposure," in D. Zillmann and J. Bryant (eds.) Selective Exposure to Communication. Hillsdale, NJ: Erlbaum.

——(in press b) "Exploring the entertainment experience," in J. Bryant and D. Zillmann (eds.) Perspectives on Media Effects. Hillsdale, NJ: Erlbaum.

——(in press c) Selective Exposure to Communication. Hillsdale, NJ: Erlbaum.

——and B. S. SAPOLSKY (1979) "The enjoyment of watching sports contests," in J. H. Goldstein ed. Sports, Games and Play: Social and Psychological Viewpoints. Hillsdale, NJ: Erlbaum.

ZILLMANN, D. and J. R. CANTOR (1976) "A disposition theory of humor and mirth," pp. 93-115 in A. J. Chapman and H. C. Foot (eds.) Humour and Laughter: Theory, Research, and Applications. London: John Wiley.

ZILLMANN, D., R. HEZEL, and N. MEDOFF (1980) "The effects of affective states on selective exposure to televised entertainment." Journal of Applied Social Psychology 10: 323-339.

ZILLMANN, D. and J. WAKSHLAG (in press) "Fear victimization and the appeal of crime drama," in D. Zillmann and J. Bryant (eds.) Selective Exposure to Communication. Hillsdale, NJ: Erlbaum.

ZUCHERMAN, M. (1979) Sensation Seeking: Beyond the Optimal Level of Arousal. Hillsdale, NJ: Erlbaum.

ABOUT THE CONTRIBUTORS

Jay G. Blumler is Director of the Centre for Television Research at the University of Leeds in England, where he also holds a Personal Chair in the Social and Political Aspects of Broadcasting, and Associate Director of the Center for Research in Public Communication, College of Journalism, University of Maryland. In addition to many works on audience uses and gratifications, his publications reflect a range of political communication concerns, including the comparative analysis of political communication systems, and an interest in similarities and differences of communication research approaches in the United States and Europe.

Michael Gurevitch is Professor and Director of the Center for Research in Public Communication at the College of Journalism, University of Maryland. His research interests are in the areas of the relationship between the media and political institutions and media portrayals of social and political issues and events. He has written on these and other topics and is coeditor of *Mass Communication and Society, Culture, Society and the Media,* and *Mass Communication Review Yearbook,* Volumes 5 and 6.

Elihu Katz is Professor of Sociology and Communication at the Hebrew University of Jerusalem and at the Annenberg School of Communications at the University of Southern California. He is currently at work on a study of major media events (with Daniel Dayan) and on the decoding of American television overseas (with Tamar Liebes). He is coeditor, with Jay G. Blumler, of *The Uses of Mass Communication* (Sage, 1974).

Mark R. Levy is an Associate Professor in the College of Journalism and a Research Associate of the Center for Research in Public Communication at the University of Maryland. Formerly a writer, editor, and associate producer with NBC News and an associate national affairs editor of *Newsweek*, he received his Ph.D. (sociology) from Columbia University in 1977. He has written extensively on mass media audiences, home communication technologies, and the content and effects of the news media. He is coeditor of *Mass Communication Review Yearbook*, Volumes 5 and 6.

James Lull is Associate Professor of Radio-Television-Film in the Department of Theatre Arts at San Jose State University, California. His theoretical and empirical work focuses on how media and music are incorporated into the rule-based worlds of their audiences. He has conducted qualitative, empirical research in order to document these activities in their natural settings.

Patricia Lum is a doctoral candidate at the Annenberg School of Communications at the University of Southern California. She is currently a research associate at the East-West Institute of Communication and Culture in Honolulu and is studying consumer attitudes toward telephone use.

Maxwell E. McCombs is Jesse H. Jones Centennial Professor in Communication and Chairman of the Journalism Department at the University of Texas at Austin. His recent publications have focused on two topics: the agenda-setting role of the press and newspaper readership. He is the coauthor of *Media Agenda-Setting in a Presidential Election* (Praeger, 1981), *Using Communication Theory* (Prentice-Hall, 1979), *Television and Human Behavior* (Columbia University Press, 1978), and *The Emergence of American Political Issues* (West, 1977). His Ph.D. is from Stanford University.

Denis McQuail is currently Professor of Mass Communication at the University of Amsterdam, Netherlands. Formerly, he taught in the Sociology Department of Southampton University, England. His main research interests have been in political communication, audience research, and media evaluation research for policy. In this connection, he worked as academic adviser to the British Royal Commission on the Press, 1974-1977 and as adviser to the Scientific Council for Government Policy in the Netherlands, 1981-1982. He is currently engaged in a cross-national study of new electronic media policymaking in Europe. His publications include *Television and the Political Image*, with J.

Trenaman (1961); *Television in Politics*, with J. Blumler (1968); *Towards a Sociology of Mass Communication* (1969); *Communication* (1975); *Communication Models*, with S. Windahl (1982); and *Mass Communication Theory* (1983).

Philip Palmgreen is Associate Professor in the Department of Communication, University of Kentucky. He received his Ph.D. in mass communication at the University of Michigan. He is primarily interested in audience uses and gratifications and theories of mass media consumption. His publications include "Uses and Gratifications: A Theoretical Perspective," in *Communication Yearbook 8.*

Amy Friedman Phillips received a Ph.D. from the Annenberg School of Communications at the University of Southern California and an M.S. in broadcasting from Boston University's College of Communications. She is currently a consultant on the social impacts of new communication technologies in the Los Angeles area.

J. D. Rayburn II is Associate Professor in the Department of Communication, Florida State University. He received his Ph.D. from Florida State University. His research interests are in the areas of audience uses of mass communication and media effects.

Karl Erik Rosengren is Professor of Communication at the University of Gothenburg, Sweden. His main research interests are in the areas of the sociology of culture and communication, media uses and gratification, and media theory.

Alan M. Rubin (Ph.D., University of Illinois, 1976) is an Associate Professor in the School of Speech Communication at Kent State University. His research interests include mass communication uses and effects. His work has appeared in the *Journal of Broadcasting, Human Communication Research, Communication Research,* the *Journal of Communication, Journalism Quarterly, Communication Yearbook,* and elsewhere. He currently serves as Editor of the *Journal of Broadcasting & Electronic Media.*

David H. Weaver is Professor of Journalism at Indiana University and Director of the Bureau of Media Research in the School of Journalism. He is the author of *Videotex Journalism* (Erlbaum, 1983), senior author of *Media Agenda-Setting in a Presidential Election* (Praeger, 1981), coauthor of *Newsroom Guide to Polls and Surveys* (American Newspaper Publishers Association, 1980), and author of numerous book chapters and articles on media agenda-setting, newspaper readership, and foreign news coverage. He received his Ph.D. in mass communication research from the University of North Carolina in 1974 after having worked as an editor and reporter on four daily newspapers. He has taught at Indiana since 1974.

Lennart Weibull is Associate Professor and Director of Studies at the Unit for Mass Communication, University of Gothenburg, Sweden. His main research interests are political communication, readership research, and media development.

Lawrence A. Wenner is an Associate Professor and the Director of the Media Studies Program in the Department of Communication Arts at Loyola Marymount University in Los Angeles. He received his Ph.D. in 1977 from the University of Iowa, where he was a University Fellow specializing in Broadcasting and Communication Research within the Department of Speech and Dramatic Art. His research has appeared in numerous journals, including *Communication Research,* the *Journal of Broadcasting, Communication Quarterly,* and the *Western Journal of Speech Communication.* His current research interests are in the areas of media theory, the social uses of media, television criticism, and political communication.

Frederick Williams is Director of the Center for Research in Communication Technology and Society and holds the Mary Gibbs Jones Centennial Chair in Communication at the University of Texas at Austin. He was formerly on the faculty of the Annenberg School of Communications at the University of Southern California, where he served as founding dean (1972-1980). In 1979-1980 he served as President of the International Communication Association. His recent books include *The Communication Revolution* (New American Library, 1983); *The New Communications* (Wadsworth, 1984); and *The Executive's Guide to Information Technology,* with H. Dordick (Wiley, 1983).